D1465997

A Special Issue of
Language and Cognitive Processes

Language and Cognitive Processes in Developmental Disorders

Edited by

Dorothy Bishop
University of Oxford, UK

Published in 2001 by Psychology Press Ltd
27 Church Road, Hove, East Sussex, BN3 2FA
www.psypress.co.uk

Simultaneously published in the USA and Canada
by Taylor & Francis Inc.
325 Chestnut Street, Suite 800, Philadelphia, PA 19106

Psychology Press is part of the Taylor & Francis Group

British Library Cataloguing in Publication Data
A catalogue record for this book is available from the British Library

ISBN 1-84169-910-1 (hbk)
ISSN 0169-0965

Cover design by Jim Wilkie
Typeset in the UK by Mendip Communications Ltd., Frome, Somerset
Printed and bound in the UK by Henry Ling Ltd., Dorchester

Contents*

---

*This book is also a special issue of the journal *Language and Cognitive Processes*, and forms issue 2 & 3 of Volume 16 (2001). The page numbers are taken from the journal and so begin with p. 113.

LANGUAGE AND COGNITIVE PROCESSES, 2001, *16* (2/3), 113–142

Mapping theories of developmental language impairment: Premises, predictions and evidence

Shula Chiat

Department of Human Communication Science, University College London, London, UK

This paper presents the case for a mapping theory of developmental language impairment, which branches into a theory that Specific Language Impairment (SLI) arises from impaired phonological processing and the consequent disruption of the mapping process through which the words and sentence structure of a language are established. The prelude to the case is that the mapping process, which is a *sine qua non* of language acquisition, is the first place to look for possible sources of deficits in language acquisition; that recent research on the mapping process points up the contribution of complex phonological processing not just in the segmentation and representation of lexical phonology, but in wider lexical and syntactic development; and that phonological processing is therefore a plausible source of the deficits observed in SLI. Detailed analysis of the mapping process and the role of phonological processing gives rise to specific predictions which are evaluated against wide-ranging research findings on children with SLI. It is argued that the phonological theory provides a better fit with this empirical evidence than theories which posit either specific grammatical deficits or low-level auditory processing deficits, and offers more far-reaching insights than theories which invoke a general limitation in processing capacity. The paper concludes with wider implications, further predictions, and further questions arising from the mapping theory of developmental language impairment and its particular instantiation in the phonological theory of SLI.

Requests for reprints should be addressed to Shula Chiat, Department of Human Communication Science, University College London, 2 Wakefield Street, London WC1N 1PF. E-mail: shula.chiat@ucl.ac.uk.

I would like to thank Maria Black for discussion and comments during the drafting of this paper; Courtenay Frazier Norbury for suggestions; and Dorothy Bishop and anonymous reviewers for their valuable comments on an earlier version.

http://www.tandf.co.uk/journals/pp/01690965.html   DOI: 10.1080/01690960042000012

INTRODUCTION

It is uncontroversial that children acquiring language acquire a specific language. It is also uncontroversial that the acquisition of a specific language entails the acquisition of mappings between form and meaning which are specific to that language. These commonplace observations are the starting point for a less commonplace argument regarding theoretical approaches to impaired language development and explanations of the specific patterns of impairment observed in children with Specific Language Impairment (SLI).

The argument runs like this. The language-acquiring child is faced with a stream of speech in a "scene" to which the speech relates in some way. In order to discover the mappings of her language, the child must segment the stream of speech into meaning-relevant chunks, and segment the scene into speech-chunk-relevant meanings. The nature of speech chunks, meaning chunks, and their relation to each other is by no means simple, and varies significantly between languages. The task of discovering mappings in a language is therefore no mean task. Yet the majority of children crack it successfully by 3 or 4 years. Logically, they could not do this unless they were equipped with powerful capacities to make connections between form chunks and meaning chunks, and so they are. The last decade has seen breakthroughs in research on speech processing and semantic processing in early infancy which cast new light on the hypothesised capacities. The flipside of this logic and evidence is that if the capacities which underpin lexical and syntactic development are defective, the repercussions for language acquisition will be significant.

This is the starting point for the two claims to be pursued in this paper. The first is the broad claim that, since the mapping process is a *sine qua non* of language acquisition, it is the first place to look for hypotheses about impairments in language acquisition. This "mapping theory" of language impairment stands in opposition to grammatical theories which attribute language impairment to deficits in specific linguistic structures, and disregard possible deficits in the mapping process which might explain these. The specifics of that mapping process lead to the second, more specific, claim advanced in this paper: that linguistic deficits observed in children with SLI are due to deficits in phonological processing and their repercussions for lexical and syntactic development. This "phonological theory" of SLI predicts patterns of difficulty with words and sentence structure which are distinct from those predicted by grammatical theories. The different theories about the nature of impaired language development can therefore be evaluated against the patterns of difficulty observed in language-impaired children.

PRECURSORS OF THE MAPPING THEORY

The mapping theory which lies at the heart of this paper draws on a strand of child language research which starts with Slobin's (1973) pioneering work on the "cognitive prerequisites for the development of grammar". The seven "operating principles" which emerged from this initial exploration represent an early attempt to characterise the cues children use to discover the mappings of their language, and remain influential. Such piecemeal strategies have, though, been superseded by more integrated approaches and hypotheses. Their emergence is apparent in Gleitman and Wanner's (1982) chapter charting the "state of the state of the art" in language acquisition. Although the issue explicitly targeted by this chapter is the process of *grammar acquisition*, the bulk of the discussion is about *mapping processes*. The question of how the child acquires the adult grammar is addressed in terms of precisely the three mapping problems identified above: how the child goes about "extracting meaning from the situation", "extracting form from the sound wave", and subsequently "projecting a system that maps between the sounds and the meanings". The discussion of the cues which children may use to solve these problems presages much of the recent research on which the present paper draws.

Bates and MacWhinney (1987) also focus on the "mapping problem", but from a rather different angle. Their "competition model" is primarily concerned with the extent to which children use different cues, rather than what those cues are. Hypotheses about the relative validity of cues in different languages leads to predictions about order of acquisition. The effects of cue validity are tempered by constraints which stem from the child: the readiness of the function to be mapped onto a form, and the cost of perceiving and integrating a cue. In common with the competition model, and in contrast with typical modular models, the mapping theory predicts effects of impairment crossing levels of language, rather than confined to specifically phonological, semantic, or syntactic modules. In contrast to the competition model, with its focus on the validity and strength of cues, the mapping theory looks to the *types of cues* which are problematic for the language-impaired child and the ramifications through the mapping process.

The broad claim embodied in this mapping theory also finds echoes in earlier approaches to language impairment. The assumption that deficits must be traced to some point in the form-meaning relationship is embedded in Bloom and Lahey's (1978) distinction between disorders of form/content/use and the interaction between these. Coming from a somewhat different tradition which sees specific levels of language such as grammar as the main means of identifying language disability, Crystal

(1987) points out that *interactions* between levels of language may be central. He proposes a "bucket" theory in which "An extra 'drop' of phonology (syntax, semantics etc.) may cause the overflow of a 'drop' of syntax (semantics, phonology etc.)" (p. 20).

What differentiates the proposals in the present paper is the *specification of the mapping process* afforded by advances in psycholinguistic theory and by a wealth of recent research on pre-linguistic and linguistic development; and the consequent *specification of possible breakdowns in the mapping process*, in particular, the specification of the "phonological theory" of SLI and its predictions for lexical and syntactic deficits. These predictions are distinct from the predictions which flow from grammatical theories of SLI. The following sections of this paper amplify each step in the argument for a mapping theory of language impairment in general, and a phonological theory of SLI in particular, and work through the empirical evidence bearing on these.

THE NON-TRIVIAL NATURE OF THE MAPPING PROCESS

Phonological segmentation

Children must discover words from the utterances they hear. These typically consist of a combination of words, rather than a word in isolation (Morgan, Shi, & Allopenna, 1996). Even when mothers are asked to teach their infant a new word, they are more than likely to present the target word within a multiword utterance (Aslin, Woodward, LaMendola, & Bever, 1996). Either way, the child has the task of segmenting the utterance into meaning-relevant phonological chunks: even given utterances of a single word, she cannot know a priori that these *are* single words. Utterances such as /'pækɪt/ and /'pæk ɪt/, /fə'gɛtɪŋ/ and /fə 'gɛtɪŋ/ do not come tagged as one or two form-to-meaning chunks. Aslin et al. (1996) point out that mothers used pairs such as "this shoe" and "tissue", where the acoustic information at the word boundary was the same as that present within the word. In the absence of explicit tagging of word boundaries, such as pausing between word forms, speech input must contain more subtle cues of a sort which pre-linguistic infants must perceive and must use to start the ball rolling. The challenge of explaining how this happens has been widely acknowledged in child language research (see for example Chiat, 1979; Cutler, 1994, 1996; Echols, 1996; Peters, 1983). It has been met with a close scrutiny of the cues to segmentation which the speech signal may provide, both within and across languages, and a plethora of investigations into whether and when infants are able to notice those cues and use them to identify units and boundaries.

Before the infant has acquired lexical forms, and as a prerequisite to their acquisition, the only possible source of information about word units lies in their *rhythmic* and *segmental* characteristics. Salient points in the rhythmic structure of speech input may act as beacons signalling the presence of a word. Accordingly, it has been proposed that children use stressed syllables to locate word units and phrase- and clause-final lengthening to locate word boundaries (Echols, 1996; Gleitman & Wanner, 1982). Cutler (1996) suggests that children exploit the characteristic rhythm of their language to identify lexically significant chunks, and that in English, this means assuming that any strong syllable in the input is a word unit. The cues provided by rhythmic structure may, on the other hand, be construed as cues provided by vowels, since it is vowels that indicate the relative weight of a syllable and therefore carry the rhythm of an utterance. Mehler, Dupoux, Nazzi, and Dehaene-Lambertz (1996) argue that "vowels are the cornerstone of prosodic representation in young infants" (p. 112).

Investigations into infants' speech perception between birth and first words have demonstrated stunning sensitivities to speech rhythm and vowel quality which are in keeping with their proposed role in word segmentation. On the basis of a variety of experiments which use habituation-dishabituation and preferential listening techniques, Mehler et al. (1996) conclude that neonates are able to distinguish sentences spoken in two different languages, and show a preference for their native language. Since they can do this even when the input is filtered so that only the information carried by the lower 400 Hz of the spectrum is available, Mehler et al. claim that the infants must be relying on the prosodic properties of the input. They report further experimental findings indicating newborns' sensitivity to the presence of vowels, which carry the prosody: newborns habituated to a string of syllables notice the addition of a new syllable if it contains a different vowel from the familiar syllables, but not if it contains a different consonant. Two-month-olds, on the other hand, notice both.

At the later age of 9 months, infants have been found to favour trochaic (strong-weak) stress patterns which are characteristic of their native English (Jusczyk, Cutler, & Redanz, 1993). Early production of words shows the same preference, reflected in typical child forms such as 'mato, 'jamas, 'raffe for targets tomato, pyjamas, giraffe. Unstressed non-final syllables are far more vulnerable to omission than stressed or final unstressed syllables (Echols, 1996).

Together, these findings depict an infant who registers complex prosodic features of speech which might serve as crucial cues to segmentation. What is the evidence that they do? Morgan and Saffran (1995) report a series of studies which investigated whether the rhythm and sequence of two syllables embedded within a trisyllabic string influence infants' grouping of those syllables. They found that 9-month-olds amalgamated the two syllables into a cohesive unit if both the sequence of syllables and their rhythmic pattern were preserved across different contexts, but not if just one of these was preserved. For 6-month-olds, on the other hand, rhythmic consistency was enough: they treated a consistently stressed pair of syllables as an amalgam even if their sequence altered.

Infants' sensitivity to rhythmic patterns and syllable sequence as cues to segmentation is not quite the end of the segmentation story as current evidence tells it. There is one more phonological cue to segmentation, which must be the ultimate arbiter of word status: segmental consistency. By their very nature, word units are phonologically cohesive units. This means that "the transitional probability from one sound to the next will generally be highest when the two sounds follow one another within a word, whereas transitional probabilities spanning a word boundary will be relatively low" (Saffran, Aslin, & Newport, 1996, p. 1927). In cases where prosodic and acoustic cues leave segmentation ambiguous, only the relative consistency of a phonological sequence can vouch for its word status. Saffran et al. presented 8-month-old infants with 2 minutes of speech consisting of a stream of syllables which provided no prosodic or acoustic cues to their grouping. However, the transitional probabilities between syllables were systematically varied, providing the only possible evidence as to whether they did or did not belong together in a "word". After the infants had been exposed to the stream of speech, a preferential listening task was used to see if listening times for "words" differed from listening times for "non-words". It was found that they did: infants listened longer to novel syllable strings (those with low transitional probabilities) than to familiar ones (whose transitional probabilities were high). This finding demonstrates not only the precision with which infants perceive and retain sequences of syllables, but their ability to track the reliability of syllable co-occurrence across contexts, and thereby distinguish cohesive sequences from accidental juxtapositions.

The picture to date is one of infants receiving speech input which provides a range of subtle cues to segmentation; registering some of these cues from birth and others not long after; integrating them with each other; and exploiting these integrated cues to discover and store word units.

Semantic cues to phonological segmentation

It might be argued that sound is not the only source of information about word units. The child hears speech in a context, and that speech typically relates to the context in which it is produced (Snow, 1995). The child's understanding of that context and of the connection between utterance and context are essential if she is to have some chance of discovering the meaning of the utterance. More than this, though, her understanding of the context might focus her attention on elements of the context to which words refer, and thereby act as a prompt to find word forms corresponding to those elements. The ideal scenario for this type of "semantic bootstrapping" is the "joint attention episode" (Moore & Dunham, 1995): the child picks up a car and the speaker says "That's a car". The child assumes the speaker is talking about the object on which they are both focused, and this leads her to search for a phonological form for that object in the speech she hears.

But even this ideal scenario has shortcomings which make it less than adequate for word acquisition. A semantically driven search for a word phonology does not automatically lead to the target phonology. This will only happen if the child recognises every other word in the utterance and can eliminate these from her search. Even if she solves the phonological segmentation problem in this way, she still faces the semantic segmentation problem. As has long been recognised by philosophers of language, the sense of a word is not the same as its reference. Discovering what *car* refers to is not the same as discovering what *car* means. It might mean "vehicle", or "car", or "thing with wheels", for example. The ideal scenario is not enough to delimit the semantic boundaries of a word.

It could help, though, if children bring more to the joint attention episode than a simple assumption that the speaker's words label what speaker and child are both looking at. Current evidence indicates that they do. Researchers have proposed a variety of principles which direct children's hypotheses about word meaning (see Clark, 1993; Markman, 1989). These principles capture the biases in conceptualisation which children bring to the discovery of word meaning, and the assumptions children make about the mapping of lexical forms onto conceptual categories. They go some way towards explaining how children segment scenes into word-size meanings, and how they come to distinguish the meanings of words which are used to label the same referent but from different points of view (see also Clark, 1997).

Equally important, though, is the emerging evidence that children are guided not just by their own biased perspectives on the scene, but by their perception of the *speaker's* focus within the scene. Using ingenious experiments which manipulate the input of novel words, researchers have shown that, in learning a new word, infants do not have to hear the word at the point where they can see its referent and are focused on it (Baldwin, 1995; Tomasello, 1995). On the contrary, they know that a word refers to the *speaker's intended focus of attention*, and they know they must discover what that focus is in order to discover the word's meaning. When the speaker says "Let's find the gazzer", picks up one object, frowns, then picks up another object with glee, the child does not assume that the word *gazzer* refers to an object in view at the moment the word is heard, or to the first object the speaker picks up (Tomasello, Strosberg, & Akhtar, 1996). Instead, she takes it to refer to the object the speaker *intended* to focus, and the speaker's frown and further search are enough to tell her this. This important finding hints at a sophistication in infants' interpretation of scenes which matches the sophistication of their speech processing, and which research has just begun to tap.

Whatever details of these early capacities eventually emerge, it is evident that they constitute a potent combination. Thanks to the convergence of phonological and semantic cues, "fast mapping" can occur after only a few exposures to a word, contributing to the rapid vocabulary acquisition observed in normally developing children (Carey, 1978). Yet this cannot be the whole story, for reasons which the next section uncovers.

Phonological cues to semantic segmentation

This rather skeletal analysis of what is involved in identifying words has already led us to attribute a great deal to the child: sensitivity to subtle phonological cues, sensitivity to the focus of attention in a scene, but also sensitivity to their co-occurrence. All this is required even where concrete nouns are the target. The challenges are compounded when it comes to other sorts of words. Consider words whose referents are not directly observable and cannot be the shared focus of attention. These include vast swathes of the vocabulary a child must acquire. Everyday verbs such as *fall, play, eat* refer to events which cannot be focused in the same way as concrete nouns (see Fisher, Hall, Rakowitz & Gleitman, 1994; Tomasello & Kruger, 1992). It is true that they have features which are open to perception, so that observation of the scenes in which these verbs occur will give some clue to their referent. But observational evidence will wildly underdetermine the boundaries of their meaning: that *fall* entails uncaused but not caused downward movement (in contrast to *drop* which can be used for both); or that *eat* entails consumption of solid but not liquid substances (in contrast to *swallow* which can be used with both). The problems are even greater with nouns and verbs which refer to non-perceptual experience. *Friend, idea, want, dream,* for example, refer to social or emotional or mental aspects of experience, none of which can be focused by shared gaze. Likewise, terms which refer to time and temporal relations have no observable correlate in scenes. The less a word meaning can be cued by observation of scenes, the more the child must depend on phonological cues to discover it. The acquisition of some aspects of verb meaning will depend on encounters with the same verb form across different scenes. The meaning of *open*, for example, entails a variety of distinct-looking events involving distinct-looking objects—jars, mouths, eyes, windows, presents. Only by encountering *open* in these different contexts can its full meaning be determined.

The clearest evidence for the underdetermination of meaning by scenes, and the role of phonology in determining meaning, lies in differences we observe across languages. These are apparent even in children's earliest words. One well-rehearsed example is children's encoding of the most basic and observable of events, those involving motion and contact (Slobin, 1996). This is found to be influenced by language. In English, children's earliest utterances typically refer to such events using verb particles such as *on*, *in*, which focus on direction of movement; subsequently they combine these with verbs which focus on manner of movement: *put on*, *push on*, *push in*. To talk about the same causation of contact, the Korean-speaking child must focus less on subtle differences in direction of movement, but must notice the tightness of fit between the objects in contact, since a different verb is required depending whether the objects are brought into tight or loose contact (Choi, 1997). The English-speaking child, of course, remains oblivious to this feature of the scene.

Presumably English- and Korean-speaking children start out with the same potential to notice specific direction of movement *and* tightness of fit of objects. It is hard to see how any *semantic* cue could alert the child to the importance of these aspects of events for the purpose of talking about them. Nothing in the scene itself or in the speaker's focus of attention within the scene could spotlight the specific direction or the tightness of fit in the motion-and-contact event. If no semantic cue is available, *phonology* must be the trigger. Only their encounter with consistent phonological forms across different contexts could lead children to search for and register that feature which is significant in their language and attached to the phonological form for the event. Given the differences in English and Korean children's first references to motion events, this phonological trigger must be operating in the earliest stages of lexical acquisition.

It must continue to operate as children go on to acquire "grammatical" or "function" morphemes. Since languages vary dramatically in number and types of function morphemes, the child cannot know in advance which distinctions she should be looking to mark (see Slobin, 1985). The English-acquiring child cannot know that she should look for past and present tense markers; that she should notice the number of the subject in the case of the present tense but not the past; and that she need not notice the gender of the subject, as the Hebrew-acquiring child must. What could enable her to discover these facts about her language? The only available cue is phonology. She can only discover that past tense is marked in English if she notices the phonological variation in familiar form-meaning pairs (*walk/walked*, *laugh/laughed*), which will prompt her to "search" for the context in which that variation occurs—a temporal context. Likewise, she can only discover the marking of present tense and agreement if she notices the occurrence of -s with these same form-meaning pairs (*walk/walks, laugh/laughs*). But in this case, her discovery of the grammatical function depends on noticing not just the phonological form and temporal context. She must also notice semantic features of a syntactically related constituent—person and number of the head of the subject NP with which the inflected form occurs—which must themselves be phonologically cued.

Empirical support for the hypothesised role of phonology in their development comes from investigations into the effects of metrical factors on children's production of function morphemes. Gerken (1991, 1994) found that 2-year-olds' imitation of articles and pronouns depended on their position within a phonological phrase, echoing the metrical biases children show within words. When a weak function morpheme such as an article preceded a strong form, as in

> he KISSED / the DOG,

children were more likely to omit it than when it followed a strong form, as in

> MAX / KISSED the DOG.

This shows that children are using phonological cues to notice and/or organise their production of function words.

Phonological and semantic cues to syntax

The phonological processing which is necessary for lexical and morphological acquisition is also a prerequisite for discovering how sentences are structured in the input language. From the perspective of the mapping theory, the acquisition of syntax is more than the grafting of syntactic structure (of whatever theoretical persuasion) onto the material provided by lexical acquisition. Even the most primitive syntactic combinations, in the form of typical two-word utterances preserving the word order and/or inflectional markers of the input language, require the child to have registered substantial prosodic chunks and phonological details within these. In addition, the child must have registered the relation within the scene which word order or inflections mark. If we take such word combinations to be rudimentary syntactic forms, the acquisition of syntax originates in the child's ability to weld together a prosodic arrangement of familiar word forms and a relation observed between the referents of those word forms. This proposal is reminiscent of the functionalist model proposed by Bates and MacWhinney (1987), who "show how the native speaker learns to map phrasal configurations onto propositions, using the same learning principles and representational mechanisms needed to map single words onto their meanings" (p. 163). It is in keeping with the evidence presented by Tomasello and Brooks (1999) that children's early combinatorial patterns are lexically specific, occurring with particular predicative terms in what they describe as "verb island" constructions. What differentiates the present proposal is the specification of these constructions as pairings between a *prosodic arrangement of words* and a semantic relation between their referents.

The accumulation of such piecemeal pairings provides the material for abstracting "commonalities of both form and function" (Tomasello & Brooks)—in terms of the mapping theory, commonalities of prosodic-semantic mapping. It is the abstraction of these commonalities which leads to abstract syntactic categories such as "subject" and "object", and equips the child with both semantic bootstraps to verb-argument structure (Pinker, 1989) and syntactic bootstraps to verb meaning (Fisher et al., 1994). This may be illustrated by considering the acquisition of verbs such as "offer" and "accept", which convey alternative perspectives on the same event:

> The clown offered a cake to the dancer/The dancer accepted a cake from the clown.

If the child has registered the correlation between "entity focused as agent in an event" and "noun occupying prosodic slot before event word" (a rudimentary notion of subject in English), this can help her gain information about these verbs. She might notice that the speaker who uses "accept" is focused on the goal (dancer) rather than the source doing something, and use this as a semantic bootstrap, inferring that "accept" will take a goal argument as its subject. Alternatively, she might notice which noun argument (dancer) occupies the subject slot with "accept", and with the help of syntactic bootstrapping, infer that the verb conveys the event from the perspective of the goal argument. Experiments carried out by Pinker and Fisher et al. have shown that children as young as 3 and 4 can exploit both types of bootstrapping.

With semantic and syntactic bootstrapping, we have brought the child full circle. Mappings between semantic relations and abstract syntactic frames which are the *product* of earlier established lexical meanings and their combinations become the *means* of establishing the semantics of verbs and the syntactic frames in which they occur. In its totality, this conception of the emergence of syntax most closely resembles the coalition model developed by Hirsch-Pasek and Golinkoff (1996). According to this model, "Comprehension begins with a strong reliance on acoustics, moves to a reliance on coordinated input cues from syntax, prosody, extra-linguistic context, and semantics ... and culminates in a reliance mainly on syntax" (p. 198).

From the analysis of the mapping process to the phonological theory of SLI

In the above analysis of the mapping process, phonology has figured as a key player. The child's sensitivity to prosodic structure and the phonological detail within this was critical in the segmentation and hence storage of lexical units, the identification of their semantics, and the identification of their syntactic combination. The allegedly pivotal role of phonological processing in lexical and syntactic development is the catalyst for the phonological theory of SLI.

THE CASE FOR THE PHONOLOGICAL THEORY OF SLI

In a broad review of opposing theories of SLI, Joanisse and Seidenberg (1998) question whether SLI is a specifically grammatical deficit, and argue that grammatical impairments are "sequelae of information processing". The gist of their argument is

> that SLI is associated with impairments in the processing of speech; that these impairments affect the development of phonological representations; and that degraded phonological representations are the proximal cause of deviant acquisition of morphology and syntax, by virtue of their roles in learning and working memory. (p. 241)

According to Joanisse and Seidenberg, disruptions in aspects of grammatical development are the end of a chain which starts with abnormal speech perception.

In a similar spirit, the phonological theory of SLI claims that impairment in phonological processing disrupts the child's progress through the mapping process outlined above, with inevitable consequences for lexical and syntactic development. It is hypothesised that children with SLI have reduced access to the phonological details within rhythmic structures which are required for the establishment of lexical forms and syntactic structures. This implies that particular syllables, and/or vowels at the core of those syllables, and/or consonants which flank those vowels will be unavailable or unstable in the child's perception, storage and/or retrieval of rhythmic chunks. The hypothesised deficit might be expected to span all levels of phonological processing, with the deficit at each level feeding into and fed by the deficit at other levels in ways which change in the course of development (see Chiat & Hunt, 1993; Constable, Stackhouse, & Wells, 1997). However, the focus of the phonological theory is the pattern of linguistic deficit arising from the proposed impairment in phonological processing rather than the way in which the impairment spreads across different levels of phonological processing.

Predicted effects on the language of children with SLI

Difficulties with phonological processing which cannot be due to semantic or syntactic factors.   This may be evidenced by purely phonological errors in lexical output, and/or by poor performance in discrimination, judgement or repetition of auditory input.

Differential disruption of lexical, morphological and syntactic forms depending on the role phonology must play in cueing their semantics (see Black & Chiat, forthcoming).   Where the semantics of a target is close to a pre-linguistic perceptually based concept, as in the case of concrete nouns, it should be least affected. The more dependent a semantic representation is on phonological triggering, the less accessible it will be to the child. Accordingly, relational categories such as verbs and prepositions should be more difficult than concrete nouns. Within relational categories, we would expect differential difficulty, for example:

(i) Verbs referring to events which are directly observable, such as *fall, eat, open*, should be easier than verbs referring to events which are not observable, such as mental state verbs *think, dream, guess*. These mental state verbs should nevertheless be accessible: assuming that the child processes mental and emotional experiences in the same way as other people, the salience of these experiences should enable her to map an appropriate concept onto the corresponding verbs without recourse to their typically complex syntactic frame. The sentential complement they take, which could serve as a syntactic bootstrap to the verb's mental state meaning (as suggested by Fisher et al., 1994), entails phonological processing which would, by hypothesis, be an obstacle for children with SLI.

(ii) Aspects of verb meaning which do not correlate closely with experience and which can only be established through phonological and syntactic bootstrapping should be more problematic. This may result in the child acquiring aspects of a verb's meaning which can be derived from the interpretation of scenes in which it occurs, and missing other aspects. For example, the child may attach the verb *open* to certain visually distinctive events such as opening a door or a jar, and use it appropriately for those events, yet not have a generalised notion of *open* stretching across visually different events to which *open* can refer. Establishing the full meaning of *open* depends on phonological bootstrapping (noticing the sameness of the phonological form of *open* across different visually distinctive contexts in which it occurs). Likewise, the verb *give* may be attached to the observable change of possession, without establishing the perspective *give* takes on possession, which differentiates it from *take*. This depends on syntactic bootstrapping (noticing the position of participants in relation to the verb).

(iii) Temporal terms should be more difficult than terms relating to experience, whether of a perceptual, mental, emotional, or social nature.

This outline of predicted effects highlights a crucial point about the hypothesised deficit in phonological processing: its disruption of the mapping process through which semantic and syntactic structure grow. The predictions of the phonological theory as construed here are therefore quite distinct from a purely phonological hypothesis under which "all similar surface forms of the utterance must be affected in a similar way" (Gopnik & Crago, 1991). Under this interpretation, the forms *nose* and *bees* and *bee's* should be treated in just the same way, even though one is a simple noun, the second a noun+plural, and the third a noun+possessive. The phonological theory, rooted in a theory of the mapping process, makes no such prediction. On the contrary, it predicts differential difficulty with these forms depending how crucial phonology is to discovering their function (see also Leonard, 1998).

Differential disruption of lexical, morphological and syntactic forms depending on their phonological complexity, with phonological factors compounding the effects of semantic factors predicted above:

(i) Within a semantic category such as temporal terms, forms which are phonologically strong ("content" words) should be easier than those which are phonologically weak ("function" words and inflections). So, temporal adverbials *now, soon, yet* should be easier than syllabic aspectual inflections *-ing* and *-en*; these should in turn be easier than contracted forms of aspectual verbs *be* and *have* and sub-syllabic tense inflections *-ed* and *-s*.

(ii) In languages and contexts where these function words and inflections are phonologically more salient, they should be less vulnerable.

Beyond the mapping process: predicted effects on "thinking for speaking"

One observation which might be made about the predicted hierarchy of difficulty is that the aspects of language most at risk are those which are least crucial to the message conveyed, for example deictic distinctions marked by determiners, tense and aspect, and perspective distinctions marked by verb pairs such as *give* and *take.* It is possible to refer to things, events, states, and even times without these. Hence the commonplace description of some of these forms as having "little" or (misleadingly) "no" meaning.

This view of the more vulnerable items masks the role they play in our construction of meaning. When we use language to convey thoughts, we are forced to "think them for speaking" (Slobin, 1996): to shape our thoughts according to the categories of our language. The meaning distinctions selected by a particular language may, in some sense, be of little consequence for the meanings we can convey or the thoughts we can think. Children using English or Korean can put across events such as putting an apple in a bowl or a plug in the bath even if their languages demand different "takes" on these events. But in a different sense, marking of distinctions may be very important for meaning and thought. It may be the packaging of experience by language which allows us to represent, attend to, and manipulate experience in the ways what we do (Jackendoff, 1997). In this case, the effects of *different* linguistic packaging may be negligible, but the effects of *missing* linguistic packaging will not. A child who has difficulty with linguistic distinctions might then be expected to show difficulties beyond language itself, in the representation and manipulation of ideas.

Empirical evidence

Independent difficulties with phonology.   A variety of studies provide evidence of difficulties with phonology *per se.* These are apparent in children's performance on repetition tasks, where semantic and syntactic demands are eliminated or reduced. Gathercole and Baddeley's finding (1990) that language-impaired children have problems repeating non-words is particularly notable. This finding has been replicated by Bishop, North, and Donlan (1996) who observed deficits even in children whose language difficulties appeared to have resolved. Single case studies of language-impaired children's lexical processing have compared repetition of words and non-words with naming and spontaneous word production and have revealed similar levels and patterns of difficulty (Chiat & Hunt, 1993; Constable et al., 1997). If phonological processing were intact, and difficulties were due to particular grammatical features or categories, we would surely expect better performance in repetition than in naming and spontaneous production.

It may be that difficulties observed in repetition are themselves the product of more fundamental difficulties in processing auditory input. The work of Tallal and colleagues (Tallal, Merzenich, Miller & Jenkins, 1998; Tallal & Piercy, 1974; Tallal & Stark, 1981) has provided ample evidence that children with SLI are impaired in their ability to perceive rapidly changing acoustic information of a sort required to discriminate, recognise, and produce certain phonological contrasts, at least in their early years. The relationship between these limitations in verbal and non-verbal auditory perception and the limitations observed in their repetition is currently a matter of debate and investigation (see Bishop et al., 1999). Tallal et al. (1998) refer to the "cascading effects that rapid integration deficits have on phonological perception and production, the building blocks on which both oral and written language depend", but the specific nature of these effects is not pursued.

Auditory difficulties such as those observed by Tallal and colleagues are not necessarily the ultimate or sole source of phonological difficulties in SLI. The evidence which has accrued on infants' early phonological processing—their sensitivity to prosodic patterns, the vowels which carry these, and the statistical probabilities of co-occurring segments—points to further possibilities. Children with SLI may have reduced sensitivity to these aspects of speech input for reasons other than a deficit in processing rapid acoustic transitions. Nor are their problems necessarily exclusive to auditory input: they may equally arise in the storage and production of phonological forms. Analysis of individual children's lexical processing by Chiat and Hunt (1993) and Constable et al. (1997), for example, revealed difficulties with phonological representation and production which could not be wholly attributed to limitations in auditory input.

Whereas difficulties with phonology are predicted by the phonological theory, it is hard to see how grammatical theories of SLI could account for them. In their defence, it may be argued that phonological difficulties are irrelevant to their claim, on the grounds that evidence of an association between phonological and grammatical difficulties does not rule out the possibility that these may be dissociated at least in some cases. Evidence for just such a dissociation is put forward by Van der Lely, Rosen, and McClelland (1998). They present a profile of AZ, a young person with SLI, arguing that this provides evidence for "a discrete developmental grammatical language deficit" on the grounds that it reveals a range of grammatical impairments in production and comprehension alongside normal performance on auditory and cognitive tasks. However, the profile of AZ makes no reference to his phonology apart from the observation that his speech is "clear and without articulation errors". We therefore lack the evidence which would be necessary to rule out a phonological deficit. The phonological theory makes the strong prediction that careful probing of phonological processing in a subject such as AZ, whose difficulties appear to be purely grammatical, *would* reveal subtle problems with phonology (which may have been more acute at crucial stages of language development). These would emerge where efficient and effective phonological segmentation and storage are required, for example in non-word repetition and in "fast mapping" or "quick incidental learning" tasks. Though we have no relevant data for AZ, findings reported by Norbury, Bishop, and Briscoe (manuscript submitted for publication) lend some credibility to the prediction that non-word repetition would reveal problems. Their study of 20 children with SLI included syntactic tests which were instrumental in identifying AZ's specific grammatical impairment *and* the Children's Test of Non-word Repetition. Significantly, Norbury et al. found that even children who were very similar to AZ and might be taken to have a specific grammatical impairment demonstrated deficits in non-word repetition. It seems that their problems were not confined to grammar.

Relative difficulty of words.   Children with SLI have problems with words, and with the "fast mapping" and "quick incidental learning" entailed in their acquisition (Rice, Buhr, & Nemeth, 1990; Rice et al., 1994), but these problems affect some words more than others. According to Leonard (1998), "Verbs, in particular, begin to show deficiencies that seem to go beyond the general lag in these children's lexical abilities" (p. 44). Children with SLI have been found to use a more limited range of verbs than language-matched controls, despite showing no difference in their *overall* lexical diversity (Watkins, Rice, & Moltz, 1993). As predicted, the use of verbs is variable in a number of respects. The verb vocabularies of the children studied by Watkins et al. were not confined to particular semantic domains, nor particular syntactic categories. Children with SLI are likely to use verbs spanning actions and perceptible states and events, but also non-perceptual events such as *think*, *pretend* (see, for example, Chiat & Hirson, 1987). Furthermore, while they show verb omissions and substitutions which do not occur in language-matched controls, these are not consistent (Chiat, 2000; Rice & Bode, 1993). Children often produce in other contexts the very verb which would have been appropriate in the context of omission or substitution. These various findings suggest that verbs pose specific problems, and are more problematic in some contexts than others, as the phonological theory predicted. Since there has been little detailed investigation into the semantic scope of the verbs these children use, or the scope of meaning which they attach to those verbs, we await further evidence to evaluate more specific predictions about the vulnerability of different aspects of verb meaning.

Relative difficulty of grammatical morphemes and syntactic relations. Even more problematic than verbs are "grammatical morphemes":

"Grammatical difficulties are one of the most striking features in the expressive language of many children with SLI ... Typically one sees omission of grammatical inflections ..." (Bishop, 1997, p. 116). Disruption of temporal markers on verbs is particularly extreme: "... serious problems with tense and agreement can persist through the school years and even into adulthood" (Leonard, 1998, p. 223). In a study by Moore and Johnston (1993), children with SLI were found to be more delayed in their use of temporal inflections such as past tense than temporal adverbials such as *yesterday*, *last night*, *ago*: "In essence, the SLI children were more like the 3-year-olds in their morphological performance and more like the 4-year-olds in their lexical performance" (Moore & Johnston, 1993, p. 525). This disproportionate difficulty with phonologically weak temporal terms is again in keeping with the predictions of the phonological theory.

However, the persistence of such difficulties also lies behind certain current theories which attribute SLI to specific grammatical deficits. Gopnik and Crago (1991), for example, explain difficulties with tense and number in terms of "a selective impairment of that component of grammar that encodes abstract morphology" (p. 47). As a result of the inability to acquire "particular abstract morphological rules", forms inflected for tense and number can only be acquired lexically. In similar vein, Goad (1998) proposes that SLI grammar lacks certain sublexical features, such as [+plural], so that plural forms can only be acquired as compound forms in which the plural is a stem, or as unanalysed chunks.

The Extended Optional Infinitive hypothesis proposed by Rice, Wexler, and Cleave (1995) represents another grammatical account of problems with tense marking. According to this hypothesis, the normal Optional Infinitive stage is prolonged, and possibly even permanent, in children with SLI. One of the arguments for this account is that it provides an explanation not only for omission of tense, but for omission of *be* and *do* which serve only to carry tense. It is also claimed to account for the finding that tensed forms are not used incorrectly.

These grammatical accounts of SLI are motivated by and consistent with observed difficulties with grammatical morphology. In some cases, they predict patterns of difficulty which are substantiated by the data. But they have nothing to say about the many other linguistic difficulties and patterns in these difficulties which are typically observed in SLI. As others have pointed out (Ingham, Fletcher, Schelleter, & Sinka, 1998; Van der Lely, 1998), SLI is not confined to problems with sublexical features.

Van der Lely provides a grammatical account which does address the wider problems (Van der Lely, 1998; Van der Lely & Stollwerck, 1997). According to the Representational Deficit for Dependent Relationships (RDDR) which she proposes, children with "Grammatical SLI" have "a deficit with building nonelementary, complex dependencies" (p. 178) which lies in the syntactic computational system. The RDDR offers a unified explanation for the apparently disparate morphological and syntactic deficits which characterise Grammatical SLI. These include problems with tense marking, thematic role assignment, anaphoric and pronominal reference, wh-movement, and embedded structures. Since all these aspects of language are argued to involve complex dependencies, all are predicted to pose problems. Van der Lely works through each aspect accounting for the patterns of optional but correct marking of morphological distinctions; problems assigning thematic roles to arguments with novel verbs and to arguments in non-canonical sentence structures; incorrect and correct interpretation of anaphors; optional movement of wh; difficulties with object wh-questions and tense marking in wh-questions; limited elaboration of phrase structure. Ingham et al. (1998) put a similar case for problems with VPs which contain a resultative predication as a complement of the verb. The commonality between these apparently distinct structures is surely significant.

However, the phonological theory provides an alternative interpretation of this commonality. Ingham et al. hint at this when they allude to a "simpler encoding of the form-meaning relation" (p. 105) in accounting for preferred structures in SLI. The point is that long-distance or complex dependencies are characterised by just the features which the phonological theory predicted to be challenging for children with SLI:

    (i) They do not relate directly to non-verbal experience: they mark functions such as timing of events (tense), perspective on events (argument structure of verbs), alternative perspective on events (non-canonical organisation of arguments); co-reference (pronouns and reflexives). They are therefore dependent on phonology to trigger the "search" for the semantic-syntactic contexts in which they occur.

    (ii) Their phonology is demanding. Some are unstressed or sub-syllabic forms (tense, agreement); some entail phonology which extends beyond the word (verb-argument structure); some further entail relationships between elements which are phonologically separate (non-canonical structures including wh-structures).

The mapping process depends on a convergence between these phonologically challenging forms and the semantic/syntactic context in which they occur.

Patterns of error suggest that a purely grammatical account is not adequate to explain difficulties with these structures. O'Hara and Johnston (1997) provide a breakdown of errors in thematic role assignment made by children with SLI in a syntactic bootstrapping experiment. This required them to act out sentences containing novel verbs, for example:

The woman soogs the bunny
The bear gebs the boy to the woman.

O'Hara and Johnston found that 30% of the errors involved either selection of an incorrect object for one of the argument roles or omission of one of the objects, and that these selection and omission errors occurred on initial and medial NPs three times as often as on final NPs. They also note that more errors occurred on three-argument than two-argument items. They suggest that these recency and length effects point to a problem with processing load.

These conclusions are corroborated by another investigation of syntactic bootstrapping (Oetting, 1999). Presented with novel verbs in simple intransitive and transitive sentences which were embedded in a story, subjects with SLI were able to use the verb's syntactic structure as a cue to its meaning, performing no differently from age-matched or language-matched control groups. But this was only true when the child's interpretation of the verb was tested directly after presentation of the cue. When they were required to *retain* a syntactic cue until the middle or end of the story, and then interpret the verb, the scores of the children with SLI were below those of both control groups, and did not exceed chance. It looks as though, given phonologically and syntactically simple input (verbs taking a maximum of two arguments), children with SLI have little problem registering and using syntactic information as a bootstrap to a verb's meaning, but even here, they struggle to retain that information. We might predict that, if the stakes were raised by using three-place-predicates, or predicates whose syntactic frame conveys less perceptually salient information (such as event perspective), difficulties would show up even in immediate interpretation of the verb.

The conclusions from these syntactic bootstrapping tasks are supported by a study of a language-impaired child reported in Chiat (2000). The child was presented with a set of tasks designed to elicit production and repetition of verb-argument structures. His responses sometimes showed omission of verbs or arguments, or substitution with unintelligible weak forms. These omissions and substitutions occurred in tasks requiring description of acted-out and pictured events, but they were most frequent in a pure repetition task. In contrast, younger vocabulary-matched children virtually never made such omissions and substitutions, and their repetition was almost flawless. The nature of the errors made by the language-impaired child, and the fact that they were most acute in repetition, point to a problem with phonological overload which has repercussions for verb syntax.

Evaluation of a phonological account for other structures highlighted by Van der Lely awaits analysis of each in terms of the mapping processes entailed in their growth. The motivation for pursuing this line of inquiry is that the phonological theory embraces the wider pattern of impairment which is not addressed by the RDDR. The predicted effects of disruptions in phonological processing mesh tightly with the observed range and hierarchy of difficulties with words, morphological structure, and syntactic structure. The RDDR may be equally compatible with the range of syntactic and morphological difficulties observed, but does not predict their hierarchy. A further advantage of the phonological theory, identified above, is that it predicts difficulties with phonology which the RDDR does not. This advantage is reinforced by Norbury et al.'s finding that their SLI group's performance on the Children's Test of Non-word Repetition was not only poor, but was significantly correlated with performance on a range of syntactic and morphological tasks. It was also found that performance on tests of syntactic structures implicated in the RDDR was not as consistent as the RDDR would predict. Norbury et al. suggest that these findings are more compatible with a "non-modular account that stresses processing limitations" than with the RDDR, and propose that "the relationship of phonological memory and processing skills to syntactic comprehension requires further investigation". This conclusion accords closely with the phonological theory of SLI developed in this paper, and with the final evidence to be advanced in its support: the observation that grammatical difficulties are subject to phonological factors.

Effects of phonological factors on grammatical difficulties.   If problems with function morphemes were purely grammatical, we would not expect these to be influenced by phonological characteristics, yet they are. Following on from Gerken's findings with normally developing children, McGregor and Leonard (1994) predicted that omission of function words by children with SLI would be influenced by phonological factors, but not by their grammatical category. They compared imitation of two categories (pronouns *you* and *he* and article *the*) in phonological phrase-initial position, where they preceded a strong syllable:

the GIRL KISSED him / you BOTH KISSED him,

and phonological phrase-internal position, where they followed a strong syllable:

JEFF BUMPED the CAT / JEFF BUMPED you BOTH.

Their prediction was borne out by the data. Subjects with SLI made significantly more omissions than MLU-matched controls, but the *pattern* of their omissions was the same, showing the influence of stress pattern rather than syntactic category. Both subject groups omitted pronouns and articles more frequently in phonological phrase-initial position than in phonological phrase-internal position, but showed no difference between the two types of functions words. McGregor and Leonard conclude that "Complexity at the phonological level resulted in deficient use at the morpho-syntactic level" (p. 177).

The effects of phonological differences within a language are mirrored by the effects of phonological differences between languages. Extensive cross-linguistic research by Leonard and colleagues has revealed that particular grammatical categories are more affected in some languages than others (see Leonard, 1998). For example, Hebrew-speaking and Italian-speaking children with SLI do not show the disproportionate difficulty with tense marking which is observed in their English-speaking counterparts. It seems that the phonological or phonetic properties of the grammatical category are responsible for these cross-linguistic differences. The same grammatical category is easier in a language where it is stressed or post-stress, syllabic, and therefore of longer duration, than a language where it is pre-stress or sub-syllabic, and therefore of shorter duration. These findings led Leonard to propose his "surface account" which attributes problems with grammatical morphemes to their phonetic properties, particularly their relatively short duration. An alternative view is that these factors reflect the cues children use to segment and store morphological units, and constraints on the phonological segmentation and/or storage process in children with SLI.

Difficulties in thinking.   The evidence of studies presented so far has proved highly consistent with the profile of difficulties predicted by the phonological theory. But that profile was not confined to phonological, lexical, and grammatical difficulties. The importance of phonological and syntactic packaging of meaning for the structuring of thought led to the further prediction that impairments in language development would affect the development of thought. This appears at odds with the very definition of SLI: for a diagnosis of SLI, children must show normal performance on non-verbal tests of intelligence, which implies that thinking in children with SLI will be normal as long as it does not demand language which they do not possess.

But this criterion of normal IQ in any case presents something of a conundrum. According to Johnston (1992), "Children with specific language impairment are, by definition, children for whom the development of language and thought is out of phase" (p. 105), yet "Research over the past decade has revealed that children with specific language impairment do, in fact, show cognitive delays and deficits across a considerable range of tasks" (p. 113). Informal clinical observation suggests that children with SLI often misunderstand situations, are pragmatically inappropriate, and socially awkward, despite intellectual and social problems figuring among the exclusion criteria. Yet they are also felt to be "normal" socially and emotionally, despite their sometimes odd pragmatic and social behaviour.

Investigations by Johnston and her colleagues have exposed cognitive differences between children with SLI and normally developing children which cannot be attributed to differences in their language. In an experiment reported by Johnston, Smith, and Box (1997), a group of SLI children (with IQ in the average or superior range) and a group of normally developing controls were presented with a referential task requiring them to identify two objects from an array of three. The two objects shared size or colour or whole identity with each other, but not with the third object. The most sophisticated way to identify the targets is by means of a "Quantitative Grouping strategy". This requires the abstraction of the dimension or identity shared by the targets, permitting reference to them as a set: "the green ones" or "the big ones" or "the trees". Alternative strategies include, for example, use of deictics ("this one and that one"), and exhaustive description of each object ("a green big one and a green little one"). The striking finding was that the children with SLI were as successful as the controls in identifying the target objects, but they were less likely to use the Quantitative Grouping strategy to do so. Their reduced use of this strategy could not be attributed to their linguistic deficit, since they demonstrated knowledge of the required terms for virtually all items. Johnston et al. suggest that it is cognitive load that distinguishes the Quantitative Grouping strategy. By inference, the reason this strategy is particularly challenging for children with SLI is that they have reduced cognitive resources. The nature of their capacity limitation, Johnston et al. acknowledge, remains uncertain.

An appeal to Slobin's notion of "thinking for speaking" may offer a way forward. "Thinking for speaking" is not co-terminous with thinking in general. It refers to the structuring of mental representations in ways which are required by language, rather than to all forms of mental representation. Differentiation between "thinking for speaking" and other sorts of thinking may provide a basis for explaining the apparent paradox of children being diagnosed with *specific* language impairment, by exclusion of intellectual disturbance, yet showing limitations which cannot be directly attributed to language, such as those observed by Johnston et al. If "thinking for speaking" is required only for certain thought processes, disruptions in "thinking for speaking" could plausibly give rise to cognitive problems such as those we have observed, while sparing other thought processes such as those engaged by typical IQ tests. The resulting cognitive impairments may in turn affect some aspects of pragmatic and social development, yet spare others such as the development of emotional attachment and the construction of self and other. Detailed evaluation of these possibilities awaits more precise formulation of "thinking for speaking", allowing more precise hypotheses about thinking in SLI and its repercussions.

Ultimately, an understanding of "thinking for speaking" may enable us to clarify differences between children who *are* experienced as pragmatically "odd", and others who present with pragmatic behaviours which are odd, yet are experienced as "pragmatically normal"—in the terms of Bishop et al. (2000), children with Pragmatic Language Impairment (PLI) and children with SLI-Typical. Perhaps the SLI-Typical group have a deficit in "thinking for speaking", i.e., in the organisation of meaning entailed in linguistic representation, while the PLI group have a deficit in the interpretation of non-verbal experience itself. Behaviours resulting from these deficits may look similar and make differential diagnosis very tricky. The lived experience of the deficits, and at least some of their observable effects are surely quite distinct (see, for example, Bishop et al., 2000).

THE CASE SO FAR: EVIDENCE, IMPLICATIONS, PREDICTIONS, QUESTIONS

This paper set out with a logical argument that the acquisition of language is fundamentally a mapping process, and that constraints on this mapping process are the most plausible source of limitations in language acquisition. The logical case was substantiated with detailed evidence of what is entailed in the mapping process which highlighted the role of complex phonological processing in lexical and syntactic development. The phonological theory of SLI is rooted in these observations about the mapping process.

The predicted effects of a phonological deficit on the child's language were highly consistent with wide-ranging research findings on SLI. This favours the phonological theory over theories which address selected linguistic features and say little about observed difficulties which fall outside their scope. Theories postulating specific grammatical deficits, for example, offer no account for the complex patterns of problems in grammatical morphology and syntactic structure, and for problems observed in other domains. They are particularly hard pressed to account for evidence that children with SLI have independent difficulties with phonology, and for correlations that have been found between some measures of phonological and grammatical deficits. Such evidence challenges even a broad-range syntactic theory of SLI such as the RDDR.

It does not, however, rule out the possibility of a dissociation between these phonological and grammatical difficulties. Conclusive evidence of such a dissociation would undermine the phonological theory, since this identifies phonological difficulties as the source, rather than a typical concomitant, of grammatical difficulties. The phonological theory predicts that children alleged to have a purely grammatical deficit will manifest problems with phonology in tasks which demand fully intact phonological processing, for example in non-word repetition and "fast mapping" tasks. Conversely, it predicts that children alleged to have purely phonological difficulties in segmenting and storing words will manifest problems in tasks which demand high-level syntactic skills. The case for the phonological theory would be strengthened by evidence which, in line with these predictions, refuted alleged dissociations.

The novelty of the proposed phonological theory lies in the *specific* connections it makes between deficits in phonological processing and deficits in lexical and syntactic development. This differentiates it from a processing theory which attributes SLI to a general limitation in processing capacity. Studies which invoke a limited processing capacity rarely map out the path from the hypothesised limitation to the particular range of deficits observed in SLI. In contrast, the phonological theory proposed in this paper targets the *whole pattern of impairment*, and provides an account for many of the findings which have emerged from diverse studies of groups and individuals meeting the standard criteria for SLI.

This construal of SLI has significant implications for further research. The hypothesis that phonological processing is the problem leads to further questions about the nature of that problem and its ramifications. Some of these questions were anticipated in the initial formulation of the hypothesis. For example, is the difficulty with phonology due to more fundamental difficulties with temporal integration of acoustic information and possibly any rapid temporal integration (as in Tallal et al., 1998), or are these independent or otherwise related impairments? Findings that peripheral auditory processing problems are not sufficient to account for problems in the representation and production of lexical phonology in at least some children with SLI (Chiat & Hunt, 1993; Constable et al., 1997) point in the direction of a more extensive deficit affecting central and output phonological processing. However, this may vary between children. Do some children show problems which can be wholly attributed to peripheral input or output processing or to central processing, or does SLI entail deficits at all stages of phonological processing and if so, are these deficits interrelated? What is the nature of the hypothesised deficit in phonology? Does it affect prosodic structure itself, or is it confined to segmental details within the prosodic structure? Are some aspects of prosodic or segmental phonology more vulnerable than others? Do children show differences in the aspects of phonology affected and/or the degree of those effects, and do these correlate with other aspects of the child's language?

Predicted effects on semantic and syntactic development invite further investigation. Current evidence is too sparse to evaluate predicted strengths and weaknesses in the semantics and syntax of verbs. In order to determine, for example, whether components of verb meaning which correlate directly with non-verbal experience (for example mental state) are easier than those which do not (for example perspective on transactions) we will need to investigate comprehension and production of different types of verbs in carefully controlled contexts. Syntactic and semantic bootstrapping tasks could yield further insights if they employed verbs and verb frames associated with different types of events. Of particular interest would be those events which can be viewed from different perspectives, for example events of the give/take and fill/pour variety, where either the specific focus in the scene or the syntactic frame is crucial in determining the verb's perspective on the event.

The focus of this paper has been the hypothesised deficit in phonological processing and its effects on the mapping process in SLI. The wider mapping theory which introduced the paper predicts that other types of language impairment may occur as a result of deficits at other points in the mapping process. Allusion was made to the possibility that deficits in the interpretation of non-verbal experience, and hence in the interpretation of scenes, may lie at the root of Pragmatic Language Impairment. The analysis of the mapping process leads to predictions regarding the effects of disruption at this point in the mapping process. One such prediction is that children with PLI, unlike those with SLI, will have a normal capacity for phonological processing and will perform normally on purely phonological tasks even where the demands of the task are high, as in non-word repetition (though difficulties in understanding or co-operating in the task could be an obstacle to obtaining evidence). This in turn predicts that children should have the phonological wherewithal to segment and store phonological units. The hypothesis that the deficit arises in the interpretation of experience leads to questions about the aspects of experience which are limited or impaired; the range and severity of impairment in different children; the effects on the meanings which they attach to lexical and syntactic forms; and the relationship between the resulting deficits in linguistic meaning and deficits in pragmatic interaction.

The phonological theory of SLI and the wider mapping theory proposed in this paper have generated a range of further hypotheses and questions, some highly specified, some inviting tighter specification. These point towards further research which might give us better insights into the experience of language-impaired children and their potential: the kinds of thoughts they can think and the kinds of language into which they can put thoughts. The theories developed in this paper also open up new directions for research into intervention. The better we understand the connections between components of the mapping process, the better we can anticipate the benefits and limitations of interventions in the mapping process. For example, suppose that manipulation of auditory input is found to be effective, as suggested by Tallal et al. (1998). The mapping theory makes predictions about how such intervention will affect particular aspects of lexical and syntactic structure. Understanding these effects may influence selection of linguistic material to be targeted in such a programme.

This paper has presented a logical and empirical case for a mapping theory of developmental language impairment and its offspring phonological theory of SLI. It concludes with a different motivation for the proposed theories: their potential as a catalyst for research which is of theoretical interest and practical consequence.

REFERENCES

Aslin, R.N., Woodward, J.Z., LaMendola, N.P., & Bever, T.G. (1996). Models of word segmentation in fluent maternal speech to infants. In J.L. Morgan & K. Demuth (Eds.), *Signal to syntax: Bootstrapping from speech to grammar in early acquisition*, pp. 117–134. Mahwah, NJ: Lawrence Erlbaum Associates Inc.

Baldwin, D.A. (1995). Understanding the link between joint attention and language. In C. Moore & P.J. Dunham (Eds.), *Joint attention: Its origins and role in development*, pp. 131–158. Hillsdale, NJ: Lawrence Erlbaum Associates Inc.

Bates, E., & MacWhinney, B. (1987). Competition, variation, and language learning. In B. MacWhinney (Ed.), *Mechanisms of language acquisition*, pp. 157–193. Hillsdale, NJ: Lawrence Erlbaum Associates Inc.

Bishop, D.V.M. (1997). *Uncommon understanding: Development and disorders of language comprehension in children.* Hove, UK: Psychology Press.

Bishop, D.V.M., Bishop, S.J., Bright, P., James, C., Delaney, T., & Tallal, P. (1999). Different origin of auditory and phonological processing problems in children with language impairment: Evidence from a twin study. *Journal of Speech, Language, and Hearing Research, 42*, 155–168.

Bishop, D.V.M., Chan, J., Adams, C., Hartley, J., & Weir, F. (2000). Conversational responsiveness in specific language impairment: Evidence of disproportionate pragmatic difficulties in a subset of children. *Development and Psychopathology, 12*, 177–199.

Bishop, D.V.M., North, T., & Donlan, C. (1996). Nonword repetition as a behavioural marker for inherited language impairment: Evidence from a twin study. *Journal of Child Psychology and Psychiatry, 37*, 391–403.

Black, M., & Chiat, S. (Forthcoming). Putting thoughts into verbs: Developmental and acquired impairments. In W. Best, K. Bryan, & J. Maxim (Eds.), *Semantic processing: Theory and practice.* London: Whurr Publishers.

Bloom, L., & Lahey, M. (1978). *Language development and language disorders.* New York: John Wiley & Sons.

Carey, S. (1978). The child as word learner. In M. Halle, J. Bresnan, & G. Miller (Eds.), *Linguistic theory and psychological reality*, pp. 264–293. Cambridge, MA: MIT Press.

Chiat, S. (1979). The role of the word in phonological development. *Linguistics, 17*, 591–610.

Chiat, S. (2000). *Understanding children with language problems.* Cambridge: Cambridge University Press.

Chiat, S., & Hirson, A. (1987). From conceptual intention to utterance: A study of impaired language output in a child with developmental aphasia. *British Journal of Disorders of Communication, 22,* 37–64.

Chiat, S., & Hunt, J. (1993). Connections between phonology and semantics: An exploration of lexical processing in a language-impaired child. *Child Language Teaching and Therapy, 9,* 200–213.

Choi, S. (1997). Language-specific input and early semantic development: Evidence from children learning Korean. In D.I. Slobin (Ed.), *The crosslinguistic study of language acquisition,* Vol. 5, pp. 41–133. Hillsdale, NJ: Lawrence Erlbaum Associates Inc.

Clark, E.V. (1993). *The lexicon in acquisition.* Cambridge: Cambridge University Press.

Clark, E.V. (1997). Conceptual perspective and lexical choice in acquisition. *Cognition, 64,* 1–37.

Constable, A., Stackhouse, J., & Wells, B. (1997). Developmental word-finding difficulties and phonological processing: The case of the missing handcuffs. *Applied Psycholinguistics, 18,* 507–536.

Crystal, D. (1987). Towards a "bucket" theory of language disability: Taking account of interaction between linguistic levels. *Clinical Linguistics and Phonetics, 1,* 7–22.

Cutler, A. (1994). Segmentation problems, rhythmic solutions. *Lingua, 92,* 81–104.

Cutler, A. (1996). Prosody and the word boundary problem. In J.L. Morgan & K. Demuth (Eds.), *Signal to syntax: Bootstrapping from speech to grammar in early acquisition,* pp. 87–99. Mahwah, NJ: Lawrence Erlbaum Associates Inc.

Echols, C.H. (1996). A role for stress in early speech segmentation. In J.L. Morgan & K. Demuth (Eds.), *Signal to syntax: Bootstrapping from speech to grammar in early acquisition,* pp. 151–170. Mahwah, NJ: Lawrence Erlbaum Associates Inc.

Fisher, C., Hall, D.G., Rakowitz, S., & Gleitman, L. (1994). When it is better to receive than to give: Syntactic and conceptual constraints on vocabulary growth. *Lingua, 92,* 333–375.

Gathercole, S.E., & Baddeley, A.D. (1990). Phonological memory deficits in language disordered children: Is there a causal connection? *Journal of Memory and Language, 29,* 336–360.

Gerken, L.A. (1991). The metrical basis for children's subjectless sentences. *Journal of Memory and Language, 30,* 431–451.

Gerken, L.A. (1994). Young children's representation of prosodic phonology: Evidence from English-speakers' weak syllable productions. *Journal of Memory and Language, 33,* 19–38.

Gleitman, L.R., & Wanner, E. (1982). Language acquisition: The state of the state of the art. In E. Wanner & L.R. Gleitman (Eds.), *Language acquisition: The state of the art,* pp. 3–48. Cambridge: Cambridge University Press.

Goad, H. (1998). Plural in SLI: prosodic deficit or morphological deficit? *Language Acquisition, 7,* 247–284.

Gopnik, M., & Crago, M.B. (1991). Familial aggregation of a developmental language disorder. *Cognition, 39,* 1–50.

Hirsh-Pasek, K., & Golinkoff, R.M. (1996). *The origins of grammar: Evidence from early language comprehension.* Cambridge, MA: MIT Press.

Ingham, R., Fletcher, P., Schelleter, C., & Sinka, I. (1998). Resultative VPs and Specific Language Impairment. *Language Acquisition, 7,* 87–111.

Jackendoff, R. (1997). *The architecture of the language faculty.* Cambridge, MA: MIT Press.

Joanisse, M.F., & Seidenberg, M.S. (1998). Specific language impairment: A deficit in grammar or processing? *Trends in Cognitive Science, 2,* 240–247.

Johnston, J.R. (1992). Cognitive abilities of language-impaired children. In P. Fletcher & D. Hall (Eds.), *Specific speech and language disorders in children: Correlates, characteristics and outcomes,* pp. 105–116. London: Whurr Publishers.

Johnston, J.R., Smith, L.B., & Box, P. (1997). Cognition and communication: Referential strategies used by preschoolers with specific language impairment. *Journal of Speech, Language, and Hearing Research, 40,* 964–974.

Jusczyk, P.W., Cutler, A., & Redanz, N.J. (1993). Infants' preference for the predominant stress patterns of English words. *Child Development, 64,* 675–687.

Leonard, L.B. (1998). *Children with specific language impairment.* Cambridge, MA: MIT Press.

Markman, E.M. (1989). *Categorization and naming in children: Problems of induction.* Cambridge, MA: MIT Press.

McGregor, K.K., & Leonard, L.B. (1994). Subject pronoun and article omissions in the speech of children with specific language impairment. *Journal of Speech and Hearing Research, 37,* 171–181.

Mehler, J., Dupoux, E., Nazzi, T., & Dehaene-Lambertz, G. (1996). Coping with linguistic diversity: The infant's viewpoint. In J.L. Morgan & K. Demuth (Eds.), *Signal to syntax: Bootstrapping from speech to grammar in early acquisition,* pp. 101–116. Mahwah, NJ: Lawrence Erlbaum Associates Inc.

Moore, C., & Dunham, P.J. (1995). *Joint attention: Its origins and role in development.* Hillsdale, NJ: Lawrence Erlbaum Associates Inc.

Moore, M.E., & Johnston, J.R. (1993). Expressions of past time by normal and language-impaired children. *Applied Psycholinguistics, 4,* 515–534.

Morgan, J.L., & Saffran, J.R. (1995). Emerging integration of sequential and suprasegmental information in preverbal speech segmentation. *Child Development, 66,* 911–936.

Morgan, J.L., Shi, R., & Allopenna, P. (1996). Perceptual bases of rudimentary grammatical categories: Toward a broader conceptualization of bootstrapping. In J.L. Morgan & K. Demuth (Eds.), *Signal to syntax: Bootstrapping from speech to grammar in early acquisition,* pp. 263–283. Mahwah, NJ: Lawrence Erlbaum Associates Inc.

Norbury, C.F., Bishop, D.V.M., & Briscoe, J. (Manuscript submitted for publication). Does impaired grammatical comprehension provide evidence for an innate grammar module?

Oetting, J.B. (1999). Children with SLI use argument structure cues to learn verbs. *Journal of Speech, Language, and Hearing Research, 42,* 1261–1274.

O'Hara, M., & Johnston, J. (1997). Syntactic bootstrapping in children with specific language impairment. *European Journal of Disorders of Communication, 32,* 189–205.

Peters, A. (1983). *The units of language acquisition.* Cambridge: Cambridge University Press.

Pinker, S. (1989). *Learnability and cognition: The acquisition of argument structure.* Cambridge, Mass: MIT Press.

Rice, M.L., & Bode, J.V. (1993). GAPS in the verb lexicons of children with specific language impairment. *First Language, 13,* 113–131.

Rice, M.L., Buhr, J.C., & Nemeth, M. (1990). Fast mapping word learning abilities of language-delayed preschoolers. *Journal of Speech and Hearing Disorders, 55,* 33–42.

Rice, M.L., Oetting, J.B., Marquis, J., Bode, J., & Pae, S. (1994). Frequency of input effects on word comprehension of children with specific language impairment. *Journal of Speech and Hearing Research, 37,* 106–122.

Rice, M.L., Wexler, K., & Cleave, P.L. (1995). Specific language impairment as a period of Extended Optional Infinitive. *Journal of Speech and Hearing Research, 38,* 850–863.

Saffran, J.R., Aslin, R.N., & Newport, E.L. (1996). Statistical learning by 8-month-old infants. *Science, 274,* 1926–1928.

Saffran, J.R., Newport, E.L., & Aslin, R.N. (1996). Word segmentation: The role of distributional cues. *Journal of Memory and Language, 35,* 606–621.

Slobin, D.I. (1973). Cognitive prerequisites for the acquisition of grammar. In C.A. Ferguson & D.I. Slobin (Eds.), *Studies of child language development,* pp. 175–208. New York: Holt, Rinehart & Winston.

Slobin, D.I. (1985). Crosslinguistic evidence for the language-making capacity. In D.I. Slobin (Ed.), *The crosslinguistic study of language acquisition*, Vol. 2, pp. 1157–1256. Hillsdale, NJ: Lawrence Erlbaum Associates Inc.

Slobin, D.I. (1996). From "thought and language" to "thinking for speaking". In J. Gumperz & S.C. Levinson (Eds.), *Rethinking linguistic relativity*, pp. 70–95. Cambridge: Cambridge University Press.

Snow, C.E. (1995). Issues in the study of input: Finetuning, universality, individual and developmental differences, and necessary causes. In P. Fletcher & B. MacWhinney (Eds.), *The handbook of child language*, pp. 180–193. Oxford: Blackwell.

Tallal, P., Merzenich, M.M., Miller, S., & Jenkins, W. (1998). Language learning impairments: Integrating basic science, technology, and remediation. *Experimental Brain Research, 123*, 210–219.

Tallal, P., & Piercy, M. (1974). Developmental aphasia: Rate of auditory processing and selective impairment of consonant perception. *Neuropsychologia, 12*, 83–93.

Tallal, P., & Stark, R.E. (1981). Speech acoustic-cue discrimination abilities of normally developing and language-impaired children. *Journal of the Acoustical Society of America, 69*, 568–574.

Tomasello, M. (1995). Joint attention as social cognition. In C. Moore & P.J. Dunham (Eds.), *Joint attention: Its origins and role in development*, pp. 103–130. Hillsdale, NJ: Lawrence Erlbaum Associates Inc.

Tomasello, M., & Brooks, P.J. (1999). Early syntactic development: A construction approach. In M. Barrett (Ed.), *The development of language*, pp. 161–190. Hove, UK: Psychology Press.

Tomasello, M., & Kruger, A.C. (1992). Joint attention on actions: Acquiring verbs in ostensive and non-ostensive contexts. *Journal of Child Language, 19*, 311–333.

Tomasello, M., Strosberg, R., & Akhtar, N. (1996). Eighteen-month-old children learn words in non-ostensive contexts. *Journal of Child Language, 23*, 157–176.

Van der Lely, H.K.J. (1998). SLI in children: Movement, economy, and deficits in the computational-syntactic system. *Language Acquisition, 7*, 161–192.

Van der Lely, H.K.J., Rosen, S., & McClelland, A. (1998). Evidence for a grammar-specific deficit in children. *Current Biology, 8*, 1253–1258.

Van der Lely, H.K.J., & Stollwerck, L. (1997). Binding theory and specifically language impaired children. *Cognition, 62*, 245–290.

Watkins, R.V., Rice, M.L., & Moltz, C.C. (1993). Verb use by language-impaired and normally developing children. *First Language, 13*, 133–143.

LANGUAGE AND COGNITIVE PROCESSES, 2001, *16* (2/3), 143–176

Past tense formation in Williams syndrome

Michael S.C. Thomas, Julia Grant, Zita Barham,
Marisa Gsödl, Emma Laing and Laura Lakusta
Neurocognitive Development Unit, Institute of Child Health, London, UK

Lorraine K. Tyler
*Department of Experimental Psychology, University of Cambridge,
Cambridge, UK*

Sarah Grice, Sarah Paterson and Annette Karmiloff-Smith
Neurocognitive Development Unit, Institute of Child Health, London, UK

It has been claimed that in the language systems of people with Williams
syndrome (WS), syntax is intact but lexical memory is impaired. Evidence
has come from past tense elicitation tasks with a small number of participants
where individuals with WS are said to have a specific deficit in forming
irregular past tenses. However, typically developing children also show
poorer performance on irregulars than regulars in these tasks, and one of the
central features of WS language development is that it is delayed. We
compared the performance of 21 participants with WS on two past tense
elicitation tasks with that of four typically developing control groups, at ages
6, 8, 10, and adult. When verbal mental age was controlled for, participants in
the WS group displayed no selective deficit in irregular past tense
performance. However, there was evidence for lower levels of generalisation
to novel strings. This is consistent with the hypothesis that the WS language
system is delayed because it has developed under different constraints,
constraints that perhaps include atypical phonological representations. The

Requests for reprints should be addressed to Michael Thomas or Annette Karmiloff-Smith,
Neurocognitive Development Unit, Institute of Child Health, 30, Guilford Street, London
WC1N 1EH, UK. Email: M.Thomas@ich.ucl.ac.uk or a.karmiloff-smith@ich.ucl.ac.uk

We would like to express our appreciation to the Williams Syndrome Foundation, UK, for
their generous help in putting us in touch with families whom we warmly thank for their
participation in this research. Thanks also to Dorothy Bishop and Marc Joanisse for helpful
comments on an earlier draft on this paper. This research was supported by MRC Programme
Grant No. G9715642 to Annette Karmiloff-Smith.

http://www.tandf.co.uk/journals/pp/01690965.html   DOI: 10.1080/01690960042000021

results are discussed in relation to dual-mechanism and connectionist computational models of language development, and to the possible differential weight given to phonology versus semantics in WS development.

INTRODUCTION

Williams syndrome (WS) is a rare neurodevelopmental disorder occurring in approximately 1 in 20,000 live births (Morris, Demsey, Leonard, Dilts, & Blackburn, 1988). It is caused by a micro-deletion on one copy of chromosome 7 (Tassabehji et al., 1999) and results in specific physical, cognitive, and behavioural abnormalities (Karmiloff-Smith, 1998; Mervis, Morris, Bertrand & Robinson, 1999). The syndrome has been of particular interest to cognitive scientists because individuals with WS exhibit an uneven cognitive-linguistic profile together with mild to moderate mental retardation (Howlin, Davies, & Udwin, 1998; Mervis et al., 1999). Thus Udwin and Yule (1990) found that 54% of their sample of 43 WS participants had a full-scale intelligence quotient (IQ) of ≤ 50 and 42% had an IQ between 51–70. However, in general the full-scale IQ score in WS masks differences in specific cognitive abilities. The syndrome is often characterised as one where verbal abilities are superior to visuospatial abilities (Mervis et al., 1999), although in both areas performance is below that expected for chronological age. This pattern of uneven abilities may be one that emerges and increases over the course of development (Jarrold, Baddeley, & Hewes, 1998; Bellugi, Lichtenberger, Mills, Galaburda, & Korenberg, 1999). The uneven profile extends to other abilities. Thus while individuals with WS often perform within the normal range on standardised tests for face recognition (Bellugi, Wang, & Jernigan, 1994), and show relatively good performance on theory of mind tasks (Karmiloff-Smith, Klima, Bellugi, Grant, & Baron-Cohen, 1995), they exhibit difficulties in numerical cognition (Karmiloff-Smith et al., 1995), and in problem solving and planning (Bellugi, Marks, Bihrle, & Sabo, 1988).

The uneven cognitive profile found in WS has been of interest because it promises to offer the potential to identify developmental *fractionations* in the cognitive system. For example, given limitations in general cognition, the largely successful acquisition of language might be taken as evidence of the developmental independence of language from cognition (see Mervis & Bertrand, 1997; Rossen, Bihrle, Klima, Bellugi, & Jones, 1996). A similar argument might be made for the developmental independence of face recognition from spatial cognition. Given the standard assumption that the adult cognitive system has a modular structure and that WS has a genetic origin, there is an additional temptation to link dissociations in the cognitive abilities of adults with WS with damage to or sparing of innate cognitive modules. This approach attempts to extend the logic of adult neuropsychology in which patterns of adult brain damage are taken to reveal (under some circumstances) the functional modules comprising the cognitive system. When extended to developmental disorders that have a genetic basis, the implication is that deficits in the endstate behaviour of individuals will reveal the *innate* modular structure of the cognitive system (see e.g., Baron-Cohen, 1998; Temple, 1997). In this paper we will seek to question whether the adult brain damage model is indeed appropriate for characterising behavioural deficits found in developmental disorders. To do so, we will examine a specific example, that of the acquisition of past tense formation in Williams syndrome.

WS and SLI: a double dissociation of innate mechanisms?

Williams syndrome has been used to support the presence of innate structure in the normal language system. This innate structure supposes the existence of two sorts of mechanism, a computational, syntactic, rule-based mechanism responsible for learning the abstract rules of grammar, and an associative memory system responsible for learning information about individual words (Pinker, 1991, 1994, 1999). We will refer to this as the dual-mechanism account, by which we specifically mean a model with one rule-based mechanism and one associative mechanism. (It is of course possible to have dual-mechanism accounts where both mechanisms are rule-based or both are associative. Debates about the quantity of mechanisms are orthogonal to those about the nature of those mechanisms.) Pinker (1991) proposed that Specific Language Impairment (SLI) and Williams syndrome together provide a developmental double dissociation between these two language mechanisms. SLI is a developmental disorder in which impairments are found in language in the absence of any apparent cognitive, social, or neurological deficits. In addition, there is a genetic component to this disorder (Bishop, North, & Donlan, 1995). Referring to evidence from Gopnik and Crago (1991), Pinker proposed that people with SLI have an impairment to the syntactic, rule-based device, but that their ability to memorise words is intact. Citing evidence from Bellugi, Bihrle, Jernigan, Trauner, and Doherty (1990), he further proposed that in Williams syndrome, there is a "selective sparing of syntax, and grammatical abilities are close to normal in controlled testing" (p. 479), but that there is an impairment to the associative memory mechanism such that individuals "retrieve words in a deviant fashion" (ibid.). In short, we have the claim that the two mechanisms can be dissociated because they can independently fail in two distinct developmental disorders, forming, as Pinker describes it, a "genetic double dissociation" (1999, p. 262).

Much of the behavioural evidence behind this proposal comes from performance on forming the English past tense. The English past tense is characterised by a rule in which the past tense of a verb is formed by adding the suffix -ed to the verb stem (e.g., talk-talked). However, there is also a minority of verbs which form their past tense in different ways (e.g., go-went, think-thought, hit-hit). These irregular or exception verbs often fall into clusters sharing a family resemblance (e.g., sleep-slept, creep-crept, leap-leapt). The English past tense is important for Pinker's dual-mechanism theory, since performance on the regular and irregular past tense formations are taken to directly index, respectively, the functioning of the rule-based and associative mechanisms. Pinker's claims about SLI and WS then translate into the following empirical predictions: (1) we should expect individuals with SLI to show a selective deficit in forming regular past tenses but not irregular past tenses; (2) we should expect individuals with WS to show a selective deficit in forming irregular past tenses but not regular past tenses. Recent work has sought to address these claims in detail.

SLI: deficit on regulars but not irregulars?

Van der Lely and Ullman (this issue) have examined English past tense formation in a sample of children with "grammatical" SLI. SLI is a heterogeneous disorder (Aram, Morris, & Hall, 1993) which may have a number of underlying causes. Van der Lely and Stollwerck (e.g., van der Lely, 1997; van der Lely & Stollwerck, 1996) have identified a subgroup of children with SLI based on behavioural measures, such that their predominant deficit is restricted to grammatical abilities. Van der Lely claims that, at least for this subgroup, their disorder can be characterised as a "primary deficit in the computational syntactic (grammatical) system" (van der Lely, 1998). Van der Lely and Ullman found that in a past tense elicitation task, the children with SLI predominantly responded by reproducing the stem without marking it, accounting for approximately 65% of all responses. In terms of correct performance, the children with SLI showed no advantage of regular over irregular verbs which, compared to controls, represented a greater deficit on regulars than irregulars. Lastly, they found frequency effects in the performance of the SLI group on regular verbs, an affect normally confined to irregular verbs. On the assumption that Pinker's dual-mechanism model is correct, van der Lely and Ullman took these results as supporting the view that in grammatical SLI, the rule-based mechanism is impaired but the associative memory is intact. Although the children with SLI provided some correct regular past tense items, these were taken as reflecting compensatory activity of the associative memory. Frequency effects are taken as a hallmark of such an associative system. Van der Lely and Ullman thus interpreted the frequency effects found in regular past tense formation as an indication that, in the absence of a rule-based mechanism, all past tenses were being treated as exceptions (see also Ullman & Gopnik, 1999).

Williams syndrome: deficit on irregulars but not regulars?

Clahsen and Almazan (1998) recently examined the performance of four children with WS (aged 11;2 to 15;4) on a range of grammatical tasks. These included an analysis of expressive language in story telling, a test of comprehension of active and passive sentences, a test of the comprehension of sentences using syntactic binding in referential dependencies between anaphoric elements, a test of inflection morphology (English past tense formation), and a test of derivational morphology (past tense formation for normal and denominal irregular verbs). The analysis of expressive language showed that the performance of the WS group was appropriate for their mental age (as measured by their overall scores on the Wechsler Intelligence Scale for Children-III; Wechsler, 1992), and that their language comprised complex syntactic structures and grammatical morphemes that were almost always correct. Performance of participants with WS on the particular tests used for passives and syntactic binding was at ceiling.

Clahsen and Almazan used the same past tense elicitation procedure as van der Lely and Ullman so the results are directly comparable. Their results pointed to a selective deficit in irregular past tense formation in two individuals with WS with mental ages (MA) of 5 years and two individuals with WS with MA of 7 years compared to MA-matched control groups. They concluded that the individuals with WS had an impaired associative memory mechanism, citing as evidence the fact these participants *irregularised* novel verbs which rhymed with existing irregular verbs (e.g., *crive-crove*, *drive-drove*) at a much lower rate than their controls. Thus participants with WS "seemed to be impaired (relative to controls) in associating phonological patterns of novel verbs to corresponding strings of existing irregular verbs" (p. 193). On the assumption that Pinker's dual-mechanism model is correct, Clahsen and Almazan concluded that in Williams syndrome, the "computational system for language is selectively spared yielding excellent performance on syntactic tasks and on regular inflection, whereas the lexical system and/or its access mechanisms required for irregular inflection are impaired" (ibid.). Their results on inflectional morphology in WS are in line with previous unpublished data for six participants with WS presented by Bromberg, Ullman, Coppola, Marcus, Kelley, and Levin (1994).

Problems with existing WS past tense data

There are two serious problems with the current data on inflection morphology in Williams syndrome. Firstly, *typically* developing children usually show poorer performance on irregular verbs than regular verbs (with the exception of the very early stages of language development where vocabulary size is small) (Bybee and Slobin, 1982; see also van der Lely & Ullman, this issue). One of the most salient characteristics of language development in Williams syndrome is that it is delayed (Mervis et al., 1999; Singer Harris, Bellugi, Bates, Jones, & Rossen, 1997; Thal, Bates, & Bellugi, 1989). Therefore, to show a selective deficit in irregular past tense formation in individuals with WS, it is not enough to demonstrate that irregular past tense formation is poorer than regular past tense formation. Rather, it must be shown that their level of past tense formation is poorer than we would expect *given their level of language development.* In the unpublished data of Bromberg et al. (1994), no such comparison is possible since participants with WS were only roughly matched to normal controls. While the comparison is possible for the Clahsen and Almazan data, their study only comprised four individuals with WS, and even for these, the data appear fairly noisy. For example, for irregular verbs, the two individuals with MA of 5 scored 14% correct on irregular verbs compared to the 57% correct scored by the two individuals with MA of 7. And when performance on irregulars was re-tested as a control condition in the derivational morphology task, the MA-5 individuals now scored 44% correct. On the evidence of this study alone, one cannot be confident that the apparent deficit on irregular verbs in the WS group is any more than a consequence of delayed language development.

Secondly, Clahsen and Almazan note a marked difference between the WS and control groups in how willing they were to extend patterns of irregular past tense formation to novel items (e.g., *crive-crove*). Levels of irregularisation were much lower in the WS group and they took this as revealing an impairment to lexical associative memory. However, the control data Clahsen and Almazan used in this comparison look very different to those collected by van der Lely and Ullman (2000) on exactly the same task. Clahsen and Almazan's two control groups irregularised novel rhymes at rates of 68% and 75%. Van der Lely and Ullman's groups, of a similar age, irregularised novel rhymes at levels of 10%, 9%, and 10%. These latter levels are much closer to the rates that Clahsen and Almazan reported for their WS group. Thus the apparent deficit shown by the WS group would seem to depend crucially on the true level of novel irregularisation in the normal population at an equivalent level of language development.

In our study, we set out to rectify these problems in order to establish whether the performance of individuals with WS in irregular past tense formation is indeed reliably poorer than would be expected for their level of language development. We did this in three ways. Firstly, we examined a much larger sample of participants with WS than the Clahsen and Almazan study. Secondly, we sought to build a normal developmental profile of performance on this particular task against which we could compare the performance of the WS group. To do so, we tested four groups of control participants, aged 6, 8, 10, and adult. Thirdly, we employed an additional past tense elicitation task to explore whether any features of the Clahsen and Almazan results were due to particular features of the task they used.

The second elicitation task was developed for use with patients with brain damage by Lorraine Tyler and William Marslen-Wilson. This task does not require participants to repeat sentences and instead provides them with the initial sound of the past tense form. Consequently, it may be seen as having a lower memory load. In addition, it employed a set of regular and irregular verbs three times as large as that used in the Clahsen and Almazan (1998) study. This larger set of verbs allowed us to explore underlying factors in the elicitation task, such as the role of verb frequency and verb imageability in past tense formation. We have already seen that frequency effects have been taken as a hallmark of lexical associative processing. Evidence of effects of imageability, a semantic dimension differing across verbs, could also be taken to implicate lexical memory in the operation of the grammatical process of past tense formation.

Two contrasting hypotheses were tested in the current study. The first represents the Pinker/Clahsen and Almazan position: Individuals with Williams syndrome show a specific deficit in irregular past tense formation. Thus if one controls for language ability, one should expect performance on regulars to be the same for the WS and control groups. On the other hand, one should expect performance on irregular verbs to be lower for the WS group than the control group. With novel items, one should expect performance on regularising novel words which do not rhyme with any existing irregular verb to be the same as controls (e.g., *stoff-stoffed*). On the other hand, one should expect performance on irregular rhyming novel verbs to be different from controls. Perhaps the WS group might show less irregularisation (e.g., *crive-crove*), in keeping with the hypothesis of an impaired associative mechanism, or more regularisation, in keeping with the hypothesis of a preserved rule-based mechanism (e.g., *crive-crived*).

The alternative hypothesis suggests that poor performance on irregular past tense formation in WS is a marker of their delayed language development. If one controls for level of language ability, performance on regulars and irregulars should be the same in participants with WS and controls. One should find a similar pattern in performance on novel items.

METHOD

Participants were tested on two tasks, both of which were designed to elicit past tense verb forms but which imposed somewhat different demands on memory. Task 1 was adapted from Ullman (1993), Ullman et al. (1997), and Clahsen and Almazan (1998). Task 2 was developed by Tyler and Marslen-Wilson.

Participants

Twenty-one children and adults with WS, 12 male and 9 female, were recruited through the Williams Syndrome Foundation UK to take part in this and other studies. Mean chronological age was 22;8 (range 10;11–53;3). Mean General Cognitive Ability (GCA; IQ equivalent as assessed by the British Abilities Scale II) was 45, (range 39 (floor)–73).

Three groups of typically developing children were also tested, with five boys and five girls in each group. Their mean ages were as follows: 5–6-year-olds = 6;0 (range 5;5–6;40), 7–8-year-olds = 8;1 (range 7;8–8;5), 9–10-year-olds = 9;10 (range 9;6–10;6). These children attended a North London primary school. A group of 16 normal adult controls were recruited by means of notices placed at Great Ormond Street Hospital and in a local community centre. Ten males and six females took part in the study, with a mean age of 30;5 (range 17;3–45;0). Participants in all groups were drawn from a range of socio-economic classes.

Materials

Task 1.   Fifty-six sentence pairs were constructed according to the form illustrated in the following two examples:

(1) *Every day I slam a door*
    Just like every day, yesterday I .... *a door*
(2) *Every day I swim in the pool*
    Just like every day, yesterday I .... *in the pool*

The verbs in these sentences were those used by Clahsen and Almazan (1998). Existing regular and irregular verbs were matched for frequency and familiarity (see van der Lely & Ullman, this issue). The stimulus set is shown in Table 1. It included 16 existing regular verbs, 14 existing irregular verbs, 12 novel verbs with stems which did not rhyme with any existing irregular verbs, and 14 novel verbs which rhymed with existing irregulars.

TABLE 1
Stimulus sets for the two past tense elicitation tasks

	Task 1			Task 2			
Regular verbs	Irregular verbs	Non-rhyme novel items	Irregular-rhyme novel items*	Regular verbs		Irregular verbs	
scowl	swim	spuff	strink (strunk)	kick	laugh	stick	shrink
tug	dig	dotch	frink (frunk)	croak	help	creep	sing
flush	swing	stoff	strise (strose)	climb	mix	mislead	draw
mar	wring	cug	crive (crove)	stay	shave	shake	learn
chop	bend	trab	shrell (shrelt)	balance	agree	deal	keep
flap	bite	crog	vurn (vurnt)	dance	drag	begin	meet
stalk	feed	vask	steeze (stoze)	trim	leak	bleed	come
scour	make	brop	shrim (shram)	chase	stop	choose	grow
slam	give	satch	cleed (cled)	graze	call	leap	ring
cross	think	grush	sheel (shelt)	share	raise	cling	dream
rush	stand	plam	blide (blid)	walk	move	sting	shine
rob	keep	scur	prend (prent)	fix	shove	hang	lose
drop	drive		shreep (shrept)	bless	save	weep	drink
look	send		drite (drote)			feed	
stir							
soar							

*possible irregularisation shown in parentheses.

In order to optimise the enunciation and audibility of past tense endings produced by participants, each verb was followed by a noun phrase or prepositional phrase whose first word began with a vowel (the past tense verb ending in a sentence such as *Yesterday I robbed a bank*, whose verb is followed by a word starting with a vowel, is often more full articulated and/or more audible than in a sentence such as *Yesterday I robbed the bank*, where a consonant follows the verb ending).

Fourteen pairs of practice sentences were also constructed, using the same format as the test sentences. These incorporated six irregular verbs, four regular verbs, and four novel verbs with stems which did not rhyme with any existing irregular verbs.

Task 2. In this task, participants received the initial phoneme of the past tense form as a cue. The stimuli consisted of 53 sentences, each paired with an incomplete sentence, for example:

(1) *The bull sometimes kicks.*
   Yesterday, it k..........
(2) *Maggie always hangs the pictures.*
   Last time, she h..........

Twenty-six regular verbs and 27 irregular verbs were used in the test sentences. These were matched for frequency and imageability. Two practice sentences were constructed using irregular verbs.

Standardised tests

The participants with WS were also tested on the British Picture Vocabulary Scale (BPVS; Dunn et al., 1982) and seven subtests of the British Abilities Scales II (BAS–II; Elliott, 1996), namely Recall of Designs, Pattern Construction, Word Definitions, Verbal Similarities, Matrices, Quantitative Reasoning and Recall of Digits Forward. Table 2 shows the individual participant scores for chronological age, BPVS, General Cognitive Ability (GCA) from BAS (a composite score based on

TABLE 2
Ages and standardised test results of participants with Williams syndrome

Subject	Chronological Age	BAS General Cognitive Ability	BPVS test age	Verbal MA (BAS subtests)	Spatial MA (BAS subtests)	Non-verbal MA (BAS subtests)
		(Floor 39)	(Floor 1;8, ceiling 19;6)	(Floor 5;0, ceiling 18;0)	(Floor 5;0, ceiling 18;0)	(Floor 5;0, ceiling 18;0)
1*	10;11	44	5;2	5;10	5;0	5;4
2	11;1	48	6;8	6;9	5;0	6;2
3	11;3	46	9;3	7;11	5;10	8;2
4	11;5	44	5;3	5;7	5;0	6;2
5	11;7	47	9;0	7;0	5;1	7;0
6*	12;6	39	5;2	5;0	5;0	5;0
7	12;9	54	8;1	8;6	5;4	7;3
8	13;11	46	5;5	7;3	5;1	7;4
9	14;4	41	8;0	7;9	5;4	6;4
10	15;6	39	8;1	6;9	5;4	5;6
11	18;7	40	8;9	6;6	6;9	6;9
12*	19;3	39	5;0	5;0	5;0	5;0
13	20;10	39	8;4	6;10	5;0	5;2
14	21;8	39	7;1	6;12	5;0	5;0
15	27;6	39	8;8	6;10	5;6	5;0
16	30;3	39	15;4	7;4	5;2	6;7
17	30;8	51	15;7	13;9	6;7	7;2
18	34;9	39	7;10	6;4	5;0	5;0
19	42;9	73	19;6	16;5	8;9	10;6
20	50;11	50	13;11	13;0	5;4	7;11
21	53;3	39	14;3	9;0	5;2	6;1
Mean	22;8	44	9;7	7;11	6;5	5;6

* Starred participants were unable to complete the past tense elicitation tasks.
BAS, British Abilities Scale; BPVS, British Picture Vocabulary Scale; MA, mental age

performance on the first six subtests listed above), as well as subscores for verbal mental age, spatial mental age, and non-verbal mental age derived from the BAS (Verbal = mean of Word Definitions and Verbal Similarities; spatial = mean of Recall of Designs and Pattern Construction; non-verbal = mean of Matrices, Quantitative Reasoning and Recall of Digits Forward). The three starred participants in Table 2 were unable to complete the elicitation tasks. The verbal subscore test age was significantly higher than both non-verbal and spatial test ages (7;11 vs. 6;5, $t = 3.42$, df = 20, $p = .003$; 7;11 vs. 5;6, $t = 4.75$, df = 20, $p < .001$). Finally, non-verbal test age was significantly higher than spatial (6;5 vs. 5;6, $t = 4.48$, df = 20, $p < .001$). Thus our sample of participants with WS reflects the usual pattern, with verbal abilities superior to visuospatial abilities.

Design and procedure

The participants with WS and adult controls were tested at the Neurocognitive Development Unit in London. One experimenter introduced the tasks and presented the stimuli while two experimenters noted the participants' responses. All sessions were audio tape-recorded using a DAT recorder. The child controls were seen by two experimenters at their school. One experimenter administered the task while the other wrote down the responses. Since one of the aims of the study was to replicate the results obtained by Clahsen and Almazan (1998), their task was always given first, followed by Task 2.

Task 1 was presented as a game called "Fill in the missing word". The experimenter said: "I'm going to say something like *Every day I eat an orange* and you have to repeat that—try that now." Once the participant had successfully repeated the sentence the experimenter went on: "Then I'll say something like *Just like every day, yesterday I .... an orange* and you have to finish the sentence to fit in with what happened yesterday. So after I say, *Just like every day, yesterday I .... an orange* you might say *Yesterday I* (brief pause in case the participant was able to complete the sentence spontaneously) *I ATE an orange*." A second practice trial was presented in the same way. Participants were then told that they might hear some words they didn't know and they should simply say what they thought sounded right. The experimenter continued with practice trials until seven had been attempted, and then presented the test sentences, unless the participant did not seem to understand the task in which case further practice sentences were provided.

The test trials were presented in two blocks of 28, usually with a brief pause between the two blocks. The second block was preceded by further practice trials if the experimenter deemed it helpful. A single pseudo-random order of sentence pairs was used for each block, with numbers of exemplars of each of the four sentence types distributed equally across the two blocks.

The second task was then introduced as a game called "Finish the word I started". One experimenter said: "I'm going to say a sentence, and then I'll start another one and stop in the middle. Your job is to finish off the word that I've started." Participants were given only the first phoneme of the past tense form as a recall cue. The two practice sentences were presented, followed by the test sentences in a single pseudo-random order.

After the session, the two experimenters who had written down the participant's responses checked for agreement. Any disagreement was resolved by listening to the audio tape.

The BPVS and BAS-II were administered to all the participants with WS by a single experimenter, either during the same visit or on a separate but closely dated occasion.

RESULTS

Three of the participants with Williams syndrome were unable to complete the past tense elicitation tasks. In two cases (participants 1 and 6), this appeared to be due to an inability to understand the metacognitive demands of the task. In at least one case (participant 12), the level of language as a whole was very poor. In this participant's spontaneous production, there was little evidence of any inflections, as well as poor syntax, missing articles and prepositions, and a large proportion of incomplete sentences. Participants 6 and 12 were at floor on all subtests of the BAS–II.

Responses for the remaining 18 participants with WS and the 46 control participants were coded according to eight categories. These were as follows (illustrated using the examples of *leak* and *creep*): regularised (leaked, creeped), irregularised (lekt, crept), unmarked (leak, creep), substitution of other real word (dripped, walked), blend (lekted, crepted), third person singular (leaks, creeps), no response, and other. All irregular verbs formed their past tense by an internal vowel change and/or the change of a final consonant. For both tasks, an irregularised response was defined according to the same template. Nonsense strings that did not fall under this definition were classed as "other".

Because some of these response categories were sparsely filled, and for reasons of space, four of the categories (blend, 3rd person, no response, other) have been pooled together in the results shown in Table 3.

Within the WS group, there was, unsurprisingly, a fair degree of between-participant variability. By comparison, the 6-year-old group showed an equivalent level of variability, but the other three control

TABLE 3
Percentages of elicited past tense forms (bold figures show correct response for existing verbs)

Task	Verb type	Response (%)				
		WS	6	8	10	Adult
Task 1	Existing regular					
	Regular	**76.7**	**73.8**	**94.4**	**97.5**	**98.0**
	Irregular	0.0	0.6	0.0	0.0	0.0
	Unmarked	17.0	18.8	2.5	0.6	1.6
	Substitution	3.5	3.1	1.3	0.0	0.0
	Other	2.8	3.8	1.9	1.9	0.4
	Existing irregular					
	Regular	18.3	23.6	28.6	20.7	3.1
	Irregular	**52.0**	**42.1**	**68.6**	**76.4**	**95.5**
	Unmarked	26.2	32.9	2.9	1.4	0.9
	Substitution	2.0	0.7	0.0	0.0	0.0
	Other	1.6	0.7	0.0	1.4	0.4
Task 2	Existing regular					
	Regular	**82.5**	**80.4**	**99.6**	**97.7**	**98.6**
	Irregular	1.7	1.2	0.0	1.2	1.0
	Unmarked	5.8	5.8	0.0	0.0	0.2
	Substitution	2.4	2.3	0.0	0.4	0.0
	Other	7.7	10.4	0.4	0.8	0.0
	Existing irregular					
	Regular	26.7	31.1	20.4	13.3	2.8
	Irregular	**54.3**	**45.2**	**77.0**	**84.4**	**97.2**
	Unmarked	5.3	5.6	0.0	0.0	0.0
	Substitution	3.5	1.5	0.0	0.4	0.0
	Other	10.1	16.7	2.6	1.9	0.0
Task 1	Novel non-rhyme					
	Regular	57.4	60.0	93.3	97.5	92.7
	Irregular	0.5	0.0	0.0	0.0	1.0
	Unmarked	22.7	12.5	5.0	1.7	3.1
	Substitution	9.3	15.8	0.0	0.0	0.0
	Other	10.2	11.7	1.7	0.8	3.1
	Novel rhyme					
	Regular	40.1	44.3	75.7	81.4	51.3
	Irregular	4.8	6.4	6.4	10.0	34.4
	Unmarked	32.1	30.0	12.9	5.0	6.7
	Substitution	12.3	9.3	1.4	0.0	1.3
	Other	10.3	10.0	3.6	3.6	6.3

WS, Williams syndrome.

155

groups much lower levels. Figure 1 shows the performance levels (% correct) for the WS group on existing verbs in Tasks 1 and 2, and the level of regularisation for novel verbs in Task 1, with participants ordered by chronological age from left to right. The pattern of this group as a whole is one of superior performance on regular past tense formations compared to irregulars. However, there are exceptions with individuals exhibiting quite different patterns to the group mean. This emphasises the difficulty of using very small sample sizes or single case studies when working with rare developmental disorders. For example, if we had used only a single WS case study and only Task 1, we could have by chance found evidence to support the claim that individuals with WS show equal levels of performance on irregular and regular past tense forms (participants 4, 9, and 11 show this pattern). If we had used both tasks, for two of these participants (4 and 11), we would have found that in Task 2, performance on regulars was now better than that on irregulars. But participant 9 still shows equal performance on regulars and irregulars in both tasks (at 55% in Task 1, at 65% in Task 2). In addition to participant 9, other "chance" WS case studies include: near perfect regulars at 94%, and very impaired irregulars at below 30% (Task 1, participant 2); regulars and irregulars both perfect at 100% (Task 1, participant 21, Task 2, participant 19); regulars and irregulars both very impaired at less than 25% (both tasks, participant 18). If we make the assumption that a syndrome such as Williams is characterised by a single cognitive architecture, masked by individual differences and task-specific factors, then these results suggest that it is as crucial as with the typical population to examine as large a population as possible, in order to adequately characterise the relevant cognitive architecture.

Comparison of the WS and control groups

An initial comparison of the WS group with the performance of individual control groups showed that their performance most resembled that of the 6-year-old group, in terms of the proportions of each response type that they produced. As a broad metric of similarity (and therefore not correcting for the number of tests), we compared the response rates for the WS group and the 6-year-olds in each of the four main response categories (regularise, irregularise, unmark, substitute) for each of the six stimulus sets (Task 1 regular, irregular, novel non-rhyme, novel rhyme, Task 2 regular, irregular), in the form of 24 between-participant t-tests. These tests showed no significant differences at the .05 level. By comparison, when the WS group was compared to the 8-year-old group across these 24 cells, there were 12/24 significant differences; in comparison to the 10-year-

Task 1 - Existing verbs

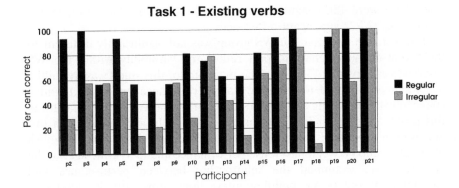

Task 2 - Existing verbs

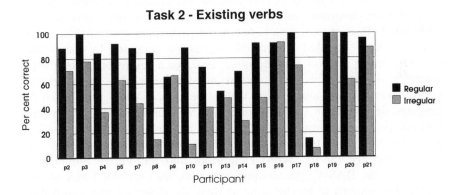

Task 1 - Novel verbs, addition of '-ed'

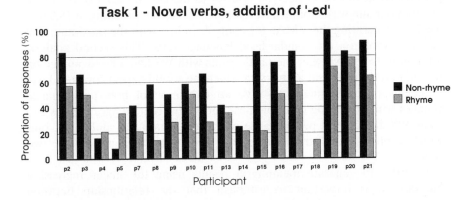

Figure 1. Performance (% correct) of participants with Williams syndrome on the past tense elicitation task for regular and irregular verbs in Task 1 and Task 2, and levels of regularisation for novel non-rhymes (e.g., brop) and novel rhymes (e.g., crive) in Task 1.

olds, there were 12/24 significant differences; and in comparison to the adult group, 17/24 significant differences.

However, the fact that the WS group was not significantly different to the 6-year-old group may in part reflect the variability within the WS responses as shown in Figure 1. The main aim of this study was to build a developmental profile to examine how performance on Tasks 1 and 2 changed with increasing age, and to see whether the WS participants fitted this profile given their level of language ability. In accordance with this aim, we ran two sets of linear regression analyses, which sought to establish the relationship between past tense performance and increasing age. In the first case, we examined the relationship between performance and chronological age (CA), building interaction terms into the model to allow us to compare the performance of the normally developing group with that of the WS group, to compare the performance on regular verbs with that on irregular verbs, and to examine whether there was a differential effect of verb type between the participant groups. (Repeated measures were handled within the regression analyses by using the criterion scaling method; see Pedhazur, 1997, for a description, along with a general discussion of linear regression techniques.) We expected the performance of individuals with WS to be poorer given their delayed language development. In the second case, we examined the relationship between performance and increasing verbal mental age (VMA), including the same interaction terms. For the WS group, VMA was taken as the average test age for the Word Definitions and the Verbal Similarities subtests of the BAS–II. As an approximation, we took the VMA of the control participants to be the same as their chronological age, given that their class teachers were asked to avoid selecting children who were either particularly advanced or delayed relative to the general level of the class, and that our aim was to build a developmental profile. A ceiling of 18;0 was used for generating the VMAs for controls in line with the maximum test age achievable on the standardised language tests. This second analysis allowed us to test whether the participants with WS had a disadvantage on irregular verbs over and above that which we would expect for their level of language development. To give an indication of how performance changes with increasing chronological and verbal mental age, Figures 2–5 show WS and control performance when sorted into CA and VMA bins which capture the distribution of the respective ages across the two samples.

In order to generate meaningful results using the linear regression analyses, it is important to establish that the relationship between performance and age is indeed a linear one. However, Figures 2–5 clearly demonstrate ceiling effects in the performance measures. In order to linearise this relationship, we took the inverse of the squares of chronological age and verbal mental age as the factors to be included in the regression analyses. Thus although for brevity we will refer to them as CA and VMA, the age factors in the following analyses were actually $1/(CA)^2$ and $1/(VMA)^2$, with age measured in months.

Existing verbs

Although correct performance in Task 2 was better than that in Task 1 by approximately 4% [related samples t-test, $t = 3.28$, df $= 127$, $p = .001$], this was a small effect. When Task was added as a factor in the regression model relating chronological age to performance in both tasks, it did not pick up a significant amount of variance [fit of model to data: $R = .98$, $N = 128$, $F(14,61) = 124.32$, $p < .001$; main effect of Task: $F(1,61) = 1.48$, $p = .229$] nor show significant interactions with participant group [$F(1,61) = 0.67$, $p = .418$]. This was also the case when verbal mental age was related to performance in both tasks [fit of model to data: $R = .98$, $N = 128$, $F(14,61) = 126.10$, $p < .001$; main effect of Task: $F(1,61) = .60$, $p = .443$; interaction of Task and participant group: $F(1,61) = .03$, $p = .866$]. For conciseness, the following section describes performance according to a single composite score on both tasks, since the pattern was the same when each task was analysed separately.

Analyses controlling for chronological age

In the following analyses, the four control groups were combined into a single typically developing control group. A linear regression analysis was carried out predicting correct performance on the basis of chronological age, verb type (regular/irregular; repeated measure), and participant group (WS/control). Two interaction terms were included which examined whether the relationship between correct performance differed between the two participant groups, and whether the difference between performance on regular and irregular verbs was affected by the group variable. This latter term should tell us whether the WS group showed a greater disparity between irregulars and regulars than that found in the control group. Figure 2 shows the distribution of the scores across CA for the two groups. The regression analysis produced a significant fit to the data [$R = .96$, $N = 128$, $F(6,61) = 106.02$, $p < .001$]. The results showed a significant relationship between increasing chronological age and correct performance [$F(1,61) = 31.02$, $p < .001$], which was significantly modulated by verb type such that irregular verbs showed poorer performance than regular verbs [$F(1,61) = 31.90$, $p < .001$]. As expected, when chronological age was controlled for, the performance of the WS group was significantly lower than that of the typically developing group [$F(1,61) = 37.00$, $p < .001$]. In addition, the difference in performance was

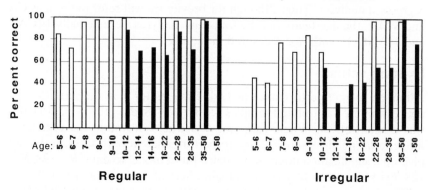

Figure 2. Comparison of levels of correct past tense production for Williams syndrome (■) and typically developing groups (□) on regular and irregular verbs for tasks 1 and 2 combined, across increasing chronological age (CA). Scores show means for a representative set of age groups across the full range.

greater for irregular verbs than regular verbs [$F(1,61) = 19.24, p < .001$]. This first analysis would seem to support the claim that participants with WS have a selective deficit on irregular verbs.

Analyses controlling for verbal mental age

The preceding analyses were repeated but now relating correct performance to increasing verbal mental age. Figure 3 shows the distribution of performances for the WS and typically developing groups across VMA. The regression model again showed a significant fit to the data [$R = .95, N = 128, F(6,61) = 97.18, p < .001$], and a significant relationship between performance and increasing VMA [$F(1,61) = 50.37, p < .001$]. The results showed that verb type once more modulated the relationship between the correct performance and age, with regular verbs demonstrating higher performance than irregular verbs [$F(1,61) = 100.16, p < .001$]. The effect of participant group was reduced but still significant [$F(1,61) = 7.04, p = .010$], such that the performance of the WS group was still worse even when matched according to our measure of VMA. Importantly, however, there was now no significant interaction of participant group with verb type [$F(1,61) = .75, p = .390$]. The WS group showed the same difference between performance on regular and irregular verbs as the typically developing group. There was no specific additional deficit for irregular verbs.

Existing verbs (tasks combined): VMA matched

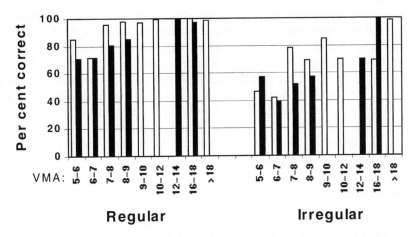

Figure 3. Comparison of levels of correct past tense production for Williams syndrome (■) and typicall developing groups (□) on regular and irregular verbs for tasks 1 and 2 combined, across increasing verbal mental age (VMA). VMA has a ceiling of the oldest test age achievable on the relevant British Abilities Scale subtests.

Analysis of errors

In this section, we will only consider errors that participants made on irregular verbs, since these are the stimuli where individuals with WS are purported to have a specific deficit. In particular, we will focus only on the two largest error types, regularisation of these verbs, and reproducing the unmarked stem. Direct comparison of the proportions of each error made by a group is compromised by the fact that these distributions are not independent, increasing the chance of Type 1 errors. Nevertheless, regression analyses showed a strong three-way interaction of task, participant group, and error type in relating rate of regularisation and unmarking errors to CA and VMA (CA: fit to model: $R = .93$, $N = 256$, $F(14,61) = 26.97$, $p < .001$, Task × Group × Error type interaction: $F(1,61) = 14.26$, $p < .001$; VMA: fit to model: $R = .93$, $N = 256$, $F(14,61) = 29.16$, $p < .001$, Task × Group × Error type interaction: $F(1,61) = 4.71$, $p = .034$). The interaction suggests that task demands had a differential effect on the two participant groups. In both groups, the shift from Task 1 to 2 reduced the levels of unmarking errors, while the overall levels of performance remained approximately the same. Thus the demands of Task 1, with its higher memory load, promoted unmarking errors over regularisation errors for irregular verbs, while Task 2 promoted regularisation errors over unmarking errors. This effect was stronger in the WS group.

However, inspection of Table 3 reveals that the WS group as a whole exhibited the same pattern of errors on irregular verbs as the 6-year-old group in both Tasks 1 and 2: more unmarking than regularisation errors in Task 1, more regularisation errors than unmarking errors in Task 2. What, then, is the source of the differential group effect? The interaction arises from the fact that half of the WS group have verbal mental ages in *excess of 6 years*. In other words, the differential effect arises because the participants with WS who have higher VMAs persist in showing an immature pattern of errors in Task 1, a pattern in which unmarking errors are produced in response to higher memory loads.

Novel verbs

The most common response to novel verbs for all participant groups was regularisation. We compared the levels of regularisation for novel verbs which did not rhyme with existing irregulars (e.g., brop) against those which did (e.g., crive), using the same regression model as with the existing verbs. Regularisation levels were predicted on the basis of chronological age, item type (non-rhyme/irregular-rhyme; repeated measure), and participant group (WS/control), with two interaction terms to check for interactions of item type with chronological age, and item type with participant group.

Figure 4 shows the distribution of the scores across CA for the two groups. The regression analysis produced a significant fit to the data [R =

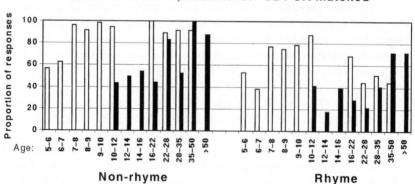

Figure 4. Comparison of levels of regularisation of novel non-rhymes (e.g., brop) and rhymes (e.g., crive) for Williams syndrome (■) and typically developing groups (□) in Task 1, across increasing chronological age (CA).

.95, $N = 128$, $F(6,61) = 91.27$, $p < .001$]. The results demonstrate a significant relationship between increasing chronological age and novel verb regularisation [$F(1,61) = 5.37$, $p = .024$]. This relationship was significantly modulated by item type such that novel items not rhyming with existing irregular verbs were regularised more than those that did rhyme [$F(1,61) = 101.05$, $p < .001$], consistent with the notion that the similarity of the novel terms to irregulars interfered with regularisation. When chronological age was controlled for, the performance of the WS group in adding "-ed" to novel verbs was significantly poorer than that of the typically developing group [$F(1,61) = 25.96$, $p < .001$]. Lastly, the WS group showed significantly greater impairment in regularising rhymes than non-rhymes [$F(1,61) = 8.92$, $p = .004$].

Figure 5 depicts the distribution of the scores across VMA for the two groups. When the analysis was performed using VMA, the same effects were found except that the trend for a greater impairment in the WS group on regularising rhymes had disappeared [$F(1,61) = .31$, $p = .578$], suggesting that this disparity was a consequence of language delay. There was still a strong main effect of participant group corresponding to poorer generalisation in the WS group [$F(1,61) = 13.92$, $p < .001$]. Interestingly, a regression model relating correct performance on existing verbs/regularisation on novel verbs to VMA showed that the disparity between the two

Task 1 Novel Verbs, addition of '-ed': VMA matched

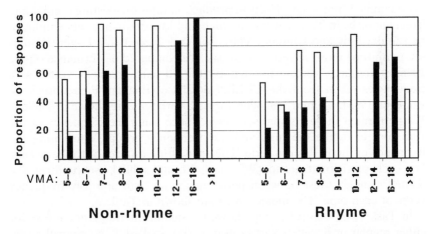

Figure 5. Comparison of levels of regularisation of novel non-rhymes (e.g., brop) and rhymes (e.g., crive) for Williams syndrome (■) and typically developing groups (□) in Task 1, across increasing verbal mental age (VMA). VMA has a ceiling of the oldest test age achievable on the relevant British Abilities Scale subtests.

groups was significantly greater for generalisation than it was for performance on existing verbs [fit of the model to data: $R = .93$, $N = 256$, $F(14,61) = 29.16$, $p < .001$; interaction of stimulus type (existing verb/novel verb) and participant group (WS/control): $F(1,61) = 4.02$, $p = 0.049$]. That is, the WS group appeared to have an additional deficit in generalising regular past tense formation to novel verbs.

Lastly, we examined the levels of irregularisation of novel rhymes. Our control groups showed low levels of irregularisation (6 years: 6.4% 8 years: 6.4%, 10 years: 10.0%, adults: 34.3%), much more in line with van der Lely and Ullman's (this issue) control data than those of Clahsen and Almazan (1998). The WS group showed lower levels of irregularisation, at 4.8%. Regression analyses which used the untransformed ages gave a better fit to the data here than the $1/age^2$ transform. These analyses showed a significant relationship between irregularisation levels and CA but also an effect of participant group, with the WS group producing less irregularisations [fit of model: $R = .63$, $N = 64$, $F(2,61) = 20.07$, $p < .001$, group effect: $F(1,61) = 21.56$, $p < .001$]. However, this difference became non-significant when VMA rather than CA was controlled for [fit of model: $R = .67$, $N = 64$, $F(2,61) = 25.45$, $p < .001$; group effect: $F(1,61) = 1.76$, $p < .190$]. Unlike with regularisation, the lower level of irregularisation in the WS group was not significant once language ability was controlled for.

Frequency and imageability effects

We examined frequency effects in production rates on existing regular and irregular verbs in Task 1 using the high and low frequency sets employed by van der Lely and Ullman (2000). For Task 2, we had a larger stimulus set, permitting more sensitive contrasts. We compared performance on the 10 most frequent verbs with that on the 10 least frequent verbs, with frequencies taken from the CELEX database (Baayan, Piepenbrock, & van Rijn, 1993). Mean frequencies for each verb type are shown in Table 4. We performed these comparisons twice, once using the frequency of the verb root to define the high and low frequency groups, once using the frequency of the past tense form. This made little difference to the results. For each participant group (WS, 6, 8, 10, and adult), we performed a related samples t-test between performance on high and low frequency verbs of each type. The mean scores are shown in Table 5.

In Task 1, no control group showed a significant frequency effect for either regular or irregular verbs (all $p > .35$). In Task 2, no control group showed a significant frequency effect for regular verbs. However, the 6-year-old, 8-year-old and 10-year-old groups showed a significant frequency effect for irregular verbs (*root frequency*: 6 years $t = 4.15$, df = 9, $p = .002$,

TABLE 4
Mean frequency and imageability ratings for the stimuli in Task 2

| | | | Frequency (per million words) | | | | Imageability (mean verb root frequency) | | |
| | | | Verb root frequency | | Past tense frequency | | | | |
		N	High	Low	High	Low	N	High	Low
Regular	mean	10	67	3	48	2	6	515 [7]	395 [42]
	std		45	1	49	1		25 [6]	39 [32]
Irregular	mean	10	42	2	45	2	7	544 [6]	342 [52]
	std		19	1	49	1		27 [3]	37 [55]

Frequency ratings are combined written and spoken frequencies taken from the CELEX database (Baayan, Piepenbrock, & Rijn, 1993). Imageability ratings are from Coltheart (1981). std = standard deviation.

TABLE 5
Effects of frequency and imageability in past tense production

| | | | Correct response (%) | | | | |
Task	Verb type		WS	6	8	10	Adult
Task 1	Existing regular	High frequency	83.3	71.3	96.3	98.8	97.7
		Low frequency	70.1	76.3	92.5	96.3	98.4
	Existing irregular	High frequency	46.5	42.5	65.0	72.5	86.7
		Low frequency	50.8	35.7	62.9	70.0	92.0
Task 2	Existing regular	High frequency+	85.0/85.0	81.0/79.0	100.0/100.0	99.0/98.0	100.0/98.8
		Low frequency+	78.9/76.1	81.0/78.0	99.0/99.0	97.0/96.0	97.5/97.5
	Existing irregular	High frequency+	52.2/55.6	49.0/50.0	84.0/88.0	87.0/90.0	98.1/98.1
		Low frequency+	49.4/51.1	30.0/29.0	64.0/65.0	77.0/76.0	95.6/95.6
Task 2	Existing regular	High imageability	77.8	81.7	100.0	96.7	97.9
		Low imageability	83.3	75.0	100.0	98.3	97.9
	Existing irregular	High imageability	65.9	55.7	87.1	88.6	98.2
		Low imageability	50.8	48.6	84.3	87.1	98.2

WS, Williams syndrome; +root frequency/past tense frequency.

8 years $t = 2.37$, df $= 9$, $p = .042$, 10 years $t = 1.46$, df $= 9$, $p = .177$; *past tense frequency*: 6 years $t = 3.28$, df $= 9$, $p = .010$, 8 years $t = 3.02$, df $= 9$, $p = .014$, 10 years $t = 2.33$, df $= 9$, $p = .045$). The presence of frequency effects for irregulars but not regulars in our younger control groups replicates the typical pattern seen in past tense elicitation tasks (Pinker, 1991, 1999).

The WS results for frequency are surprising. The WS group showed no frequency effect for irregulars in either task (all $p > .3$). However, they displayed a frequency effect for *regular* verbs in both Task 1 ($t = 2.64$, df $=$ 17, $p = .017$) and Task 2 (*root frequency*: $t = 2.27$, df $= 17$, $p = .037$; *past tense frequency*: $t = 2.41$, df $= 17$, $p = .028$). Non-parametric sign tests on these three comparisons yielded p-values of .002, .073, .073. Thus they remained at least as trends using tests with much reduced statistical power. This pattern of frequency effects for regular but not irregular verbs is very unusual.

Established imageability ratings were only available for a subset of the verbs in Task 2 (Coltheart, 1981). Mean performance on the six most and six least imageable regular verbs (high: *kick, dance, leak, laugh, graze, walk*; low: *raise, call, move, stay, save, balance*) and the seven most and seven least imageable irregular verbs (high: *weep, ring, drink, sing, stick, sting, hang*; low: *grow, lose, learn, keep, come, chose, deal*) was compared across the control groups. Mean imageability scores are given in Table 4. The results showed no effect of imageability for regular or irregular verbs in any control group (all $p > .25$). The WS group did not show an effect of imageability on regular verbs. However, there was a significant effect of imageability for irregular verbs, whereby past tense forms for high imageability verbs were produced more accurately than those for low imageability verbs (high: 65.9%; low: 50.8%: $t = 2.37$, df $= 17$, $p = .030$). Note that frequency could not explain this effect since low imageability verbs had higher frequency than high imageability verbs. Significantly, the WS group made more regularisation errors on the low imageability verbs than on the high (high: 19.8%; low: 36.5%; $t = 2.62$, df $= 17$, $p = .018$). Sign tests for these two comparisons yielded p-values of .059 and .011. These results seem to imply that semantic representations were playing a role in the production of irregular past tense forms in the WS group, but not in typical controls. These effects may be important clues to the nature of the WS language system. It should nonetheless be noted that small item sets were used, and imageability ratings were made by typical adults which (as with frequency ratings) may have limited validity for atypical populations.

DISCUSSION

The main result of this study is that, in contrast to the findings of Clahsen and Almazan (1998) and Bromberg et al. (1994), individuals with WS showed no selective deficit in their production of irregular English past tense forms. We compared the performance of 21 individuals with WS against that of a normal developmental profile constructed using 46 control participants with ages varying from 5;5 to 45;0. When the verbal mental age of the WS group was controlled for, the difference in performance levels between the groups was very much reduced and importantly, the WS group now showed the same relation between performance on regular and irregular verbs as the typically developing group. Controlling for verbal mental age (VMA) did leave a residual effect of worse overall performance in the WS group. However, this may be because the standardised tests we employed overestimated these participants' language ability, since the tests measured vocabulary rather than syntax. A number of studies have shown that standardised tests of vocabulary with individuals with WS produce test ages in advance of those found on tests of grammar (Clahsen & Almazan, 1998; Grant et al., 1997; Karmiloff-Smith, Grant, Berthoud, Davies, Howlin, & Udwin, 1997; Volterra, Capirci, Pezzini, Sabbadini, & Vicari, 1996). Controlling for syntax rather than vocabulary would have placed the WS group lower on the control profile and it is possible the overall difference in performance would have disappeared.

The second important finding was that, when VMA had been controlled for, the WS group showed an additional deficit in generalising the "add - ed" past tense rule to novel forms, a deficit greater than the residual disparity between the groups for existing verbs. The deficit in general-isation appeared to be over and above that caused by a delay in development. With regard to the irregularisation of novel verbs rhyming with existing irregulars, both the WS group and the control group showed low levels of such generalisation. When VMA was controlled for, irregularisation of rhymes in the WS group was lower but not significantly discernible from the control group ($p = .190$). This again contrasts with the findings of Clahsen and Almazan, a disparity which appears largely due to the much higher rates of irregularisation reported for the control participants in that study than in any other published study on normal controls.

Thirdly, we found a significant effect of task demands in determining the patterns of errors produced for irregular verbs. A between-task compari-son revealed that Task 1 promoted errors of unmarking in young controls, but that Task 2 promoted errors of regularisation. However, participants with WS persisted in showing unmarking errors in Task 1 at VMAs when they had disappeared in the control group. Responses in Task 1 involved repetition of at least a sentence fragment whereas those in Task 2 only required completion of a single word when the initial sound had been provided. It is possible, then, that in younger control participants, the additional memory component in Task 1 caused errors of omission that became errors of commission in Task 2. Participants with WS remained sensitive to the memory component of Task 1 at levels of language ability when they had ceased to affect the control group. It is not clear whether this difference reflects a deficit specific to WS or is linked to the general mental retardation in this syndrome. Nevertheless, the role of task demands in determining error types in this study demonstrates that one should be cautious in reading too much into the results of a single procedure, particularly in research with atypical populations where working memory and metacognition may be weaker than in the typically developing population.

Fourthly, the results of this study highlighted how potentially misleading single case studies may be. We found a number of patterns of behaviour in our WS sample, including very high performance on both regulars and irregulars, very low levels on both regulars and irregulars, equal intermediate performance on both verb types, and very high regular performance with low irregular performance (as with the controls, no participant showed much higher irregular verb performance then regular performance). Each of the above patterns, if used as a case study, would have led to totally different conclusions about the WS language system. Yet inspection of Figures 2–5 is persuasive evidence that we are predominantly witnessing a delayed system, rather than a normal one with a selective deficit in irregular past tense formation.

However, several pieces of evidence suggest that it would be wrong to characterise the WS language system as simply delayed. We have already seen the additional deficit in generalisation compared to performance on existing verbs. Examination of factors underlying past tense production, specifically verb frequency and verb imageability, also produced unusual patterns. Effects of frequency have been taken as a marker for associative lexical memory processes in the production of past tense forms (Pinker, 1991, p. 532). For example, when van der Lely and Ullman (2000) found frequency effects in regular past tense formation of participants with SLI, they interpreted the results in terms of Pinker's dual-mechanism model. They took the frequency effect to imply that, lacking the rule-mechanism to perform *-ed* suffixation, the SLI group was memorising regular past tense forms as well as irregulars. Given that Pinker (1991) and Clahsen and Almazan (1998) take WS to represent the opposite case—a system with an intact rule-mechanism but impaired lexical memory—we should *definitely not* expect to find frequency effects in the formation of regular past tense in our WS sample. However, unlike controls, participants with WS were significantly more accurate at forming high frequency regular past tenses than low frequency. Just as surprisingly, the WS group showed no frequency effects for irregular verbs, in contrast to control participants. This pattern of frequency effects is not readily explained by any current model, but particularly strains the straightforward logic of the dual-mechanism model.

With regard to imageability, an effect of this semantic dimension on the accuracy of past tense formation would seem to implicate lexical memory in this grammatical process. The control group, however, showed no effect of this variable. While the WS group also showed no effects of imageability on regular verbs, they did demonstrate superior performance on high rather than low imageability irregular verbs. In addition, low imageability irregular verbs showed greater levels of regularisation errors. If we assume that high imageability verbs generate a more robust semantic representation, these findings imply that in WS, semantics is playing a role in preventing the regularisation of irregular verbs.

The position we wish to argue for in the rest of this discussion is that WS does not merely represent a case of delayed language development, but a case of language development following an atypical developmental trajectory. We will outline what we believe that trajectory to be shortly. Firstly, however, we wish to emphasise the contrast that exists between viewing developmental disorders as atypical trajectories of development and viewing them as if they were cases of normal development with specific deficits (in the way that cases of adult brain damage are described).

Karmiloff-Smith (1998) has argued that to conceive of developmental disorders as if they were cases of selective deficits to processing modules identified in the adult system omits the essential role of development in producing behavioural deficits in these disorders. The disordered system is one that has followed a long trajectory of development shaped by both initial low-level neurocomputational impairments and subsequent interaction with the environment. If there are behavioural deficits in the outcome of development, these are likely to be the result of a cognitive system which has developed under a different set of constraints. The *neuroconstructivist approach* (Elman et al., 1996; Karmiloff-Smith, 1998) views developmental disorders in terms of different developmental trajectories, caused by initial differences at a neurocomputational level (see also Karmiloff-Smith & Thomas, in press; Mareschal & Thomas, in press; Oliver et al., 2000; Thomas & Karmiloff-Smith, 2000). Thus there might be differences in the local connectivity of the brain or the firing properties of neurons, as opposed to discrete lesions to particular large-scale brain structures or pathways. In this view, development is an interactive process in which the cognitive system self-organises in response to interactions with a structured environment. A deficit at the behavioural level may not imply damage to a particular mechanism in an otherwise normal system. Rather, it may point to a system that has developed throughout in a qualitatively different fashion in response to different initial constraints. Indeed, neuroconstructivism suggests that even when behaviour is equivalent across normal and abnormal phenotypes, this may mask different underlying cognitive processes. The notion that an ability is "intact" or "spared" because there is no apparent deficit at the behavioural level employs terminology from the adult brain damage model that may be misleading in the case of developmental disorders.

In the case of the WS language system, there is (as yet circumstantial) evidence to suggest that the constraints under which this system has developed involve a different balance between semantic and phonological information, specifically a greater reliance on phonology and relatively weaker semantics. The following evidence is consistent with this view. Children with WS display auditory sensitivity and (relative to their other capacities) good short-term memory for words and digits from as young as 2;6, the youngest age tested (Mervis & Bertrand, 1997). During vocabulary acquisition in WS, the naming spurt precedes fast-mapping ability, whereas in typical development these two are associated, suggesting vocabulary growth in WS is more reliant on phonology (Mervis & Bertrand, 1997). Furthermore, the naming spurt in WS is not associated with exhaustive category sorting, a marker of maturing semantic representations, once more suggesting that vocabulary growth is less reliant on semantics (Mervis & Bertrand, 1997). Although local semantic organisation seems normal in WS in terms of priming effects (Tyler et al., 1997) and category fluency (Mervis et al., 1999), global semantic organisation remains immature (Johnson & Carey, 1998). A reduced contribution of semantics was also apparent in a study that looked at sentence processing. Karmiloff-Smith et al. (1998) found that when WS participants were monitoring sentences for a target word, they did not show sensitivity to subcategory violations (e.g., "The burglar was terrified. He continued *to struggle the dog* but he couldn't break free.") The authors took this to suggest that in WS, semantic information may become available too slowly to be integrated with the on-line processing of syntax. In WS, phonological encoding displays the normal patterns, but again there is a claim with respect to a reduced contribution of semantic information to short term-term memory for words (Vicari, Brizzolara, Carlesimo, Pezzini, & Volterra, 1996; Vicari, Carlesimo, Brizzolara, & Pezzini, 1996). Lastly, a recent study of reading in WS came to similar conclusions about the role of phonology over weaker constraints from semantics (Laing, Hulme, & Karmiloff-Smith, 2000). In this study, the WS group, but not the controls, showed equal levels of reading for concrete and abstract words.

Taken together, these studies paint a picture of WS in which, unlike in typical development, phonology plays a greater role than semantics during early language development. Moreover, as a consequence of early auditory sensitivity, the phonological representations themselves may be atypical. Reduced levels of generalisation of inflectional patterns in the current study and in a French gender task by Karmiloff-Smith et al. (1997) are consistent with the view that in WS, phonological representations may be too specific to support robust generalisation. However, it has also been argued that WS is characterised by impaired semantic lexical representations (e.g., Rossen et al., 1996). That is, the differential constraints in WS language development may involve both atypical phonology and weaker semantics. Therefore, we have two possible candidates to explain the performance of the WS group in past tense formation.

Computational modelling has allowed us to explore the relative merits of each account. In contrast to the dual-mechanism model, an alternative theory suggests that past tense performance may be achieved by a single device which learns associations between the phonological forms of verb stems and past tense forms (Daugherty & Seidenberg, 1992; Joanisse & Seidenberg, 1999; MacWhinney & Leinbach, 1991; Plunkett & Juola, 1999; Plunkett & Marchman, 1991, 1993; Rumelhart & McClelland, 1986; see Thomas & Karmiloff-Smith, 2000, for a recent comparison of the two theories). Connectionist models of the development of past tense formation embody this alternative theory. These computational models are learning systems which readily allow us to address the effect of initial system constraints on the subsequent developmental trajectory.

In this way, Thomas and Karmiloff-Smith (2000) have explored how changes in the initial constraints of a connectionist model of past tense formation in the normal population (Plunkett & Marchman, 1991) affect its endstate performance. This model focused on the implications of acquiring the past tense with atypical phonological representations. In particular, in line with evidence of an early (relative) strength in auditory short-term memory and the reported hypersensitivity of the auditory system in adults with Williams syndrome (McDonald, 1997; Neville, Mills, & Bellugi, 1994), the initial phonological representations were altered to increase the discriminability between the sounds making up each word. When the system was trained at the normal rate using these altered representations, the network showed delayed development, a consequent apparent deficit for irregular verbs, and reduced generalisation to novel items. Many other initial constraints were varied, but the phonological manipulation alone produced a robust fit to all three features of the WS data. Importantly, when the model was simply run with a slower rate of development, a reduction in generalisation to novel past tense forms did not result. In short, our model supported the viability of the account that atypical phonology might explain the three performance deficits of individuals with WS in past tense formation.

A similar model by Hoeffner and McClelland (1993) has captured some aspects of past tense performance in SLI. In contrast to the WS model, the SLI model showed poorer performance on regular than irregular verbs. The SLI model also used atypical phonological representations throughout training, but in this case, phonological representations that were *impoverished* rather than overly-detailed. In some senses, then, these two models retain the opposite relationship of WS and SLI proposed by Pinker (1991), but now within a developmental computational framework rather than an adult deficit framework. In addition, taken together, these two *single system* models demonstrate a developmental double dissociation between regular and irregular verb performance. The fact that performance on regular and irregular verbs can dissociate in models which do not include separate structures for each verb type undermines the inference that developmental double dissociations necessarily reveal structure within the cognitive system, let alone innate structure (see Thomas & Karmiloff-Smith, 2000, for further discussion).

The Thomas and Karmiloff-Smith (2000) model did not include semantics, however, so that it could not account for the imageability effects in the WS group in the current study. Could a weak semantic system form an alternative account of WS past tense deficits? Joanisse and Seidenberg (1999) developed a connectionist model of past tense formation including semantics, designed to account for how adults with brain damage could show differential degrees of impairment in either regular or irregular past tense formation. They proposed that the association between the phonological forms of stem and past tense is mediated by semantic information. The primary role of semantic information in this system is to aid production of irregular forms (an idea also proposed in models of word reading, see Plaut, McClelland, Seidenberg, & Patterson, 1996). If the semantic representations in this model are damaged, the result is greater impairment for irregular forms, capturing the pattern of deficits found in some patients with Alzheimer's disease and posterior aphasics (Ullman et al., 1997). The model suggests a role for semantics in the production of irregular past tense forms in normal development. If our hypothesis concerning the reduced efficiency of semantics in WS is correct, then the expression of imageability effects in the WS group's production of irregular verbs becomes readily interpretable. Low imageability verbs provide a weaker semantic input to the system so that the chance of over-regularisation increases. Paradoxically, the presence of a semantic effect in the WS group but not the control group may reflect a *weaker* semantic system than in the control group.

However, it is not clear from the Joanisse and Seidenberg (1999) model that weaker semantics alone would be sufficient to account for the delayed development and the reduction in generalisation we find in WS past tense formation, or that semantics would play the same role in the atypical case as the typical case if it were impaired at the outset of development rather than the end. Further computational modelling work remains to be done that perhaps combine aspects of both the phonological and semantic models.

CONCLUSION

Previous approaches have suggested that in terms of language, WS is a syndrome where syntax is "intact". Thus an apparent deficit in irregular past tense formation was attributed not to syntactic mechanisms but to a specific deficit in a mechanism responsible for storing information about lexical entries in an otherwise normally developing language system (Clahsen & Almazan, 1998; Pinker, 1991). In two past tense elicitation tasks with a sample of 21 participants with WS and 46 typically developing controls, we have demonstrated that (a) much if not all of the apparent deficit in irregular past tense formation is in fact a consequence of delayed language development (when verbal mental age is controlled for the selective deficit disappears); and (b) participants with WS show a number of underlying differences in generalisation, frequency effects and image-ability effects, which may be clues as to why their language development is delayed. We suggested an account of language development in WS in which development occurs under different constraints, with greater weight placed on phonological information and less weight on semantic information. Computational models of the developmental process in inflectional morphology are encouraging with regard to the viability of such an account. In addition, they are consistent with a theoretical framework which, unlike the adult brain damage model, places development centre stage in explaining behavioural deficits in developmental disorders.

REFERENCES

Aram, D., Morris, R., & Hall, N. (1993). Clinical and research congruence in identifying children with specific language impairment. *Journal of Speech and Hearing Research, 36,* 580–591.

Baayan, H., Piepenbrock, R., & van Rijn, H. (1993). *The CELEX lexical database (CD-ROM).* University of Pennsylvania, Philadelphia: Linguistic Data Consortium.

Baron-Cohen, S. (1998). Modularity in developmental cognitive neuropsychology: Evidence from autism and Gilles de la tourette syndrome. In J.A. Burack, R.M. Hodapp, & E. Zigler (Eds.), *Handbook of mental retardation and development* (pp. 334–348). Cambridge: Cambridge University Press.

Bellugi, U., Bihrle, A., Jernigan, T., Trauner, D., & Doherty, S. (1990). Neuropsychological, neurological, and neuroanatomical profile of Williams syndrome. *American Journal of Medical Genetics Supplement, 6,* 115–125.

Bellugi, U., Lichenberger, L., Mills, D., Galaburda, A., & Korenberg, J.R. (1999). Bridging cognition, the brain and molecular genetics: evidence from Williams syndrome. *Trends in Neurosciences, 22,* 197–207.

Bellugi, U., Marks, S., Bihrle, A., & Sabo, H. (1988). Dissociation between language and cognitive functions in Williams syndrome. In D. Bishop & K. Mogford (Eds.), *Language development in exceptional circumstances* (pp. 177–189). London: Churchill Livingstone.

Bellugi, U., Wang, P., & Jernigan, T.L. (1994). Williams syndrome: An unusual neuropsychological profile. In S. Broman & J. Grafman (Eds.), *Atypical cognitive deficits in developmental disorders: Implications for brain function* (pp. 23–56). Hove, UK: Lawrence Erlbaum Associates Ltd.

Bishop, D.V.M., North, T., & Donlan, C. (1995). Genetic basis of specific language impairment. *Developmental Medicine and Child Neurology, 37*, 56–71.

Bromberg, H., Ullman, M., Coppola, M., Marcus, G., Kelley, K., & Levine, K. (1994). A dissociation of lexical memory and grammar in Williams Syndrome: Evidence from inflectional morphology. Paper presented at the Sixth International Professional Conference of the Williams Syndrome Association, San Diego, CA.

Bybee, J. & Slobin, D. (1982). Rules and schemas in the development and use of the English past. *Language, 58*, 265–289.

Clahsen, H., & Almazan, M. (1998). Syntax and morphology in Williams syndrome. *Cognition, 68*, 167–198.

Coltheart, M. (1981). The MRC psycholinguistic database. *Quarterly Journal of Experimental Psychology, 33A*, 497–505.

Daugherty, K. & Seidenberg, M.S. (1992). Rules or connections? The past tense revisited. In *Proceedings of the Fourteenth Annual Conference of the Cognitive Science Society* (pp. 259–264). Hillsdale, NJ: Lawrence Erlbaum Associates Inc.

Dunn, L.M., Dunn, L.M., & Whetton, C. (1982). *British Picture Vocabulary Scale.* London: NFER-Nelson.

Elliott, C.D. (1996). *British Abilities Scales II.* London: NFER-Nelson.

Elman, J.L., Bates, E.A., Johnson, M.H., Karmiloff-Smith, A., Parisi, D., & Plunkett, K. (1996). *Rethinking innateness: A connectionist perspective on development.* Cambridge, MA: MIT Press.

Gopnik, M. & Crago, M.B. (1991). Familial aggregation of a developmental language disorder. *Cognition, 39*, 1–50.

Grant, J., Karmiloff-Smith, A., Gathercole, S.A., Paterson, S., Howlin, P., Davies, M., & Udwin, O. (1997). Phonological short-term memory and its relationship to language in Williams syndrome. *Cognitive Neuropsychiatry, 2*, 81–99.

Hoeffner, J.H. & McClelland, J.L. (1993). Can a perceptual processing deficit explain the impairment of inflectional morphology in developmental dysphasia? A computational investigation. In E.V. Clark (Ed.), *Proceedings of the 25th Child language research forum.* Stanford: Stanford University Press.

Howlin, P., Davies, M., & Udwin, O. (1998). Cognitive functioning in adults with Williams syndrome. *Journal of Child Psychology and Psychiatry, 39*, 183–189.

Jarrold, C., Baddeley, A.D., & Hewes, A.K. (1998). Verbal and nonverbal abilities in the Williams syndrome phenotype: Evidence for diverging developmental trajectories. *Journal of Child Psychology and Psychiatry, 39*, 511–523.

Joanisse, M.F., & Seidenberg, M.S. (1999). Impairments in verb morphology following brain injury: A connectionist model. *Proceedings of the National Academy of Science USA, 96*, 7592–7597.

Johnson, S. & Carey, S. (1998). Knowledge enrichment and conceptual change in folk biology: Evidence from Williams syndrome. *Cognitive Psychology, 37*, 156–184.

Karmiloff-Smith, A. (1998). Development itself is the key to understanding developmental disorders. *Trends in Cognitive Sciences, 2*, 389–398.

Karmiloff-Smith, A., Grant, J., Berthoud, I., Davies, M., Howlin, P., & Udwin, O. (1997). Language and Williams syndrome: How intact is "intact"? *Child Development, 68*, 246–262.

Karmiloff-Smith, A., Klima, E., Bellugi, U., Grant, J., & Baron-Cohen, S. (1995). Is there a social module? Language, face processing, and theory of mind in individuals with Williams syndrome. *Journal of Cognitive Neuroscience, 7*, 196–208.

Karmiloff-Smith, A. & Thomas, M.S.C. (in press). Developmental disorders. In M.A. Arbib & P.H. Arbib (Eds.), *Handbook of brain theory and neural networks, 2nd edition.* Cambridge, MA: MIT Press.

Karmiloff-Smith, A., Tyler, L.K., Voice, K., Sims, K., Udwin, O., Howlins, P., & Davies, M. (1998). Linguistic dissociations in Williams syndrome: evaluating receptive syntax in on-line and off-line tasks. *Neuropsychologia, 36*, 343–351.

Laing, E., Hulme, C., & Karmiloff-Smith, A. (2000). *Beyond reading scores: The process of learning to read in atypical development.* Manuscript submitted for publication.

MacWhinney, B. & Leinbach, J. (1991). Implementations are not conceptualizations: Revising the verb learning model. *Cognition, 40*, 121–157.

Mareschal, D. & Thomas, M.S.C. (in press). Self-organization in normal and abnormal cognitive development. To appear in A.F. Kalverboer & A. Gramsbergen (Eds.), *Brain and behaviour in human development. A source book.* Dordecht: Kluwer Academic Publishers.

McDonald, J.L. (1997). Language acquisition: The acquisition of linguistic structure in normal and special populations. *Annual Review of Psychology, 48*, 215–241.

Mervis, C., & Bertrand, J. (1997). Development relations between cognition and language: Evidence from Williams Syndrome. In L.B. Adamson & M.A. Romski (Eds.), *Research on communication and language disorders: Contributions to theories of language development* (pp. 75–106). New York: Brookes.

Mervis, C.B., Morris, C.A., Bertrand, J., & Robinson, B.F. (1999). Williams Syndrome: Findings from an integrated program of research. In H. Tager-Flusberg (Ed.), *Neurodevelopmental disorders* (pp. 65–110). Cambridge, MA: MIT Press.

Morris, C.A., Demsey, S.A., Leonad, C.O., Dilts, C., & Blackburn, B.L. (1988). The natural history of Williams syndrome: Physical characteristics. *Journal of Pediatrics, 113*, 318–326.

Neville, H.J., Mills, D.L., & Bellugi, U. (1994). Effects of altered auditory sensitivity and age of language acquisition of the development of language-relevant neural systems: Preliminary studies of Williams syndrome. In S. Broman and J. Grafman (Eds.), *Atypical cognitive deficits in developmental disorders: Implications for brain function* (pp. 67–83). Hove, UK: Lawrence Erlbaum Associates Ltd.

Oliver, A., Johnson, M.H., Karmiloff-Smith, A., & Pennington, B. (2000). Deviations in the emergence of representations: A neuroconstructivist framework for analysing develop-mental disorders. *Developmental Science, 3*, 1–40.

Pedhazur, E.J. (1997). *Multiple regression in behavioural research: Explanation and prediction, 3rd Edition.* London: Harcourt Brace.

Pinker, S. (1991). Rules of language. *Science, 253*, 530–535.

Pinker, S. (1994). *The language instinct.* Penguin Books.

Pinker, S. (1999). *Words and rules.* London: Weidenfeld & Nicolson.

Pinker, S., & Prince, A. (1988). On language and connectionism: Analysis of a parallel distributed processing model of language acquisition. *Cognition, 28*, 73–193.

Plaut, D.C., McClelland, J.L., Seidenberg, M.S., & Patterson, K. (1996). Understanding normal and impaired word reading: Computational principles in quasi-regular domains. *Psychological Review, 103*, 56–115.

Plunkett, K., & Juola, P. (1999). A connectionist model of English past tense and plural morphology. *Cognitive Science, 23*, 463–490.

Plunkett, K., & Marchman, V. (1991). U-shaped learning and frequency effects in a multi-layered perception: Implications for child language acquisition. *Cognition, 38*, 1–60.

Plunkett, K., & Marchman, V. (1993). From rote learning to system building: acquiring verb morphology in children and connectionist nets. *Cognition, 48*, 21–69.

Rossen, M., Bihrle, A., Klima, E.S., Bellugi, U., & Jones, W. (1996). Interaction between language and cognition: Evidence from Williams syndrome. In J.H. Beitchman, N. Cohen, M. Konstantareas, & R. Tannock (Eds.), *Language learning and behaviour* (pp. 367–392). New York: Cambridge University Press.

Rumelhart, D.E., & McClelland, J.L. (1986). On learning the past tense of English verbs. In J.L. McClelland, D.E. Rumelhart, & the PDP Research Group (Eds.), *Parallel distributed processing: Explorations in the microstructure of cognition, Vol. 2: Psychological and biological models* (pp. 216–271). Cambridge, MA: MIT Press.

Singer Harris, N.G., Bellugi, U., Bates, E., Jones, W., & Rossen, M. (1997). Contrasting profiles of language development in children with Williams and Down syndromes. *Developmental Neuropsychology, 13*, 345–370.

Tassabehji, M., Metcalfe, K., Karmiloff-Smith, A., Carette, M.J. Grant, J., Dennis, N., Reardon, W., Splitt, M., Read, A.P., & Donnai, D. (1999). Williams syndrome: Use of chromosomal micro-deletions as a tool to dissect cognitive and physical phenotypes. *American Journal of Human Genetics, 64*, 118–125.

Temple, C. (1997). *Developmental cognitive neuropsychology*. Hove: Psychology Press.

Thal, D., Bates, E., & Bellugi, U. (1989). Language and cognition in two children with Williams syndrome. *Journal of Speech and Hearing Research, 32*, 489–500.

Thomas, M.S.C., & Karmiloff-Smith, A. (2000). *Modelling language acquisition in atypical phenotypes.* Manuscript submitted for publication.

Tyler, L., Karmiloff-Smith, A., Voice, J.K., Stevens, T., Grant, J., Udwin, O., Davies, M., & Howlin, P. (1997). Do individuals with Williams syndrome have bizarre semantics? Evidence for lexical organization using an on-line task. *Cortex, 33*, 515–527.

Udwin, O., & Yule, W. (1990). Expressive language of children with Williams syndrome. *American Jornal of Medical Genetics, Suppl. 6*, 109–114.

Ullman, M.T. (1993). *The computation of inflectional morphology.* Unpublished doctoral dissertation, Massachusetts Institute of Technology, Cambridge, MA.

Ullman, M.T., Corkin, S., Coppola, M., Hickok, G., Growdon, J.H., Koroshetz, W.J., & Pinker, S. (1997). A neural dissociation within language: Evidence that the mental dictionary is part of declarative memory, and that grammatical rules are processed by the procedural system. *Journal of Cognitive Neuroscience, 9*, 266–276.

Ullman, M.T., & Gopnik, M. (1999). Inflectional morphology in a family with inherited specific language impairment. *Applied Psycholinguistics, 20*, 51–117.

Van der Lely, H.K.J. (1997). Language and cognitive development in a grammatical SLI boy: Modularity and innateness. *Journal of Neurolinguistics, 10*, 75–107.

Van der Lely, H.K.J. (1998). SLI in children: Movement, economy and deficits in the computational syntactic system. *Language Acquisition, 7*, 161–192.

Van der Lely, H.K.J., & Stollwerck, L. (1996). A grammatical specific language impairment in children: An autosomal dominant inheritance? *Brain and Language, 52*, 484–504.

Vicari, S., Brizzolara, D., Carlesimo, G., Pezzini, G., & Volterra, V. (1996). Memory abilities in children with Williams syndrome. *Cortex, 32*, 503–514.

Vicari, S., Carlesimo, G., Brizzolara, D. & Pezzini, G. (1996). Short-term memory in children with Williams syndrome: A reduced contribution of lexical-semantic knowledge to word span. *Neuropsychologia, 34*, 919–925.

Volterra, V., Capirci, O., Pezzini, G., Sabbadini, L., & Vicari, S. (1996). Linguistic abilities in Italian children with Williams syndrome. *Cortex, 32*, 663–677.

Wechsler, D. (1992). *Wechsler Intelligence Scale for Children, 3rd Edition*. London: The Psychological Corporation.

LANGUAGE AND COGNITIVE PROCESSES, 2001, *16* (2/3), 177–217

Past tense morphology in specifically language impaired and normally developing children

Heather K.J. van der Lely

Birkbeck College, University of London, London, UK

Michael T. Ullman

Department of Neuroscience,
Georgetown University, Washington, DC, USA

This study evaluates the input-processing deficit/single system and the grammar-specific deficit/dual system models to account for past tense formation in impaired and normal language development. We investigated regular and irregular past tense formation of 60 real and novel regular and irregular verbs in "Grammatical (G)-SLI" children (aged 9:3 to 12:10) and morphological- or vocabulary-matched younger control children. The G-SLI children and language ability (LA) controls showed quantitatively and qualitatively different patterns of performance. The LA controls, but not the

Requests for reprints should be addressed to H.K.J. van der Lely, Department of Psychology, Birkbeck College, University of London, Malet Street, London WC1E 7HX, UK. Email: h.vanderlely@psyc.bbk.ac.uk, or to M.T. Ullman, Department of Neuroscience, Georgetown University, 3900 Reservoir Road N.W., Washington, DC 20007, USA. Email: michael@giccs.georgetown.edu

We thank Linda Stollwerck, Stephen Long, and Marie Coppola for help with data collection, coding, and analysis; the staff and children from Dawn House School and St. Georges School for their help and co-operation, and Steven Pinker for his encouragement and for facilitating this collaboration. We appreciate helpful comments by audiences at presentations of this research: at the 20th Boston University Annual conference for Language development, Oxford University, and Birkbeck College, and also comments from Ram Frost and three anonymous reviewers. The study was supported by a project grant (G9325311N) from the British Medical Research Council, and a career development research fellowship from the Wellcome Trust (044179/Z/95/Z) for van der Lely; by the McDonnell–Pew Centre for Cognitive Neuroscience at MIT for Ullman, NIH grant HD 18381 and NSF grant BNS 91-09766 for Steven Pinker at MIT, and DOD grant DAMD17-93-V-3018 for Ullman at Georgetown University.

Ram Frost acted as editor for this manuscript.

http://www.tandf.co.uk/journals/pp/01690965.html   DOI: 10.1080/01690960042000076

G-SLI children, showed a significant advantage of regular over irregular past tense marking for real and novel verbs. Past tense frequency affected the G-SLI children, but not the controls' production of regular verbs, even with stem access controlled for. The G-SLI children's production of regular forms was significantly lower than that of the control groups. Frequency and phonological properties had a similar and significant effect on the G-SLI and LA controls' irregular formation. The G-SLI children's irregular past tense production did not differ from that of the morphological controls, but was lower than that of the vocabulary controls. We argue that the dual mechanism/grammar-specific deficit provides a parsimonious explanation for normal and impaired performance, and suggest that grammatical computations underlying regular past tense formation in normal grammar are impaired (not missing) in G-SLI grammar.

INTRODUCTION

Specific language impairment (SLI) is a heterogeneous disorder of language acquisition in children who do not have any other apparent cognitive, social, or neurological deficit that can obviously account for their impairment (Menyuk, 1964). The impairment affects around 7% of children (Leonard, 1998). Problems with inflectional morphology are frequently reported and are a prototypical characteristic of children with SLI (Bishop, 1994; Gopnik, 1990; Leonard, 1998; Oetting & Rice, 1993; Rice, Wexler, & Cleave, 1995). However, there is considerable controversy concerning the cause of the disorder and the nature of their inflectional morphology deficit. The controversy revolves around whether an input processing deficit (Bishop, 1997; Joanisse & Seidenberg, 1998b; Leonard, 1998; Tallal et al., 1996) or a grammar-specific deficit (Clahsen, 1989; Gopnik, 1990; Rice & Wexler, 1996; van der Lely, Rosen, & McClelland, 1998) causes SLI and whether or not representation of inflectional morphology is qualitatively different from that of normally developing children. One reason for this controversy is the variation in linguistic and cognitive characteristics found across different groups of children with SLI (Aram, Morris, & Hall, 1993; Bishop, Bishop, Bright, James, & van der Lely, 2000). The heterogeneity of SLI could reflect different causes of the disorder. To provide insight into this issue we investigated the production of real and novel regular and irregular verbs in a selected homogeneous SLI subgroup, 'Grammatical(G)-SLI children' (van der Lely, et al., 1998). Van der Lely and colleagues have claimed that G-SLI children have a primary deficit of the computational grammatical system (van der Lely, 1994, 1997a,b, 1998; van der Lely et al., 1998; van der Lely & Stollwerck, 1997). The apparent pure form of G-SLI found in this subgroup (van der Lely et al., 1998), but not in all subgroups of children with SLI (cf. Vargha-Khadem, Watkins, Alcock, Fletcher, & Passingham, 1995), makes them particularly well-suited to exploring the nature of their linguistic deficit and testing the opposing theories of SLI.

Grammatical(G)-SLI

Van der Lely and colleagues have identified a subgroup of SLI subjects who they claim have a primary and disproportionate grammatical impairment—'Grammatical(G)-SLI children' (van der Lely, 1994, 1997,a,b, 1998; van der Lely et al., 1998; van der Lely & Stollwerck, 1997). G-SLI affects between 10–20% of children with a persisting SLI and IQ > 85, and is consistent with an autosomal (non-sex linked) dominant inheritance (van der Lely & Stollwerck, 1996). Investigations of auditory, articulatory, and cognitive abilities, thought by some researchers to explain SLI (Leonard, 1998; Tallal & Piercy, 1973; Tallal et al., 1996; Wright et al., 1996), did not reveal the co-occurring deficits that have been found in some children with SLI (van der Lely et al., 1998). Linguistically, G-SLI children show that they inconsistently manipulate core aspects of syntax, including tense and agreement marking (*My Dad go to work*), assigning thematic roles in passive sentences and embedded phrases and clauses (*The boy was pushed by the girl; The dog with the bone is …*), assigning reference to pronouns or reflexives (*Mowgli says Baloo is tickling him/himself*), and producing Wh-questions (*Who Tom see some-one in the kitchen?*) (van der Lely 1994, 1996a,b, 1998; van der Lely & Battell, 1998; van der Lely & Hennessey, 1999, van der Lely & Stollwerck, 1997). Thus, while G-SLI children share many grammatical inflectional characteristics with other SLI children (Bishop, 1997; Leonard, 1998), investigations also show that they make syntactic structural errors. However, aspects of language outside grammar, such as pragmatic inference and verbal logical reasoning are not impaired in G-SLI children (van der Lely et al., 1998; cf. Bishop, 1997). For example, G-SLI children show the appropriate pragmatic knowledge needed to determine conversational inferences, use pronouns in narratives, and to facilitate sentence comprehension (Surian, Baron-Cohen, & van der Lely, 1996; van der Lely, 1997b; van der Lely & Dewart, 1986; van der Lely & Stollwerck, 1997). The validity of G-SLI as a qualitatively distinct subgroup is an empirical issue to which this paper contributes.

Regular and irregular inflectional morphology in children with SLI

The morphological representation and processing of regular and irregular morphology in children with SLI is of particular relevance to this study. Previous investigations of regular and irregular plural and past tense morphology in different groups of SLI children have revealed conflicting findings. On the one hand, the findings for young children with SLI indicate the relatively appropriate use of irregular morphology but abnormal use of regular morphology in comparison to language- or age-matched peers (Leonard, McGregor, & Allen, 1992; Oetting & Rice, 1993; Oetting & Horohov, 1997; Rice et al., 1995). This impairment is evinced in first, a greater number of omissions of past tense marking in obligatory contexts than language control children (Leonard, 1998). Second, there is less frequent use of over-regularisations of irregular words (*felled*; *mices*) and regularisations of novel words (*bips*) for SLI children than for children developing normally (Leonard, 1989; 1998; Marchman & Weismer, 1994; Marchman, Wulfeck, & Weismer, 1999). Third, frequency effects are reported in several studies for regularly inflected plural nouns and past-tense verbs for children with SLI but for normally developing children (Oetting & Horohov, 1997; Oetting & Rice, 1993; Ullman & Gopnik, 1999). An atypical frequency effect is also evident in German-speaking children with SLI. Normally developing German-speaking children over-generalise the regular-default, but relatively infrequent *-s* plural affix, whereas some children with SLI overgeneralise the most frequent *-en/n* plural affix (Bartke, 1998; Clahsen, Rothweiler, Woest, & Marcus, 1992). Finally, Marchman et al.'s (1997, 1999) analysis of children's regular and irregular error patterns of regular and irregular verbs, demonstrated that SLI children were more sensitive to frequency and phonological characteristics of stem and past tense forms than age-matched control children. However, Marchman's (1999) analysis did not focus on whether frequency and phonological patterns were having a different or similar effect on the proportion of correct regular and irregular forms, or on whether the SLI children's performance was qualitatively different from younger children of similar language abilities. Thus, to understand further the nature of inflectional morphology in SLI and normally developing children, this study investigates whether frequency is having a qualitatively different effect on the G-SLI and younger normally developing children's correct production of regular and irregular forms as well as on unmarked forms.

Alternatively, some researchers argue that some 5- to 8-year-old SLI children have normal representation of irregular and regular inflections (Clahsen et al., 1992; Marchman & Weismer, 1994; Marchman et al., 1999; Oetting & Horohov, 1997; Oetting & Rice, 1993). Oetting and Rice's (1993) study of noun compounds revealed that 5-year-old SLI children use irregular plurals inside compounds (*mice-eater*) but not regular plurals (**rats-eater*) – a pattern similar to that found in normally developing children (Gordon, 1985; Oetting & Rice, 1993; van der Lely & Christian, 2000). Moreover, Oetting and Horohov's (1997) data from 6-year-old SLI children indicated a normal distinction between past tense production of irregular and regular forms for irregular and denomalised verbs (*fly-flew/flied*). The SLI children produced 80% irregular past tense forms for the irregular verbs, while the age- and MLU-matched controls produced 85% and 41% irregular forms, respectively. For the denominal verbs, for which a regular past tense form is expected, the SLI children produced 46% regular inflections, whereas the age and MLU controls produced 77% and 67%. Thus, while the SLI children showed a distinction between the production of regular and irregular morphology, they appeared to use regular morphology less than their age or language peers did.

However, investigations of older SLI subjects indicate that the distinction between regular and irregular morphology found in normally developing children is not evident in their performance (Ullman & Gopnik, 1994, 1999; van der Lely & Christian, 2000). Ullman and Gopnik's (1994, 1999) study of a large family (the 'KE' family) found that impaired family members produced correct regular and irregular past tense forms at a similar rate, which in turn was worse than that of control subjects. Vargha-Khadem et al. (1995) reported a similar finding for the same impaired KE family members. Furthermore, van der Lely and Christian's (2000) study of 10–18-year-old subjects with G-SLI revealed a significant use of regular plurals inside compounds (**rats-eater*), unlike age- or language-matched control groups of children. However, both the G-SLI subjects and the control groups produced irregular plurals inside compounds (van der Lely & Christian, 2000). Note, although Oetting and Rice's (1993) investigation revealed that the majority (80%) of their 5-year-old SLI subjects showed the 'normal' regular-irregular distinction with irregular plurals but not regular plurals occurring inside compounds, three of the subjects (20%) used regular plurals inside compounds.

In sum: there appear to be qualitative differences in the nature of the SLI deficit in different populations of subjects. Although some children with SLI evidence a regular-irregular distinction found in normally developing children, suggesting normal morphological representations, a large number of studies report some impairment with regular morphology. One explanation for these different findings is that the full extent of the SLI deficit is not apparent until the child is older. Alternatively, the linguistic characteristics and the underlying nature of SLI may vary in different populations. This opens up the possibility that group means from heterogeneous groups of SLI children could hide potentially interesting differences. The contrasting findings emphasise the need for careful subject description in all investigations of SLI subjects and comparisons between findings of different studies if we are to shed light on these issues. This investigation of regular and irregular past tense production in the G-SLI subgroup provides an important step towards this goal and enables us to evaluate the alternative theories of SLI with respect to the nature of this subgroup's performance.

The cause of G-SLI

The input-processing account hypotheses that impaired input processes and limited processing capacity causes SLI (Bishop, 1997; Elman et al., 1996; Joanisse & Seidenberg, 1998b; Leonard, 1998; Tallal et al., 1996). Tallal and colleagues claim that SLI can be traced to a deficit in the rate of auditory processing that is not language-specific (Bishop, 1997; Leonard, 1998; Tallal & Piercy, 1973; Tallal et al., 1996; Wright et al., 1996). Leonard et al. (1992) argues that this auditory perceptual deficit causes SLI children to have problems perceiving morphemes such as -ed or -s, which have 'low perceptual salience'. Therefore, additional resources are required to perceive such morphemes, which causes further difficulties learning morphological paradigms (Leonard, 1998; Leonard et al., 1992). Moreover, they claim that these children's general processing capacity limitations affect short-term (phonological) memory, the production of consonant clusters, the speed of processing and retrieving words such that consonants and final morphemes may be lost in the production process, and cause delay in lexical development which is seen as central to problems with inflectional morphology (Bishop, 1997; Conti-Ramsden & Jones, 1997; Elman et al., 1996; Gathercole & Baddeley, 1990; Joanisse & Seidenberg, 1998; Leonard, 1998; Marchman et al., 1999).

The different variants of the input-processing deficit hypothesis are consistent with the view that a single mechanism underlies regular (*rob-robbed*) and irregular (*give-gave*) past tense inflection (Bates & Mac-Whinney, 1987; Elman et al., 1996; Marchman, 1997; Plunkett & Marchman, 1991, 1993). The 'single system' account proposes that regular and irregular forms are represented and processed by a single associative memory system (Bates & MacWhinney, 1989; Elman et al., 1996; Joanisse & Seidenberg, 1998b; Plunkett & Marchman, 1991, 1993; Rumelhart & McClelland, 1986). Rule-like generalisations, such as the regular -ed inflectional rule, are thought to emerge over the course of learning associations between verb stems and past tense forms. Specifically, both regular and irregular mappings are learned by a constraint-satisfaction learning system that exploits the way in which surface-level features predict the relations between stem and past-tense forms (Marchman et al., 1999). Thus, the acquisition and productivity of inflectional morphology is based on lexical processing and development whereby lexical factors, such as item frequency and phonological attributes of 'neighbouring' verbs, are seen as central to the acquisition process (Bates & MacWhinney, 1989;

Daugherty & Seidenberg, 1992; Elman et al., 1996; Hare, Elman, & Daugherty, 1995; MacWhinney & Leinbach, 1991; MacDonald et al., 1994; McClelland et al., 1986; Marchman, 1993; Plunkett & Marchman, 1991; Rumelhart & McClelland, 1986). Therefore, based on the input-processing/single mechanism view comparisons between morphological productions of children with G-SLI with those of a younger group of children matched on their vocabulary development are of particular relevance.

The grammar-specific deficit account claims that impairments of mechanisms and/or representations specific to the grammatical system cause SLI (Clahsen, 1989; Gopnik, 1990; Gopnik & Crago, 1991; Rice & Wexler, 1996; Ullman & Gopnik, 1994, 1999; van der Lely, 1994; van der Lely et al., 1998). Therefore, aspects of language that rely on grammatical processes may be impaired while those that rely on other processes, such as associative learning and memory, may be spared. The grammar-specific deficit hypothesis assumes that cognitive mechanisms are specialised for particular functions, such as grammar, and so can be differentially impaired (Chomsky, 1986; Fodor, 1983; Pinker, 1994). Thus, this hypothesis is consistent with the dual-mechanism view of past-tense morphology which proposes that different mechanisms underlie regular and irregular inflectional morphology (Marcus et al., 1992; Pinker, 1999, 1991; Pinker & Prince, 1988, 1992). According to the 'dual-system' framework, irregular forms are stored in and retrieved from an associative lexical memory—similar to that proposed by the single system view to account for regular as well as irregular inflections (Pinker, 1991; Pinker & Prince, 1992). Thus, both the dual and single system accounts claim that irregular verbs are subject to lexical memory effects, such as frequency and phonological neighbourhood effects (Prasada & Pinker, 1993; Ullman, 1993, 1999). In contrast, dual system models propose that regular forms are computed by a grammatical rule, which underlies the -ed suffixation of the verb stem. Retrieval of an irregular past tense form blocks the rule (gave pre-empts gived). When an irregular form is not successfully retrieved, the rule may be applied, resulting in an over-regularisation (Marcus et al., 1992; Pinker, 1991). According to the dual system framework, lexical factors such as frequency or phonological properties of regular past tense should not affect their formation and thus, lexical development is not expected to strongly predict performance of regular past tense forms.

Therefore, in this study, the comparison between the production of regular and irregular past tense forms in G-SLI children and younger children matched on vocabulary ability enables us to test the contrasting predictions from the two accounts of G-SLI and the role of vocabulary in inflectional morphology development. The comparison between G-SLI children and children matched on vocabulary or morphological abilities enables us to evaluate whether the pattern of performance found for the

G-SLI children could be expected in normally developing children at a similar stage of vocabulary or morphological development.[1]

Predictions

According to the single system account, for normally developing children lexical factors such as frequency and phonological similarity should account for much if not all of any differences between the use of regular and irregular forms (Marchman, 1997). Their production rate of novel irregularised past tense forms (*crive-crove*) should increase with age as memory traces of similar stem-past pairs strengthen (e.g., *drive-drove*, *dive-dove*). Therefore, frequency effects may be expected for both regular and irregular forms. However, frequency effects might not be found for regular verbs if the *-ed* mappings have been sufficiently learnt, such that memory traces of individual past tense forms are overwhelmed (Daugherty & Seidenberg, 1992; Seidenberg, 1992).

For the G-SLI children, the input-processing deficit hypothesis would predict a general impairment for their chronological age across regular and irregular past tense forms. However, as lexical development should predict inflectional morphological performance (Marchman et al., 1999), G-SLI children's performance should not differ from that of the vocabulary-matched control children. Moreover, the pattern of performance across regular and irregular real and novel verbs should be similar to the pattern found for normally developing children (Marchman & Weismer, 1994). However, should any differences be found between regular and irregular forms for the normally developing children, these may be exaggerated for the G-SLI children. Our logic for predicting this is based on Leonard's (1988) proposal that perceiving and producing the regular *-ed* morpheme requires extra processing capacity (Leonard et al., 1992). Therefore, we may expect all the children, and particularly G-SLI children, to be worse at producing regular than irregular past tense forms. With respect to frequency, to our knowledge no existing single-system model predicts that the type of damage leading to G-SLI should result in frequency effects for regulars, where they are not found for normal children. Therefore, the

---

[1] The Grammar-specific deficit account and the dual system models (and similarly the input-processing deficit and single system accounts) are independent, but share underlying theoretical assumptions about how the brain develops and functions. The accounts of SLI (e.g., van der Lely, 1998; Leonard, 1998) provide (a) a characterisation of SLI and (b) explicit predictions as to which aspects of language will or will not be impaired in children with SLI. The single/dual mechanism models are more general theories about how the mental lexicon is organised and while they should be able to accommodate both normal and impaired language development, they do not provide the level of explanatory detail of language breakdown as the specific hypotheses of SLI.

single system/input-processing deficit framework predicts that a similar frequency effect will be found for G-SLI children and normally developing children (Marchman & Weismer, 1994).

The dual system account predicts that normally developing children should be better at producing regular past tense forms, which are rule-produced, than irregulars, which are retrieved from memory. Differences between correct production of regular and irregular past tense verb forms may be particularly evident with low frequency verbs, which are less likely than high frequency verbs to be stored forms. This is because, according to the dual mechanism model, failure to retrieve a past tense form is likely to result in the default regular rule being applied (Marcus et al., 1992; Pinker, 1991). This would result in correct regular forms but incorrect over-regularised irregular forms. The dual-system model makes a clear prediction with respect to frequency effects. For normal children, frequency effects should be found for irregulars, but not for regulars. If past tense forms are computed by the application of a rule to their stems (e.g., *rob* + *-ed* = *robbed*), then once access to the stem (*rob*) is held constant, the frequency of the past tense form (*robbed*) should not predict the likelihood of the form's correct production. However, if past tense forms are retrieved from memory, their frequency should predict the likelihood of their correct retrieval, even with access to the stem held constant.

The grammar-specific deficit hypothesis predicts that G-SLI children should have particular difficulties computing the past tense *-ed* rule. Therefore, they may memorise both regular and irregular forms in the lexicon. This leads to the prediction that G-SLI children, unlike normally developing children, should show a similar performance on regular and irregular past tense production, and frequency effects for both past tense types. Furthermore, the G-SLI and normally developing children should evince a qualitatively different pattern of performance across regular and irregular past tense formation for real and novel verbs. G-SLI children should be particularly impaired in relation to the control children with regular but not irregular past tense formation. In addition, among the G-SLI children, the default regular rule may not be applied in the event of failure to retrieve an irregular form. However, some productivity of regular and irregular forms through associative mechanisms may be expected. Note, independently, the Grammar-specific deficit hypothesis predicts a general grammatical impairment affecting syntactic tense marking (Rice & Wexler, 1996; van der Lely 1998). Thus, this would result in a general increase in unmarked forms being produced in past tense contexts.

In sum: according to the input processing deficit/single system account lexical processing and development will predict both regular and irregular inflectional marking for the G-SLI children and controls. Conversely the grammar-specific deficit/dual system account predicts that lexical development and processing will account for irregular but not regular inflectional marking. Moreover, for the G-SLI children, in contrast to the control children, lexical factors are also predicted to affect regular past tense formation, as their grammatical rule-system is impaired. Thus, the clearest distinction between the input-processing deficit/single system and the grammar-specific deficit/dual system accounts may be found in the production of regular inflection and comparisons between the G-SLI and vocabulary-matched control children. Therefore, we will pay particular attention to these aspects of the data.

METHODS

Subjects

Four subject groups participated in the experiment: a subgroup of 12 G-SLI children and three groups of younger children with normally developing language. The three younger groups provided control groups for different aspects of language and allowed us to access developmental changes in children from ages 5:5 to 8:9.

Grammatical(G)-SLI children

The 12 G-SLI children had a mean age of 11:3 (range 9:3–12:10). There were 10 boys and 2 girls. The selection criteria and procedure for the G-SLI subgroup have already been well documented (van der Lely 1996a,b; van der Lely & Stollwerck, 1996, 1997). Therefore, only a summary will be provided here. We excluded two types of children. First, we excluded any children without the grammatical deficits that form our selection criteria. Second, we excluded any children with co-occurring problems of speech production (dyspraxia), pragmatic aspects of language (Adams & Bishop, 1989) attention, or non-verbal abilities. It is emphasised that approximately only 20% of children with a persisting SLI and IQ >85 meet our G-SLI criteria (van der Lely & Stollwerck, 1996)

The G-SLI subjects' non-verbal cognitive abilities were assessed by performance subtests of standardised IQ tests (e.g., The British Ability Scales, Elliott et al., 1978). All the children's scores fell within normal limits for their chronological age (i.e., IQ >85, +/−1.0 SD). They had a mean IQ of 99.09 (11.46 SD). They were assessed on a battery of tests, which tapped a range of comprehension and expressive language abilities. The tests provided six standardised measurements of different aspects of language abilities in relation to the children's chronological ages. The six tests were used in the initial selection process, and four of them for matching the G-SLI children with control subjects. The G-SLI children's scores fell at least -1.5 *SD* below the expected sore for their chronological age on at least one standardised language test. In addition, each child made at least 20% subject-verb agreement or tense errors in obligatory contexts in spontaneous speech (Goellner, 1995; van der Lely, 1996b), and also 20% 'reversal errors' when assigning thematic roles in reversible full passive sentences (van der Lely, 1996a). Ten of the twelve children performed at chance when assigning reference to pronouns and reflexives when syntactic knowledge of binding principles was required (van der Lely & Stollwerck, 1997). All the children showed a required persistent and disproportionate impairment of grammatical abilities, compared to single word comprehension and expression, sentence length, and information content in their expressive language. A summary of the overall G-SLI group's subject details can be found in Table 1. Appendix A provides individual subjects' test scores on the six selection tests.

Language ability control groups

Three groups of 12 normally developing younger children provided language ability matched (LA) control groups. Four of the standardised language tests, used for selecting and assessing the G-SLI children, were used for matching purposes. The youngest group (LA1 controls, mean age 5:9) were matched to the G-SLI children on two tests which tapped morpho-grammatical abilities:[2] The Grammatical closure subtest from the Illinois Test of Psycholinguistic Abilities (Kirk, McCarthy, & Kirk, 1968)—a test of morphological production which includes regular and irregular morphology;

TABLE 1

Subject details: Chronological ages and raw scores from the four standardised tests, which were used for matching the G-SLI children with the control children

	G-SLI children (n=12) Mean (SD)	LA1 controls (n=12) Mean (SD)	LA2 controls (n=12) Mean (SD)	LA3 controls (n=12) Mean (SD)	Summary of analysis between groups
Chronological age	11:2 (1:1)	5:9 (0:4)	6:11 (0:4)	7:11 (0.5)	
Range	9:3–12:10	5:5–6:4	6:5–7:4	7:5–8:9	
TROG	13.08 (1.78)	14.41 (8.56)	16.00 (1.75)	17.33 (1.23)	LA1=G-SLI<(LA2=LA3)
GC-ITPA	20.00 (3.56)	21.25 (3.16)	26.25 (4.08)	28.91 (2.19)	LA1=G-SLI<(LA2=LA3)
BPVS	78.83 (8.93)	56.25 (8.91)	71.67 (9.71)	80.00 (9.62)	LA1<G-SLI=(LA2<LA3)
NV-BAS	17.91 (1.17)	15.67 (1.61)	17.17 (1.27)	17.50 (0.90)	LA1<G-SLI=(LA2=LA3)

TROG, Test for Reception of Grammar (Bishop, 1983); GC-ITPA, Grammatical Closure sub-test, Illinois Test of Psycholinguistic Abilities (Kirk et al., 1968); BPVS, British Picture Vocabulary Scales (Dunn et al., 1982); NV-BAS, Naming Vocabulary, British Ability Scales (Elliott et al., 1978).

---

[2] Note, these morpho-grammatical tests tap non-grammatical abilities, such as lexical-conceptual knowledge, as well as grammatical knowledge.

and the Test of Reception of Grammar (Bishop, 1983)—a test of sentence comprehension. The LA1 controls scored significantly lower than the G-SLI children on expressive and receptive tests of single word vocabulary knowledge. The two older control groups (the LA2 controls, mean age 6:11, and LA3 controls, mean age 7:11) were matched to the G-SLI children on their expression and comprehension of single words: Naming Vocabulary from the British Ability Scales (Elliott, Murray, & Pearson, 1978) and The British Picture Vocabulary Scales (Dunn, Dunn, Whetton, & Pintilie, 1982). However, the LA2 and LA3 controls scored significantly higher than the G-SLI children on the two tests of morpho-grammatical abilities. Table 1 provides a summary of the details. Further details can be found in van der Lely (1996a) and van der Lely and Stollwerck (1997).

Materials

Each subject was presented with 60 verbs in the past tense production task. The verbs were drawn from the stimuli developed by Ullman (1993, 1999) and Ullman and Gopnik (1994, 1999). The verbs belonged to four classes. (1) 16 irregular verbs (*give-gave*), which take only an irregular past tense form. Thus 'doublet' verbs, such as *dive-dove/dived*, which take an irregular and a regular form, were excluded. (2) 16 regular verbs (*rob-robbed*), which take only a regular past tense form. Their stems were phonologically dissimilar to the stems of all irregular verbs. (3) 16 'novel irregular' verbs whose stems were phonologically similar to the stems of real irregular verbs, and which can take irregular or regular past tense forms (e.g., *crive-crove/crived, cf. drive-drove*). (4) 12 'novel regular' verbs (e.g., *brop-bropped*), whose stems were phonologically dissimilar to the stems of all irregulars, and phonologically similar to the stems of regular verbs. One irregular verb (*split*) and two novel irregular verbs (*ret, scrit*) were excluded from all analyses because their actual or likely past tense forms are identical to their stems.

Half of the real irregulars and half of the real regulars had high past tense frequencies (e.g., *gave, robbed*) and half had low past tense frequencies (e.g., *dug, stalked*). Frequency counts were drawn from the 17.9 million word British English COBUILD corpus of the University of Birmingham, by the Centre for Lexical Information (CELEX) at the University of Nijmegen. Individual verb frequencies were augmented by 1 and ln-transformed (see Appendix B1). A 2×2 verb type (regular/irregular) by frequency (low/high) ANOVA was carried out on the items' past tense COBUILD frequencies. The past tense frequencies for the irregular verbs overall were significantly higher than the regular verbs, $F(1, 27) = 9.50, p < .005$. A significant effect of frequency was found, $F(1, 27) = 43.78, p < .001$, but there was no significant interaction.

In order to ensure that the verbs selected for the task were familiar to the children, and that the children's familiarity reflected the frequencies provided by the COBUILD frequency counts, we carried out a stem familiarity task. All 12 G-SLI and 36 control children were asked to give a familiarity rating of the verb stems for all real and novel verbs. This task was carried out approximately 2 months after the past tense production task. Details of the stem familiarity procedure can be found in Appendix C. The children's mean stem familiarity ratings can be found in Table 2.

A correlation was carried out between the stem frequencies provided by the COBUILD counts and the G-SLI and control children's stem familiarity ratings. A high and significant correlation was found, $r(57) = .852$, $p < .0001$. This indicates that the COBUILD stem and past tense frequencies are an appropriate estimate of the familiarity and frequency of the verbs for our children.

The task was based on Berko's (1958) "Wug test". The verbs were presented in the context of two spoken sentences, such as "Every day I rob a bank. Just like every day, yesterday I _____ a bank". The introductory and elicitation sentences for each verb shared the same two-word complement or adjunct; both of these words were morphologically simple and of relatively high frequency. The sentences were drawn from those developed by Ullman (1993) and Ullman and Gopnik (1994, 1999), but were slightly modified for our British children. A full list of verbs and their accompanying arguments can be found in Appendix B.

Procedure

Subjects were tested individually in a quiet room, and were seated beside the experimenter, who spoke the following instructions: "This is a game

TABLE 2

Mean stem familiarity ratings (0 to 4) for each subject group (standard deviations calculated over items)

Verb class	Example		G-SLI		LA1		LA2		LA3	
			Mean	SD	Mean	SD	Mean	SD	Mean	SD
Regulars			1.95	0.59	2.16	0.77	2.10	0.90	2.60	0.86
High frequency	rob	n=8	2.01	0.45	2.42	0.77	2.42	0.61	2.88	0.69
Low frequency	flap	n=8	1.90	0.73	1.90	0.73	1.77	1.05	2.33	0.98
Irregulars			2.51	0.65	2.69	0.58	2.65	0.60	3.24	0.28
High frequency	give	n=7	2.77	0.61	2.98	0.41	2.94	0.49	3.39	0.24
Low frequency	dig	n=8	2.25	0.61	2.40	0.61	2.36	0.58	3.24	0.25
Novel regulars	brop	n=12	1.16	0.33	0.97	0.34	0.61	0.17	0.63	0.23
Novel irregulars	crive	n=14	1.37	0.45	1.21	0.30	0.43	0.22	0.65	0.27

with some words. First I'll say something like 'Every day I **go** to work', and you have to repeat it. Then I'll give you a sentence describing the same event, but in the past: 'Just like every day, yesterday I _____'. You have to say the missing word and finish off the sentence. Just say the first thing you think of that sounds right. In some sentences you might not know some of the words. For example, 'Every day I **prame** quite well'. Just do the best you can." Further encouragement was given to the child if necessary (e.g., "What would you say for the missing word?"). The child was given three practice items: the item in the instructions, and two additional items – one real verb (Every day I **weep** over her) and one novel verb (Every day I **scrig** over there). When the experimenter was reasonably confident that the child understood the task, the test sentences were administered. All subjects received the same pseudo-randomised version of each task: The item order was randomised and then gone over by hand to ensure that similar-sounding forms were not ordered too close to each other. All sessions were audio-recorded with a Sony DAT recorder using an Electret condenser microphone (ECM-959), which was positioned on a stand approximately 20 cm to the side of the child's mouth. This provided a high quality recording, from which a detailed transcription was made. The past tense production task was given to 11 of the 12 G-SLI children; one subject (AT) was unavailable for testing.

Coding of responses.   Subjects' responses to the missing past tense form (Just like every day, yesterday I _____) were assigned to one of four categories. (1) Unmarked form (e.g., *rob*, *give*, *crive*, *brop*). (2) Regularised *-ed*-suffixed past tense form (e.g., *robbed*, *gived*, *crived*, *bropped*). (3) Irregularised past tense form (e.g., *rob-rab*, *give-gave*, *crive-crove*, *brop-brap*). For novel irregular verbs, the categorisation of a response as an irregularisation was based on the similarity of its stem-past phonological transformation to the transformations of existing irregulars. For real and novel regular verbs (*rob*, *brap*), a response was categorised as an irregularisation if it entailed a vowel change (*rob-rab*, *brop-brap*). Thus there was more than one possible irregularised past for some verbs – e.g., *frink-frank/frunk/frought*). (4) 'Other responses', which included phono-logical errors as well as the use of an incorrect suffix (*-ing*, *-s*, *-er*), an irregular past participle (*break-broken*), or a semantically related word (*grind-corn*, *bend-broke*, *rush-ran*).

RESULTS AND DISCUSSION

The majority of the G-SLI and control children's responses fell into three categories: unmarked, regularised, and irregularised (see coding above and

TABLE 3
Mean responses rates (as % of items) for high and low frequency regular and irregular verbs (standard deviations calculated over subjects)

Verb class	Response	Example	G-SLI Mean	SD	LA1 Mean	SD	LA2 Mean	SD	LA3 Mean	SD
Regular verbs										
High frequency	Unmarked	*rob*	60.2	15.6	29.2	27.9	22.9	20.5	19.8	24.1
(rob)	Irregularised	*rab*	0		0		1.0	3.6	0	
n=8	Regularised	*robbed*	33.0	18.8	66.7	27.9	71.9	20.8	80.2	24.1
Low frequency	Unmarked	*flap*	70.5	17.0	39.6	27.1	22.9	29.1	16.7	30.3
(flap)	Irregularised	*flup*	0		0		0		0	
n=8	Regularised	*flapped*	11.4	14.2	48.9	25.0	72.9	28.1	76.0	28.6
Irregular verbs										
High frequency	Unmarked	*give*	67.5	28.6	35.7	30.8	7.1	16.7	19.0	29.4
(give)	Irregularised	*gave*	19.9	22.9	34.5	32.5	70.3	25.4	59.5	34.9
n=7	Regularised	*gived*	10.4	12.9	28.6	25.8	19.0	19.6	17.9	21.2
Low frequency	Unmarked	*dig*	73.9	23.4	51.0	31.3	21.9	27.2	25.0	30.6
(dig)	Irregularised	*dug*	13.6	22.0	18.6	26.0	42.7	20.3	41.7	31.7
n=8	Regularised	*digged*	5.7	12.9	21.9	17.0	25.0	19.2	24.0	23.5

Tables 3 and 4). There were a small number of 'other' responses, which we shall discuss first. This will be followed by the main analyses, which consider the unmarked, regularised, and irregularised responses to the real and novel verbs. ANOVAs were carried out by subject (F_1) and by item (F_2).

Other responses

Phonological errors were extremely rare for real verbs (e.g., *bend-spend*) and accounted for less than 3% of responses for any group. There were no significant differences in the four subject groups' phonological errors for real verbs, $F_1(3, 43) = 0.38, p = .76; F_2(3, 93) = 0.63, p = .60$. However, for novel verbs, phonological errors for all types of responses (unmarked, regularised, irregularised forms) were more numerous (e.g., *plam-plang*, *trab-strab*, *brop-brok*, *vurn-vured*, *strink-skwinked*). Overall, responses containing phonological errors accounted for 17.25% of the G-SLI children's productions, and 11.45%, 5.10%, and 5.85% of the LA1, LA2 and LA3 controls' responses respectively. Analysis revealed that, for the novel verbs, the G-SLI children produced significantly more phonological errors than the LA1 controls, $F_1(1, 43) = 4.45, p = .041;$

TABLE 4
Mean responses rates (as % of items) for the novel verbs for the four subject groups
(standard deviation calculated over subjects)

Verb class	Response	Example	G-SLI		LA1		LA2		LA3	
			Mean %	SD	Mean %	SD	Mean %	SD	Mean %	SD
Novel regular	Unmarked	brop	56.8	17.4	33.3	25.1	20.1	28.1	15.3	28.2
	Irregular	brap	1.5	3.4	6.3	5.2	2.8	5.4	2.1	3.8
	Regular	brapped	6.8	9.0	31.3	17.1	66.7	30.8	73.6	27.7
Novel irregular	Unmarked	crive	59.1	12.8	39.9	22.9	28.0	32.7	29.8	25.8
	Irregular	crove	3.9	5.9	9.5	18.6	8.9	14.6	9.5	12.3
	Regular	crived	7.1	7.1	22.6	14.9	55.4	34.5	50.6	26.3

$F_2(1, 27) = 4.63, p = .040$, and than the LA2 and LA3 controls, $F_1(1, 43) = 23.62, p < .001; F_2(1, 27) = 22.77, p < .001.$[3]

There were three semantic errors for the real verbs: *grind-corn* and *bend-broke*, produced by two G-SLI children, and *rush-run*, produced by an LA1 control child. Both the G-SLI children and control children produced real words for the novel verbs. There was often some phonological similarity between the novel word and the word produced by the child (e.g., *satch-sat, plam-plant, spuff-splashed*). Finally, there were a small number of forms with incorrect suffixes; -*s*-suffixed forms were produced by G-SLI subjects AZ (*thinks, splits*) and RJ (*flaps*), and the progressive -*ing* suffix was used once by G-SLI subject BS (*rushing*). The normal control children did not produce any inappropriately suffixed forms.

Regular and irregular real verbs

The groups' mean number of unmarked, regularised and irregularised responses to the real verbs are shown in Table 3.

Unmarked verb responses

The G-SLI subjects produced a large number (mean range 60 to 75%) of unmarked responses for the real verbs (*rob, give*) (see Table 3). The

---

[3] To ensure that possible phonological deficits leading to such errors among the G-SLI children were not significantly influencing the results, we carried out all the main analyses for the novel verbs (reported below) with such phonological errors included – for example, *frink-finked* was counted as an acceptable regular past tense response. The phonological errors were not found to affect the results. These analyses yielded the same pattern of results as when the phonological errors were excluded.

unmarked forms for the groups were analysed in a 4 (Group: G-SLI, LA1, LA2, LA3) × 2 (Verb type: regular, irregular) × 2 (Frequency: high, low) ANOVA. A significant main effect of group was found, $F_1(3, 43) = 11.29$, $p < .001$; $F_2(3, 81) = 87.52$, $p < .0001$. Further planned comparisons confirmed that the G-SLI children produced significantly more unmarked forms than the morphology-matched LA1 controls, $F_1(1, 43) = 9.15$, $p = .004$, $F_2(1, 30) = 48.26$, $p < .001$) and the older LA2 and LA3 vocabulary-matched controls,[4] $F_1(1, 43) = 33.37$, $p < .0001$; $F_2(1, 30) = 173.45$, $p < .0001$. In addition the LA1 controls produced significantly more unmarked forms than the LA2 and LA3 controls, $F_1(1, 43) = 5.66$, $p = .022$; $F_2(1, 30) = 35.20$, $p < .0001$.

The main effect of verb type was significant by subject, $F_1(1, 43) = 15.21$, $p < .001$, but not by item, $F_2(1, 29) = 0.43$, $p = .516$. This reflected a trend for a greater number of unmarked forms for the irregular verbs than the regular verbs over all subject groups (see Table 3). No other main effects were significant nor were any interactions significant.

In summary, the G-SLI children produced significantly more unmarked forms than each group of control children but the pattern of unmarked forms for the regular and irregular verbs was similar to that of the LA controls. Verb frequency did not significantly affect any of the groups' production of unmarked forms. Whilst the results suggest that more unmarked responses may be produced for irregular than regular verbs, this finding was not robust. Finally, the results suggest that in normally developing children there is some developmental change between 5 years and 6–8 years, with the older children producing fewer unmarked forms when using this elicitation paradigm.

Correct responses (*rob-robbed, give-gave*)

A 4 (Group) × 2 (Verb type: regular, irregular) × 2 (Frequency: High, Low) ANOVA was used to analyse the correct responses of the G-SLI and control groups. The triple interaction was significant, $F_1(3, 43) = 5.42$, $p = .003$; $F_2(3, 81) = 3.79$, $p = .013$, indicating that frequency and verb type are differentially affecting the groups' correct responses. To investigate this further, we carried out two additional ANOVAs on the correct responses – first on the irregular verbs, and second on the regular verbs.

For the irregular verbs a 4 (Group) × 2 (Frequency) ANOVA revealed significant main effects for group, $F_1(3, 43) = 7.01$, $p < .001$; $F_2(3, 39) = 28.49$, $p < .001$, and frequency, $F_1(1, 43) = 26.08$, $p < .001$; $F_2(1, 13) =$

---

[4] We analysed the LA2 and LA3 control groups together in the planned comparisons when comparing their performance with the G-SLI children because both of these groups were matched on vocabulary scores to the G-SLI children.

6.64. $p = .023$. However, the interaction was not significant by subject or by item, $F_1(3, 43) = 1.80$, $p = .162$; $F_2(3, 39) = 1.55$, $p = .216$. This indicates that frequency played a similar role in the production of irregular verbs for all four groups of children.

Planned comparisons revealed that the G-SLI children's percentage of correct irregular verb responses was not significantly different from that of the LA1 controls for either the high frequency irregular verbs, $F_1(1, 43) = 1.50$, $p = .227$; $F_2(1, 6) = 3.84$, $p = .098$, or low frequency irregular verbs, $F_1(1, 43) = 0.26$, $p = .616$; $F_2(1, 7) = 1.26$, $p = .29$. However, their percentage of correct responses was significantly lower than the LA2 and LA3 controls for both the high frequency irregular verbs, $F_1(1, 43) = 17.99$, $p < .001$; $F_2(1, 6) = 48.45$, $p < .001$, and the low frequency irregular verbs, $F_1(1, 43) = 10.48$, $p = .002$, $F_2(1, 7) = 11.33$, $p = .012$. The LA1 controls' correct responses were also significantly lower than the LA2 and LA3 controls responses on the high frequency, $F_1(1, 43) = 8.53$, $p = .006$; $F_2(1, 6) = 38.83$, $p < .001$, and low frequency irregular verbs, $F_1(1, 43) = 7.49$, $p = .009$; $F_2(1, 7) = 14.31$, $p = .007$. Thus, the percentage of correct irregular responses for the G-SLI children was not significantly different from that of the morphology-matched controls but was significantly lower than the older vocabulary-matched control children. Verb frequency had a similar and significant effect on both the G-SLI children and the control children's performance, with high frequency verbs produced significantly better than low frequency irregular verbs.

For the regular verbs, the 4 (Group) $\times$ 2 (Frequency) ANOVA revealed a significant main effect of group, $F_1(3, 43) = 14.35$, $p < .001$; $F_2(3, 42) = 54.51$, $p < .001$. Planned comparisons revealed that, for both high frequency and low frequency verbs, the G-SLI children performed significantly worse than the younger, LA1 control subjects, $F_1(1, 43) = 12.10$, $p < .001$; $F_2(1, 7) = 19.79$, $p = .003$ high frequency; $F_1(1, 43) = 13.26$, $p < .001$; $F_2(1, 7) = 13.51$, $p = .008$ low frequency, and the older, LA2 and LA3, control groups, $F_1(1, 43) = 25.97$, $p < .001$; $F_2(1, 7) = 73.15$, $p < .0001$ high frequency; $F_1(1, 43) = 49.10$, $p < .001$, low frequency. The LA1 control children's correct regular responses were also significantly lower than the LA2 and LA3 controls on the low frequency verbs, $F_1(1, 43) = 8.51$, $p = .006$; $F_2(1, 7) = 10.36$, $p = .015$, but was significant by items but not by subject on the high frequency verbs, $F_1(1, 43) = 1.30$, $p = .260$; $F_2(1, 7) = 7.99$, $p = .026$.

For the regular verbs, the Group $\times$ Frequency interaction was significant by subject, $F_1(3, 43) = 4.39$, $p = .009$, and a trend in the same direction was found by item, $F_2(3, 42) = 2.50$, $p = .072$, suggesting that frequency differentially affected the groups' performance. This was confirmed by t-tests, which were used to investigate each group's correct responses for the high and low frequency regular verbs. The G-SLI children produced significantly more correct responses to the high frequency regular verbs (*robbed*) than the low frequency verbs (*flapped*), $t_1(10) = 4.2$, $p = .002$; $t_2(10) = 2.2$, $p = .042$. Whilst the LA1 controls showed some frequency effect for the regular verbs, this was significant by subject, $t_1(11) = 2.8$, $p = .018$, but not by item, $t_2(14) = 1.4$, $p = .17$. The older control groups showed no frequency effects for the regular verbs (see Table 3). Finally to investigate whether the children's familiarity with the verb stem, rather than the frequency of the past tense form, caused the different effects of frequency on regular verbs for the G-SLI children and the control groups, we carried out a correlation between the children's production rate of correct past tense forms and the past tense frequency, partialling out the children's own stem ratings. A high and significant correlation was obtained for the G-SLI children, $r(13) = 0.66$, $p = .008$. In contrast, the correlations for all three control groups accounted for only between 1.9% to 14.4% of the variance and were non-significant (LA1: $r(13) = 0.30$, $p = .284$; LA2: $r(13) = 0.38$, $p = .162$; LA3: $r(13) = 0.14$, $p = .625$). Thus, frequency had a stronger effect on the production of correct regular past tense forms for the G-SLI children and accounted for 43.6% of the variance – that is, at least three times as much as that of the control children.

In order to assess fully the groups' relative performance on the regular and irregular verbs, for each group we compared the percentage of correct past tense responses for the two verb types for both high frequency (*robbed* vs. *gave*) and low frequency (*flapped* vs. *dug*) verbs. The G-SLI children's correct regular and irregular responses were not significantly different for either high frequency verbs, $t_1(10) = 1.74$, $p = .112$; $t_2(13) = 1.18$, $p = .26$, or low frequency verbs, $t_1(10) = 0.31$, $p = .762$; $t_2(14) = -0.42$, $p = .678$. In contrast, the LA1 controls produced significantly more correct regular than irregular responses for both the high frequency verbs, $t_1(11) = 2.68$, $p = .021$; $t_2(13) = 3.24$, $p = .006$, and low frequency verbs, $t_1(11) = 4.14$, $p = .002$; $t_2(14) = 3.06$, $p = .008$. The LA2 controls' correct regular and irregular responses did not differ for the high frequency verbs, $t_1(11)$ 0.20, $p = .844$; $t_2(13) = 0.18$, $p = .857$, but regular responses were significantly better than irregular responses for low frequency verbs, $t_1(11) = 3.39$, $p = .006$; $t_2(14) = 2.58$, $p = .022$. Analysis also revealed that the LA3 controls performed consistently better on regular than irregular verbs for both the high frequency verbs, $t_1(11) = 2.41$, $p = .035$; $t_2(13) = 2.43$, $p = .030$, and low frequency verbs, $t_1(11)$ 4.65, $p < .001$, $t_2(13) = 14.02$, $p < .001$.

Over-regularisations (*give-gived*)

Normal children sometimes produce 'over-regularisations' – forms like *gived*, which are inappropriate regularisations of irregular verbs. On the dual system, view, over-regularisations occur when children fail to retrieve the correct irregular past tense form (*gave*), and therefore resort to rule-based -*ed*-suffixation (Marcus et al., 1992; Pinker, 1991, 1999). On this view, if G-SLI children have a dysfunctional rule, they should over-regularise less than their controls. Note that the G-SLI children had more chances than the control children to over-regularise, because they made more errors on the irregular verbs. Nevertheless, analysis revealed the G-SLI children produced significantly fewer over-regularisations than the younger LA1 control children, $t_1(21) = 2.5, p = .021; t_2(29) = 4.6, p < .001$, and than the vocabulary matched LA2 and LA3 control children,[5] $t_1(29.35) = 2.63, p = .013; t_2(14) = 5.90, p < .001$.

Summary

The results revealed that frequency of regular and irregular verbs had qualitatively different effects on the G-SLI children's and the vocabulary-matched control groups' performance. Furthermore, differences were evident between the pattern of performance of the G-SLI children and children matched on expressive morphology and sentence comprehension. For the irregular verbs, frequency had a similar and significant effect for both the G-SLI children and all the LA control groups' production, with high frequency past tense forms being produced more successfully than low frequency past tense forms. For the regular verbs, frequency differentially affected the G-SLI and control groups' performance, as indicated by the significant interaction. The G-SLI children showed a strong and consistent effect of frequency. In contrast, frequency did not significantly affect the LA2 and LA3, vocabulary-matched control childrens' responses (see Table 3). For the morphology-matched, LA1 controls the difference between high and low frequency regular verbs was significant in the analyses by subject but not by item, indicating a weak or inconsistent frequency effect. However, when the children's own stem familiarity ratings were taken into consideration, the correlation between the children's regular correct responses and past tense frequency was high and significant for the G-SLI children but was substantially lower and not significant for the LA1 controls as well as the vocabulary control groups. Thus, the LA1 controls' knowledge of the stem forms rather than the frequency of the past tense forms can largely account for the weak frequency effect found for them.

For the irregular verbs, the G-SLI children's rate of correct past tense responses did not differ from that of the LA1 controls for either high or low frequency verbs. However, the G-SLI children's rate of correct

---

[5] The degrees of freedom are adjusted for unequal groups.

responses was significantly lower than those of the LA2 and LA3 controls. In contrast, for the regular verbs and G-SLI children produced significantly fewer correct responses than all three LA control groups for both the high and low frequency verbs. This difference was most marked for the low frequency verbs.

The LA control children showed an advantage for regular over irregular correct responses. This regular verb advantage was generally significant for high frequency verbs and was consistently significant for low frequency verbs. Thus, any explanation for these data must take into account that although the overall frequency of the irregular verbs was higher than that of the regular verbs, normally developing children perform worse on irregular than regular verbs. In contrast, the G-SLI children did not show this regularity advantage, and no significant difference was found between their correct regular and irregular responses for high or low frequency verbs. It can be seen from Table 3, the G-SLI children's responses for the low frequency verbs do not even show a trend for regular past tenses to be produced more successfully than irregular past tense forms. Finally, the G-SLI children produced significantly fewer over-regularisations than the LA controls, despite the increased opportunity to produce overgeneralisation because of their low number of correct irregular responses.

Novel verbs

The mean numbers of unmarked (*crive, brop*), regularised (*crived, bropped*), and irregularised (*crove, brap*) responses to the novel irregular and regular verbs can be found in Table 4.

Unmarked forms

As with the real verbs, the G-SLI children produced a large number of unmarked forms for the novel verbs (see Table 4). A 4 (Group $\times$ 2 (Novel verb type: novel irregular, novel regular) ANOVA carried out on the unmarked responses revealed a significant main effect of group, $F_1(3, 43) = 5.44$, $p = .003$; $F_2(3, 72) = 38.08$, $p < .001$. A significant main effect for novel verb type was found by subject but not by item, $F_1(1, 43) = 10.55$, $p = .002$; $F_2(1, 24) = 3.22$, $p = .085$, indicating, as with the real verbs, a tendency for more unmarked forms to be produced for irregular than regular sounding verbs. The interaction was not significant, $F_1(3, 43) = 1.10$, $p = .36$; $F_2(3, 72) = 0.70$, $p = .55$. Follow-up planned comparisons revealed that the G-SLI children produced significantly more unmarked forms than the LA1 controls, $F_1(1, 43) = 4.68$, $p = .036$; $F_2(1, 25) = 23.41$, $p < .0001$, and the LA2 and LA3 controls, $F_1(1, 43) = 16.21$, $p < .001$; $F_2(1, 25) = 96.73$, $p < .0001$. The production rate of unmarked forms for the LA1 control was significantly lower than that of the LA2 and LA3 control groups by item but not by subject, $F_1(1, 43) = 2.54$, $p = .118$; $F_2(1, 25) = 16.93$, $p < .0001$.

Novel irregular verbs

The regularised (*crived*) and irregularised (*crove*) responses to the novel irregular verbs were analysed in a 4 (Group) × 2 (Response type; regularised, irregularised) ANOVA. This revealed a significant interaction, $F_1(3, 43) = 5.67$, $p < .002$; $F_2(3, 39) = 27.01$, $p < .001$. To investigate this interaction further, we compared past tense production rates of regularised and irregularised responses (*crived* vs. *crove*) within each group. The LA control groups produced more regularised than irregularised past tense forms for the irregular novel verbs, even though these were phonologically similar to real irregular verbs (see Table 4). This difference was significant for the older LA control groups (LA2: $t_1(11) = 3.9$, $p < .002$; $t_2(13) = 8.7$, $p < .001$; LA3: $t_1(11) = 4.3$, $p < .001$; $t_2(13) = 5.9$, $p < .001$. For the LA1 controls the difference was not significant by subject but approached significance by item, $t_1(11) = 1.7$, $p = .117$; $t_2(13) = 2.1$, $p = .057$. In contrast, the G-SLI children's production rates were not significantly different for the two types of past tense forms, $t_1(10) = 1.50$, $p = .176$; $t_2(13) = 0.8$, $p = .431$.

In the production of regularisations (*crived*), the G-SLI children produced significantly fewer forms than each of the three control groups (LA1: $t_1(21) = 3.1$, $p = .005$; $t_2(13) = 3.9$, $p = .002$; LA2: $t_1(21) = 5.4$, $p < .001$; $t_2(13) = 9.7$, $p < .001$; LA3: $t_1(21) = 5.34$, $p < .001$; $t_2(13) = 7.8$, $p < .001$). In contrast, in the production of irregularisations (*crove*), the G-SLI children's performance was significantly different from that of the controls only for the *t*-tests with items as the error term, and not for the *t*-tests with subjects as the error term (LA1: $t_1(21) = 1.0$, $p = .349$; $t_2(13) = 4.0$, $p < .001$; LA2: $t_1(21) = 1.1$, $p = .300$; $t_2(13) = 3.6$, $p = .003$; LA3: $t_1(21) = 1.4$, $p = .183$; $t_2(13) = 2.4$, $p = .034$).

Novel regular verbs

Analysis of the novel regular verb responses in a 4 (Group) × 2 (Response type: regularised [*bropped*], irregularised [*brap*]) ANOVA also revealed a significant interaction, $F_1(3, 43) = 20.69$, $p < .001$; $F_2(3, 33) = 46.37$, $p < .001$). Follow-up *t*-tests revealed that each of the three control groups produced significantly more regularised (*bropped*) than irregularised (*brap*) past tense forms (LA1: $t_1(11) = 4.7$, $p < .001$; $t_2(11) = 2.7$, $p = .019$; LA2: $t_1(11) = 7.3$, $p < .001$; $t_2(11) = 21.6$, $p < .001$; LA3: $t_1(11) = 8.8$, $p < .001$; $t_2(11) = 12.1$, $p < .001$). In contrast, for the G-SLI children the advantage of regularisations over irregularisations was inconsistent – no significant difference was found by subject but was by item, $t_1(11) = 1.6$,

$p = .132$; $t_2(11) = 2.2$, $p = .046$. Note, that the lack of significant by-subject difference may be partially attributed to the G-SLI children's overall low response rate (see Table 4).

In between-group analyses, the G-SLI children were significantly worse than each of the three control groups at producing regularised forms (*brop-bropped*) (LA1: $t_1(21) = 4.2$, $p < .001$; $t_2(11) = 4.3$, $p < .001$; LA2: $t_1(21) = 6.2$, $p < .001$; $t_2(11) = 28.0$, $p < .001$; LA3: $t_1(21) = 5.34$, $p < .001$; $t_2(13) = 7.6$, $p < .001$), but were not generally worse at producing irregularised forms (*brop-brap*), LA1: $t_1(21) = 2.6$, $p = .018$. For all other analyses $t < 0.9$, $p = .398$ and, therefore, these were not significant.

Summary

For novel irregular verbs (*crive*), the control children generally produced significantly more regularisations (*crived*) than irregularisations (*crove*). In contrast, the G-SLI children produced regularisations and irregularisations at similar rates. For novel regular verbs all the groups produced fewer irregularisations than regularisations. Therefore, it appears that the G-SLI children and the control children are sensitive to the phonological characteristics of the verb when producing novel irregularisations. The G-SLI children's production rate of regularisations was significantly lower than that of the control children's production rate of regularisations. In contrast the G-SLI children's production rate of irregularisations did not consistently differ from that of the LA controls.

GENERAL DISCUSSION

The results from this investigation into the production of regular and irregular past tense formation in children developing normally and in children with G-SLI reveal quantitative and qualitative differences in the groups' performance. The responses of the G-SLI children and the LA2 and LA3 controls were remarkably distinct in their pattern of regular and irregular production, the effect of frequency on regular past tense marking, and their level of production of past tense marking on verbs. While some similarities are found between the G-SLI children and the LA1 controls – not surprisingly as they were matched on morphological abilities – differences in the pattern of performance and the effects of frequency are also found between these groups.

We will now consider how well the input-processing deficit hypothesis and the grammar-specific deficit hypothesis can account for the findings from this study and, more generally, how well the single mechanism and dual mechanism frameworks can account for impaired and normal performance.

The input-processing deficit/single mechanism account

Lexical effects were clearly influencing all the children's production of irregular forms, as predicted by single mechanism accounts, with significant frequency effects being found for irregular verbs and the phonological characteristics of the novel verbs determining irregular past tense use. Thus, the control groups, generally produced irregularisations for irregular rhyming novel verbs. In addition, performance on irregular verbs increased with age and vocabulary development. Conversely, for normally developing children, few lexical effects were evident for regular past tense marking. While no frequency effects were found for the older vocabulary-matched LA2 and LA3 control children for regular verbs, a weak frequency effect was found for the younger LA1 controls. One explanation for this weak frequency effect among the LA1 controls is that their stem-past mappings have not yet been sufficiently learnt to eliminate frequency effects. This suggestion is consistent with the predictions put forward by Daugherty and Seidenberg (1992). However, when access to the stem was controlled for by partialling out stem frequency, past tense frequency did not significantly predict performance. Furthermore, if the LA1 controls had not yet learnt general regular stem-past mappings, it is unclear why they showed the same advantage for regulars over irregulars for both high and low frequency verbs and novel verbs as the older children. One possibility for the general lack of regular frequency effects among the control children is that such effects were harder to find for regular than irregular verbs because the difference between high and low frequency was smaller for regular (1.7) than irregular (3.0) verbs. However, this seems unlikely, as the G-SLI children showed a clear and significant frequency effect for regular verbs, suggesting that the difference between high and low frequency verbs was sufficient to reveal an effect, if it was there to be found.

The advantage for regular over irregular past tense marking found for the LA controls is difficult to accommodate within a single mechanism view of inflectional morphology. The irregular verbs in this study were of an overall higher frequency than the regular forms, yet regular verbs were produced significantly better than irregular verbs and regular past tense marking was strongly favoured for even irregular rhyming novel verbs, as well as regular sounding novel verbs. One possibility is that the high type frequency for regular verbs could account for the regularity advantage found in this experiment. However, while frequency and regularity are conflated in the English inflectional system this is not so in other languages. In German, for example, a suffix added to a stem can form both irregular and regular inflectional forms for past participle and plural forms of words.

However, the less frequent plural -*s*, and the participle -*t*, which has a similar frequency as the irregular -*n* are preferentially produced as the default (regular) forms (Clahsen et al., 1992; Clahsen, 1999; Marcus et al., 1995). Thus, type frequency does not appear to be the crucial factor determining the selection and use of default forms, and therefore for reasons of parsimony we will not pursue this line of reasoning.

Finally, analysis of unmarked forms did not reveal that significantly more unmarked forms were produced for low frequency verbs than high frequency verbs, in contrast to Marchman et al.'s (1999) previous findings. However, a tendency to produce more unmarked forms for the real and novel irregular verbs than for the real and novel regular verbs was found. This suggests that the phonological characteristics of the verb stem-past mappings were affecting the children's productions to a limited extent, as unmarked forms may be acceptable as past tense forms for some irregular verbs (e.g., *hit*). However, it should be noted that we excluded no-change verbs such as *split*, *ret* and *scrit* from the analyses. Furthermore, although the irregular and regular novel verbs were carefully selected to control for irregular and regular neighbourhood size (Ullman, 1993) only a weak effect of the phonological characteristics was found. Thus, this is inconsistent with the strong claim that regular as well as irregular past tense patterns are primarily determined by a phonologically based constraint satisfaction system (Marchman, 1997).

We will now turn to the findings from the G-SLI children and evaluate the ability of the input-processing deficit within a single mechanism framework to account for impaired and normal performance. The G-SLI children's use of unmarked forms in past tense contexts, their particularly impaired production of regular past tense marking in comparison to the control children, and their limited ability to generalise the regular past tense marker to novel forms can be taken to support the single mechanism framework. First, the large number of unmarked forms found in this study for G-SLI children is consistent with the predictions of impaired input-processing in a single system model (Hoeffner & McClelland, 1993; Leonard, 1998; Marchman & Weismer, 1994; Marchman, 1997). Furthermore, the G-SLI children showed a tendency to produce more unmarked forms for the irregular real and novel verbs than for the regular real and novel verbs. This suggests that the G-SLI children, like their LA-matched peers, are sensitive to the phonological characteristics of the stem-past mappings when producing unmarked forms. However, the more detailed analysis reveals some inconsistencies with the input-processing deficit account. The input-processing deficit account predicts that more unmarked forms should be found for low frequency verbs (Marchman & Weismer, 1994). In the event, frequency did not have a significant effect on unmarked forms for either the G-SLI, or the LA control children. In addition, one might expect the G-SLI children to produce more uninflected forms for the regular known and novel verbs if they have problems perceiving or processing the -*ed* morpheme, but they did not. The production pattern of unmarked forms across known and novel regular and irregular verbs was similar for the G-SLI children and LA controls. Moreover, the very large number of unmarked forms found in this study of 9–13-year-old G-SLI children in contrast to the production of plural inflections (van der Lely & Christian, 2000) is difficult to account for by an input-processing deficit alone and suggests that other factors are significantly contributing to these errors.

The G-SLI children's significant deficit in regular past tense formation, and poor generalisation of the regular inflection to novel verbs is also consistent with the input-processing deficit account, whereby SLI children are thought to have particular problems perceiving and producing the regular past tense morphemes (Joanisse & Seidenberg, 1998*b*; Leonard, 1998). Conversely, the G-SLI and control children's qualitatively different patterns of performance reflected by the relative productivity of regular and irregular forms, and the effects of frequency on correct regular and irregular past tense forms of verbs, particularly in relation to the vocabulary control children, is inconsistent with the input-processing/ single mechanism framework. Single mechanism accounts predict that the same factors affect regular and irregular forms for all children (Marchman & Weismer, 1994; Marchman et al., 1999). Therefore, it is unclear why an input-processing deficit should cause a frequency effect for regular past-tense verbs as well as irregular verbs for the G-SLI children, whereas this effect was only found for irregular verbs for the control children. Moreover, our findings do not support Marchman et al.'s (1999) prediction that children with SLI would perform in qualitatively and quantitatively similar ways to children matched on language abilities. The G-SLI children were matched on two tests tapping morphological expression and sentence understanding to a younger group of control children and on tests of vocabulary comprehension and expression to two older groups of control children. However, the G-SLI children's overall pattern of use of irregular and regular morphology does not appear to match that of children at any stage of normal language development. Therefore although, according to some accounts of the past tense morphology, vocabulary development predicts the use and pattern of past tense marking found in acquisition (Plunkett & Marchman, 1993), the results from this study indicate that vocabulary development is insufficient to predict the pattern of past tense formation found in normally developing and SLI children.

In conclusion, an input-processing deficit may account for some of the findings for the G-SLI children, such as their poor performance on regular verbs, their use of unmarked forms in past tense contexts, and their sensitivity to phonological characteristics when producing irregularisations. However, the contrasting patterns of performance in the use of regular and irregular forms and the contrasting effects of frequency for the G-SLI children and the control groups of children matched on different aspects of language are inconsistent with the input-processing deficit account and the theoretical framework underlying this account.

The grammar-specific deficit/dual mechanism account

The dual-mechanism explanation for the lexical effects of frequency and phonological properties affecting the LA control groups' use of irregular past tense forms for real and novel verbs, and the development with age for correct irregular production is similar to the single-mechanism account. That is, irregular verbs are retrieved from a pattern associator memory, which can yield some productivity. Although this productivity is relatively limited, it can account for the production of irregular past tense novel forms (Prasada & Pinker, 1993; Xu & Pinker, 1995). Furthermore, the data indicate that this memory system for irregular verbs improves with age as predicted by both single and dual system accounts. However, in contrast to the single mechanism account, the dual mechanism account can provide a parsimonious explanation for the general regularity advantage and the lack of frequency effects for regular verbs found for the LA control children. The data indicate that for normally developing children regular past tense forms are rule products and so are not significantly affected by the properties of lexical memory (frequency and their sound patterns). Therefore, the regular rule applied as the default whenever memory access fails, can account for the greater number of regularisations than irregularisations produced for novel verbs – which was found even for those novel verbs that do not sound like existing regular verbs (i.e., for a subset of the irregular novel verbs). However, if all regular forms are rule produced it is unclear why a weak frequency effect was found for the youngest LA1 controls, although they still showed a clear regularity advantage. One possible explanation is that memorised forms are causing this weak effect by facilitating access to and keeping in memory the stem form during the process of adding the affix. This explanation is supported by the finding that, when stem frequency was partialled out of the analysis, the correlation between past-tense frequency and correct production of regular forms was no longer significant for the LA1 controls. Past-tense frequency accounted on average for 8.4% of the variance of the LA control groups' productions (range 1.9%–14.4%), whereas on average it accounted for five times as much for the G-SLI children (43.6%). The apparent support of a long-term memory system to facilitate recalling stem forms in the LA1 control group but not the older control groups is consistent with the view that phonological short-term memory develops with age and vocabulary ability (Gathercole, Service, Hitch, Adams & Martin, 1999). Thus, the older children's more advanced vocabulary abilities and we presume short-term memory abilities, may have made relying on long-term memory to recall low frequency stem forms redundant. In sum, the different pattern of regular and irregular past-tense marking for regular and irregular verbs and the differential effects of frequency found for the LA control children are consistent with the predictions of the dual mechanism account of past tense formation.

The lexical effects of frequency and phonological characteristics for irregular forms found for the G-SLI children, like the LA controls, is consistent with the predictions of the grammar-specific account of SLI in which the primary deficit is thought to be located in the grammatical system. However, it may have been expected that the G-SLI children would have performed as well as the vocabulary control children on irregular past tense formation if their associative-memory system is not impaired. There are several factors which could individually or collectively account for why this was not so. First, according to grammar-specific accounts of SLI, morphological deficits may be only one manifestation of their grammatical impairment. Therefore, problems with the syntactic representation of tense may cause infinitival or unmarked stem forms to be produced in a past tense context (Rice, Wexler, & Cleave, 1995; van der Lely, 1998). Thus, this can account for the general impairment in performance of the G-SLI children due to the large number of unmarked forms produced in past-tense contexts. Secondly, G-SLI children's verb development, particularly learning to structure lexical links between morphological variants of the same form—e.g., linking verb stem and past-tense forms—may be significantly impaired by their deficit in using syntactic cues (syntactic bootstrapping) to learn words (O'Hara & Johnston, 1997; van der Lely, 1994). This explanation is supported by the finding that the same G-SLI child, like many SLI children (Leonard, 1998), can produce and accept both the correct form (e.g., *fell*) and incorrect forms (*fall, falled*) in similar syntactic contexts (van der Lely, 1997a, b, 1998; van der Lely & Ullman, 1996). These errors suggest that G-SLI children store the past tense forms of irregular verbs but that the blocking mechanism, which normally prevents a regular inflection being affixed to a stem (Marcus et al., 1992) is not functioning appropriately. Further investigation of this possibility is warranted.

The differences in the production of regular forms found between the G-SLI children and the control children provide further support for the grammar-specific deficit account, whereby G-SLI children are impaired in the grammatical computations underlying the *-ed* suffixation rule, so that they tend to memorise regular as well as irregular past tense forms. Therefore, according to this view, lexical-associative properties should affect the G-SLI children's performance for regular and irregular formation. Consistent with this prediction was the significant effect of frequency on regular verbs, even when stem frequency was controlled for, found for the G-SLI children but not the control children. In addition, the absence of a regularity advantage for the G-SLI children, in contrast to the LA controls provides further support for the grammar-specific deficit account. However, although the difference between the G-SLI children's production of regular and irregular forms was not significant, there was a trend for more regular than irregular forms to be produced for high frequency (but not low frequency) known verbs and the regular and irregular novel verbs (see Tables 3 and 4). Furthermore, the question arises as to why the G-SLI children make any over-regularisations, if they are impaired in regular rule formation.

There are several factors that may contribute to an explanation of these findings. First, if G-SLI children are primarily memorising regular forms as indicated by the results, then the high token frequency of regular verbs could be contributing to the G-SLI children's performance, whereas it does not appear to be doing so to any great extent in normally developing children. The effect of frequency on regularly inflected verbs and nouns for children with SLI but not for normally developing children is a consistent finding in the literature (Leonard, 1998; Marchman et al., 1999; Oetting & Horohov, 1997; Oetting & Rice, 1993; Ullman & Gopnik, 1994, 1999). Moreover, if frequency is the cause of G-SLI children's pattern of use of regular forms and this is independent of the "normal" factors determining the default form, then we would expect that in languages where the default form is not the most frequent form, G-SLI children should incorrectly select the most frequent form, regardless of its morpho-syntactic properties. The atypical selection of the most frequent plural -en as the default form by German children with SLI but not by normally developing children (Bartke, 1998; Clahsen et al., 1992; Marcus et al., 1995), lends further support for the view that SLI children and normally developing children are using a different basis on which to form regular inflections. Thus, there is cross-linguistic evidence to suggest that, in contrast to normally developing children, frequency is largely determining the default inflectional form for children with SLI.

Second, productivity within the associative memory system (Xu & Pinker, 1995), although relatively limited, can account for the over-regularisations of irregular verbs. The poor ability of our children with G-SLI to overgeneralise to novel words is consistent with the resistance of associative models to overgeneralise to novel inputs, particularly when they do not sound like known forms (Prasada & Pinker, 1993).

A third possible explanation for the G-SLI children's performance is that the grammatical mechanism thought to underlie the regular rule formation is "impaired" rather than missing (cf. Ullman & Gopnik, 1994, 1999). In other words, the rule per se is not missing, but the implementation of the rule is impaired. This view concurs with van der Lely's "Representational Deficit in Dependent Relations" (RDDR) hypothesis which contends that G-SLI children's syntactic deficits are caused by a deficit in the computational grammatical system such that grammatical-structural rules, by definition obligatory in normal grammar, are optional in G-SLI grammar (see van der Lely, 1998). Thus, grammatical rules may function to a limited extent and facilitate to some minor degree the formation of regular past tense forms. Furthermore, it is evident that G-SLI children have considerable knowledge of the inflectional rule system generally, as they rarely produce inflected forms in appropriate contexts (Bishop, 1994; Leonard, 1998; Rice & Wexler, 1996). However, impaired rule functioning may cause G-SLI children to store regular forms like irregular forms and primarily rely on their associative memory system for producing known regular forms and even overgeneralising regular forms. This position may be contrasted with the missing rule hypothesis put forward by Gopnik and Crago (1991) to account for the regular and irregular production of real and novel verbs from the KE family of whom half suffer from SLI.

Finally, the effect of therapy, in which the regular rule is explicitly taught, may also contribute to the G-SLI children's tendency to produce more regularisations than irregularisations, especially in older children with SLI who have undergone years of intensive remedial training. A meta-linguistic rule, learned years after it is generally acquired in normally developing children may not reflect the same underlying mechanisms and representations as when it is learned "on-time". Further investigations which encompass derivational as well as inflectional morphology are required to distinguish whether G-SLI children's rule system is impaired or missing. In either case, it appears from these data that in functional terms their regular morphological system is qualitatively different from that of normally developing children.

In conclusion the predictions of the grammar-specific account are largely confirmed in this experiment. The grammar-specific deficit along with the underlying framework to this account provides a parsimonious and comprehensive explanation of the contrasting patterns of performance found for G-SLI children and younger normally developing children.

Conclusion

The hypothesised grammar-specific deficit/dual mechanism model was found to explain the regular and irregular past tense production of normally developing and G-SLI children. In contrast to normally developing children, G-SLI children showed a consistent effect of past tense frequency for regular verbs, independent of stem frequency and produced regular and irregular forms at a similar rate. All of the groups showed effects of frequency and phonological characteristics in irregular past tense production. Moreover, the G-SLI children's performance on regular verbs was qualitatively different from that of the LA control groups, in particular the vocabulary control groups. The LA controls showed a consistent regularity advantage for real and novel verbs. The input-processing deficit account cannot account for this qualitative difference between the G-SLI children and the vocabulary control children in overall performance on regular and irregular past tense forms. The findings conflict with the predictions of the input-processing account, and the theoretical framework underlying this account which posits that the development of inflectional morphology is determined by vocabulary development and processing (Elman et al., 1996; Leonard, 1998; Marchman et al., 1999; Tallal et al., 1996). Conversely, the grammar-specific deficit/dual system account of past tense morphology provides a parsimonious explanation for both findings from G-SLI children and normally developing children. In addition, the findings from this study for G-SLI children, such as the frequency effects, the large number of unmarked forms, and similar performance on regular and irregular past tense verbs, generally concur with the findings from many studies of younger and older children with SLI (Bishop, 1994; Oetting & Horohov, 1997; Oetting & Rice, 1993; Leonard, 1998; Marchman & Weismer, 1994; Ullman & Gopnik, 1994, 1999; Vargha-Khadem et al., 1995). The fact that such similarities are found between these different studies, although some of the other children with SLI have co-occurring speech or more general auditory or cognitive deficits, questions whether such co-occurring deficits explain their language impairments, such as those found in inflectional morphology. Thus, contrary to some views of SLI (Elman et al., 1996, Joanisse & Seidenberg, 1998b) it appears that more general deficits do not have a significant effect on the nature of grammatical deficits as the same grammatical deficits are found in children without co-occurring impairments.

This study along with previous findings for G-SLI (van der Lely & Christian, 2000) indicates that their deficit affects mechanisms and/or representations underlying regularly inflected words as well as syntactic structures (van der Lely, 1994, 1996a, b, 1998; van der Lely & Stollwerck, 1997). The data provide further support for the view that G-SLI children are defective in forming and/or computing a grammatical rule for regular inflection that requires an abstract representation of the verb stem and past tense affix (cf. Gopnik & Crago, 1991; Ullman & Gopnik, 1994, 1999).

However, in this paper we advocate an impaired, rather than a missing, rule system. Moreover, while this impairment may account for the findings, there is likely to be more than one source for this deficit. One may involve the morphological ability to identify a verb stem and apply the *-ed* suffixation rule. (Gopnik & Crago, 1991; Ullman & Gopnik, 1994, 1999). In addition, grammatical knowledge may facilitate lexical links between morphological variants of the same word and facilitate vocabulary development through the use of syntactic cues (van der Lely, 1994; van der Lely & Christian, 2000). Such lexical morpho-grammatical links may be particularly important in facilitating the decrease in over-regularisations of irregular words in development. Another source for the impairment may be in the phonological representations of words. Phonological "knowledge" and the ability to form a detailed phonological representation of a word's structure may provide the distinction between a stem and its affix. For example, the novel word [pri:kt] (like *streaked*) could only be an inflected form of the word [pri:k] because there are no comparable mono-morphemic forms which end in [–i:kt] (Harris, 1994). Thirdly, the ability to form appropriate syntactic relationships between constituents in the sentence is needed to determine when a tense marker must be obligatorily used. Thus, a grammatical deficit may impinge on all of these levels of grammar and may contribute to the G-SLI children's pattern of performance in different ways.

Finally, the findings from this study of children developing normally and children with grammatical deficits provide a valuable source of data that need to be accounted for in further developments of models of the past tense inflectional system.

REFERENCES

Adams, C., & Bishop, D. (1989). Conversational characteristics of children with semantic-pragmatic disorder. *British Journal of Disorders of Communication, 24,* 211–240.

Aram, D., Morris, R., & Hall, N. (1993). Clinical and research congruence in identifying children with specific language impairment. *Journal of Speech and Hearing Research, 36,* 580–591.

Bartke, S. (1998). *Experimentalle studien sur flexion und wortbildung: Pluralmorphologie und lexikalische komposition im unauffaellingen spracherwerb und im Dysgrammatismus.* Tübingenwen: Niemeyer Verlag.

Bates, E., & MacWhinney, B. (1987). Competition, variation, and language learning. In B. MacWhinney (Ed.), *Mechanisms of language acquisition,* pp. 157–193. Hillsdale, NJ: Lawrence Erlbaum Associates Inc.

Bates, E., & MacWhinney, B. (1989). Functionalism and the competition model. In B. MacWhinney & E. Bates (Eds), *The cross linguistic study of sentence processing,* pp. 3–76. New York: Cambridge University Press.

Berko, J. (1958). The child's learning of English morphology. *Word, 14,* 150–177.

Bishop, D.V.M. (1983). *Test for Reception of Grammar.* [Available from author. University of Manchester.]

Bishop, D.V.M. (1994). Grammatical errors in specific language impairment: Competence or performance limitations? *Applied Psycholinguistics, 15*, 507–550.

Bishop, D.V.M. (1997). *Uncommon understanding: Comprehension in specific language impairment.* Hove, UK: Psychology Press Ltd.

Bishop, D.V.M., Bishop, S., Bright, P., James, J. & van der Lely, H.K.J. (2000). Grammatical SLI: A distinct subtype of developmental language impairment? *Applied Psycholinguistics, 21*, 159–181.

Chomsky, N. (1986). *Knowledge of language: Its nature, origin and use.* New York: Praeger.

Clahsen, H. (1989). The grammatical characterization of developmental dysphasia. *Linguistics, 27*, 897–920.

Clahsen, H. (1999). Lexical entries and rules of language: A multidisciplinary study of German inflection. *Brain & Behavior Science, 22*, 991–1060.

Clahsen, H., Rothweiler, M., Woest, A., & Marcus, G. (1992). Regular and irregular inflection in the acquisition of German noun plurals. *Cognition, 45*, 225–255.

Conti-Ramsden, G., & Jones, M. (1997). Verb use in specific language impairment. *Journal of Speech, Language and Hearing Research, 40*, 1298–1313.

Daugherty, K., & Seidenberg, M. (1992). Rules or connections? The past tense revisited. *Proceedings of the Fourteenth Annual Conference of the Cognitive Science Society,* pp. 259–264. Hillsdale, NJ: Lawrence Erlbaum Associates Inc.

Dunn, L., Dunn, L., Whetton, C., & Pintilie, D. (1982). *The British Picture Vocabulary Scales.* Windsor: NFER-Nelson.

Elliott, C., Murray, D., & Pearson, L. (1978). *British Ability Scales.* Windsor: NFER-Nelson.

Elman, J., Bates, E., Johnson, M., Karmiloff-Smith, A., Parisi, D., & Plunkett, K. (1996). *Rethinking innateness: A connectionist perspective on development.* Cambridge, MA: MIT Press.

Fodor, J. (1983). *The modularity of mind.* Cambridge, MA: MIT Press.

Gathercole, S., & Baddeley, A. (1990). Phonological memory deficits in language disordered children: Is there a causal connection? *Journal of Memory and Language, 29*, 336–360.

Gathercole, S., Service, E., Hitch, G., Adams, A-M., & Martin, A. (1999). Phonological short-term memory and vocabulary development: Further evidence on the nature of the relationship. *Applied Cognitive Psychology, 13*, 65–77.

Goellner, S. (1995). *Morphological deficits of children with specific language impairment: Evaluation of tense marking and agreement.* MA thesis, University of Essex.

Gopnik, M. (1990). Feature blindness: A case study. *Language Acquisition, 1*, 139–164.

Gopnik, M. (1994). The family. *The McGill working papers in linguistics: Linguistic aspects of familial language impairment.* Vol. 10, pp. 1–5. Montreal: McGill University.

Gopnik, M., & Crago, M.B. (1991). Familial aggregation of a developmental language disorder. *Cognition, 39*, 1–50.

Gordon, P. (1985). Level-ordering in lexical development. *Cognition, 21*, 73–93.

Hare, M., Elman, J.L., & Daugherty, K.G. (1995). Default generalisation in connectionist networks. *Language and Cognitive Processes, 10*, 601–630.

Harris, J. (1994). *English sound structure.* Oxford, UK: Blackwell.

Hoeffner, J.H., & McClelland, J.L. (1993). Can a perceptual processing deficit explain the impairment of inflectional morphology in development dysphasia? A computational investigation. In E. Clark (Ed.), *Proceedings of the 25th Annual child language research forum,* pp. 38–49. Stanford University, CA: Center for the Study of Language and Information.

Joanisse, M.F., & Seidenberg, M.S. (1998a). Dissociations between rule-governed forms and exceptions: A connectionist account. Poster presented at the *1998 Annual Meeting of the Cognitive Neuroscience Society,* San Francisco.

Joanisse, M., & Seidenberg, M. (1998b). Specific language impairment: a deficit in grammar or processing? *Trends in Cognitive Sciences, 2,* 240–247.

Kirk, S., McCarthy, J., & Kirk, W. (1968). *Illinois Test of Psycholinguistic Abilities.* Urbana, IL: University Press.

Leonard, L.B. (1989). Language learnability and specific language impairment in children. *Applied Psycholinguistics, 10,* 179–202.

Leonard, L.B. (1998). *Children with specific language impairment.* Cambridge, MA: MIT Press.

Leonard, L.B., McGregor, K.K., & Allen, G.D. (1992). Grammatical morphology and speech perception in children with specific language impairment. *Journal of Speech and Hearing Research, 35,* 1076–1085.

MacDonald, M.C., Pearlmutter, N.J., & Seidenberg, M.S. (1994). Lexical nature of syntactic ambiguity resolution. *Psychological Review, 101,* 676–703.

MacWhinney, B., & Leinbach, J. (1991). Implementations are not conceptualizations: Revising the verb learning model. *Cognition, 40,* 121–157.

Marchman, V.A. (1993). Constraints on plasticity in a connectionist model of the English past tense. *Journal of Cognitive Neuroscience, 5,* 215–234.

Marchman, V. (1997). Children's productivity in the English past tense: The role of frequency, phonology and neighbourhood structure. *Cognitive Science, 21,* 283–304.

Marchman, V., & Weismer, S. (1994). Patterns of productivity in children with G-SLI and NL: A study of the English past tense. Poster presented at the SRCLD 1994. [Available from the author, Dept. of Psychology, University of Wisconsin, Madison, USA.]

Marchman, V., Wulfeck, B., & Weismer, S. (1999). Morphological productivity in children with normal language and SLI: a study of English past tense. *Journal of Speech, Language and Hearing Research, 42,* 206–219.

Marcus, G., Brinkman, U., Clahsen, H., Wiese, R., & Pinker, S. (1995). German inflection: The exception that proves the rule. *Cognitive Psychology, 29,* 189–256.

Marcus, G.F., Pinker, S., Ullman, M., Hollander, M., Rosen, T.J., & Xu, F. (1992). Overregularization in language acquisition, *Monographs of the Society for Research in Child Development Series.* Vol. 57, pp. 1–182. Chicago: University of Chicago Press.

McClelland, J.L., Rumelhart, D.E., & PDP Research Group (Eds). (1986). *Parallel distributed processing: Explorations in the microstructure of cognition: Psychological and biological models.* (Vol. 2). Cambridge, MA: MIT Press.

Menyuk, P. (1964). Comparison of grammar of children with functionally deviant and normal speech. *Journal of Speech and Hearing Research, 7,* 109–121.

Oetting, J., & Horohov, J. (1997). Past tense marking in chldren with and without specific language impairment. *Journal of Speech and Hearing Research, 40,* 62–74.

Oetting, J., & Rice, M. (1993). Plural acquisition in children with specific language impairment. *Journal of Speech and Hearing Research, 36,* 1236–1248.

O'Hara, M., & Johnston, J. (1997). Syntactic bootstrapping in children with specific language impairment. *European Journal of Disorders of Communication, 2,* 189–205.

Pinker, S. (1991). Rules of language. *Science, 253,* 530–535.

Pinker, S. (1994). *The language instinct.* New York: William Morrow.

Pinker, S. (1999). *Words and rules: The ingredients of language.* London: Weidenfeld & Nicolson.

Pinker, S., & Prince, A. (1988). On language and connectionism: Analysis of a parallel distributed processing model of language acquisition. *Cognition, 28,* 73–193.

Pinker, S., & Prince, A. (1992, February 15–18). *Regular and irregular morphology and the psychological status of rules of grammar.* Paper presented at the 17th Annual Meeting of the Berkeley Linguistics Society.

Plunkett, K., & Marchman, V. (1991). U-Shaped learning and frequency effects in a multi-layered perceptron: Implications for child language acquisition. *Cognition, 38*, 43–102.

Plunkett, K., & Marchman, V. (1993). From rote learning to system building: Acquiring verb morphology in children and connectionist nets. *Cognition, 48*, 21–69.

Prasada, S., & Pinker, S. (1993). Similarity-based and rule-based generalizations in inflectional morphology. *Language and Cognitive Processes, 8*, 1–56.

Renfrew, C. (1988). *Action Picture Test* (3rd edn). Oxford: Oxford Medical Illustration.

Renfrew, C. (1991). *The Bus Story: a test of continuous speech.* (2nd edn). Oxford: Published by author.

Rice, M. & Wexler, K. (1996). A phenotype of specific language impairment. In M. Rice (Ed.), *Toward a genetics of language*, pp. 215–238. Mahwah, NJ: Lawrence Erlbaum Associates Inc.

Rice, M.L., Wexler, K., & Cleave, P.L. (1995). Specific language impairment as a period of extended optional infinitive. *Journal of Speech and Hearing Research, 38*, 850–863.

Rumelhart, D.E., & McClelland, J.L. (1986). On learning the past tenses of English verbs. In J.L. McClelland, D.E. Rumelhart, & PDP Research Group (Eds), *Parallel distributed processing: Explorations in the microstructures of cognition* (Vol. 2). Cambridge, MA: Bradford/MIT press.

Seidenberg, M. (1992). Connectionism without tears. In S. Davis (Ed.), *Connectionism: Theory and practice*, pp 84–137. New York: Oxford University Press.

Surian, L., Baron-Cohen, S., & Van der Lely, H.K.J. (1996). Are children with autism deaf to Gricean Maxims? *Cognitive Neuropsychiatry, 1*, 55–71.

Tallal, P., Miller, S., Bedi, G., Byma, G., Wang, Z., Nagarajan, S., Schreiner, W., Jenkins, W., & Merzenich, M. (1996). Language comprehension in language-learning impaired children improved with acoustically modified speech. *Science, 217*, 81–84.

Tallal, P., & Piercy, M. (1973). Deficits of non-verbal auditory perception in children with developmental aphasia. *Nature, 241*, 468–469.

Ullman, M.T. (1993). *The computation of inflectional morphology.* Unpublished doctoral dissertation. Cambridge, MA: Massachusetts Institute of Technology.

Ullman, M.T. (1999). Acceptability ratings of regular and irregular past tense forms. Evidence for a dual-system model of language from word frequency and phonological neighbourhood effects. *Language and Cognitive Processes, 14*, 46–67.

Ullman, M.T., & Gopnik, M. (1994). The production of inflectional morphology in hereditary specific language impairment. *The McGill working papers in linguistics: Linguistic aspects of familial language impairment.* Vol. 10, pp. 81–118. Montreal: McGill University.

Ullman, M.T., & Gopnik, M. (1999). The production of inflectional morphology in hereditary specific language impairment. *Applied Psycholinguistics, 20*, 51–117.

van der Lely, H.K.J. (1994). Canonical linking rules: Forward versus reverse linking in normally developing and specifically language-impaired children. *Cognition, 51*, 29–72.

van der Lely, H.J.K. (1996a). Specifically language impaired and normally developing children: Verbal passive vs. adjectival passive sentence interpretation. *Lingua, 98*, 243–272.

van der Lely, H.K.J. (1996b). Language modularity and grammatically specific language impaired children, *Child Language*, pp. 188–201. UK: Multilingual Matters Ltd.

van der Lely, H.J.K. (1997a). Narrative discourse in grammatical specific language impaired children: A modular language deficit? *Journal of Child Language, 24*, 221–256.

van der Lely, H.K.J. (1997b). Language and cognitive development in a grammatical G-SLI boy: Modularity and innateness. *Journal of Neurolinguistics, 10*, 75–107.

van der Lely, H.K.J. (1998). G-SLI in children: Movement, economy and deficits in the computational syntactic system. *Language Acquisition, 7*, 161–193.

van der Lely, H.K.J., & Battell, J. (1998). Wh-movement in specifically language impaired children. Paper presented at the 23rd Boston University Conference on Language Development. November 6–8, 1998. Boston, MA.

van der Lely, H.K.J., & Christian, V. (2000). Lexical word formation in children with grammatical SLI: a grammar-specific versus and input-processing deficit? *Cognition, 75,* 33–63.

van der Lely, H.K.J., & Dewart, H. (1986). Sentence comprehension strategies in specific language impairment. *British Journal of Disorders of Communication, 21,* 291–306.

van der Lely, H.K.J., & Hennessey, S. (1999). Linguistic determinism and theory of mind: Insight from children with SLI. The 24th Boston University Conference on Language Development. November 5–7, 1999. Boston, MA.

van der Lely, H.K.J., Rosen, S., & McClelland, A. (1998). Evidence for a grammar-specific deficit in children. *Current Biology, 8,* 1253–1258.

van der Lely, H.K.J., & Stollwerck, L. (1996). A grammatical specific language impairment in children: An autosomal dominant inheritance? *Brain and Language, 52,* 484–504.

van der Lely, H.K.J., & Stollwerck, L. (1997). Binding theory and specifically language impaired children. *Cognition, 62,* 245–290.

van der Lely, H.K.J., & Ullman, M. (1996). The computation and representation of past-tense morphology in normally developing and specifically language impaired children. In A. Stringfellow, D. Cahan-Amitay, E. Hughes, & A. Zukowski (Eds.), *Proceedings of the 20th Annual Boston University Conference on Language Development* (pp. 816–827). Somerville, MA: Cascadilla Press.

Vargha-Khadem, F., Watkins, K., Alcock, K., Fletcher, P., & Passingham, R. (1995). Praxic and non-verbal cognitive deficits in a large family with a genetically transmitted speech and language disorder. *Proceedings of the National Academy of Sciences USA, 92,* 930–933.

Wright, B., Lombardino, L., King, W., Puranik, C., Leonard, C., & Merzenich, M. (1996). Deficits in auditory temporal and spectral resolution in language impaired children. *Nature, 387,* 176–178.

Xu, F., & Pinker, S. (1995). Weird past tense forms. *Journal of Child Language, 22,* 531–556.

APPENDIX A

G-SLI children's individual raw scores, z-scores or standard scores (based on subjects' age) and equivalent age score provided by the published tests used for the matching and selection procedure.

G-SLI subjects	Age	BPVS		TROG		NV-BAS		GC-ITPA	
		Raw score (z-score)	Equivalent age	Raw score (z-score)	Equivalent age	Raw score	Equivalent age	Raw score (z-score)	Equivalent age
JW	9:3	60 (−1.7)	6:5	10 (−2.2)	5:3	17 *	7:9	17 (−3.7)	6:0
WL	9:5	72 (−0.9)	7:9	12 (−1.7)	5:9	17 *	7:9	18 (−3.8)	6:3
JS	9:10	89 (0.0)	9:9	13 (−1.5)	6:0	19 *	>7:11	17 (−4.6)	6:0
AZ	10:3	72 (−1.3)	7:9	12 (−1.9)	5:9	19 *	>7:11	16 (−5.5)	5:10
RJ	10:11	87 (−1.4)	8:2	16 (−0.8)	9:0	19 *	>7:11	16 *	5:10
AZ	11:0	72 (−1.7)	7:9	12 (−2.1)	5:9	18 *	>7:11	24 *	7:11
CT	11:11	86 (−1.1)	9:0	13 (−2.2)	6:0	18 *	>7:11	21 *	7:0
SB	12:0	90 (−0.7)	9:5	15 (−1.6)	8:0	17 *	7:9	24 *	7:11
AT	12:1	80 (−1.6)	9:0	13 (−2.2)	6:0	16 *	6:3	17 *	6:0
BS	12:2	78 (−1.8)	8:5	12 (−2.5)	5:9	20 *	>7:11	22 *	7:3
AW	12:2	84 (−1.5)	9:3	16 (−1.2)	9:0	17 *	>7:11	22 *	7:3
MP	12:10	87 (−1.4)	7:9	13 (−2.2)	6:0	18 *	>7:11	26 *	8:6

BPVS, British Picture Vocabulary Score (Dunn et al., 1982); TROG, Test of Reception of Grammar (Bishop, 1983); NV-BAS, Naming Vocabulary, British Ability Scales (Elliott et al., 1978); GC-ITPA, Grammatical Closure sub-test from Illinois Test of Psycholinguistic Abilities (Kirk et al., 1968). *, z-score not available.

APPENDIX A cont'd.

G-SLI subject	Language tests					Non-language
	Bus story			Action picture test		BAS: IQ
	Info. (age)	Sentence length (age)	Sub-clause (age)	Info (age)	Grammar (age)	Visual performance score
JW	28(6:1)	14(8:2)	2(4:8)	34(6:9)	23(5:3)	105
WL	23(5:1)	10(6:4)	1(4:2)	26.5(4:2)	20(4:3)	115
JS	29(6:4)	11(6:10)	1(4:2)	33.5(6:6)	26(6:3)	90
AZ	42(5:3)	13(7:10)	2(4:8)	28(4:8)	20(4:3)	119
RJ	27(5:10)	8(4:7)	1(4:2)	34.5(7:0)	22(5:0)	110
AZ	22(4:11)	11(6:10)	1(4:2)	34.5(7:0)	25(6:0)	105
CT	33(7:4)	12(7:4)	2(4:8)	38(8:5)	24(5:9)	86
SB	20(4:7)	12(7:4)	3(5:10)	35.5(7:6)	23(5:3)	92
AT	29(6:4)	11(6:10)	1(4:2)	34.5(7:0)	26(6:3)	90
BS	30(6:7)	11(6:10)	2(4:8)	35(7:3)	26(6:3)	99
AW	25(5:5)	9(5:7)	2(4:8)	35(7:3)	25(6:0)	92
MP	32(7:1)	9(5:7)	1(4:2)	35(7:3)	28(6:9)	86

Action Picture Test/Bus Story (Renfrew, 1988, 1991): Info, information score; sub-clause, number of subordinate clauses; age, equivalent age score; BAS, British Ability Scales.

APPENDIX B1

Individual verb stems and past tense forms for regular and irregular verbs, together with their past tense frequencies (raw frequencies augmented by 1 and then ln-transformed), and the complement/adjuncts used in sentences for their presentation.

	Verb	Past tense form	Past tense freq COBUILD	Verb complement/ Adjunct
Regular verbs				
High frequency	slam	slammed	3.6	my door
	cross	crossed	5.1	Oxford Street
	rush	rushed	4.4	over there
	rob	robbed	3.1	a bank
	drop	dropped	5.6	my brush
	look	looked	7.5	at Susan
	stir	stirred	4.0	my soup
	soar	soared	2.5	over this
Mean			4.5	
SD			1.6	
Range			2.5–7.5	
Low frequency	scowl	scowled	2.3	at Joe
	tug	tugged	2.9	at it
	flush	flushed	3.9	the toilet
	mar	marred	2.1	its beauty
	chop	chopped	3.7	some garlic
	flap	flapped	2.6	my wings
	stalk	stalked	2.7	a rabbit
	scour	scoured	2.1	my pan
Mean			2.8	
SD			.7	
Range			2.1–3.9	
Irregular verbs				
High frequency	make	made	8.2	my lunch
	give	gave	7.2	away money
	think	thought	7.2	about you
	stand	stood	6.7	over here
	keep	kept	6.6	my food
	drive	drove	5.0	a car
	send	sent	6.3	a letter
Mean			6.7	
SD			1.0	
Range			5.0–8.2	
Low frequency	swim	swam	5.0	a mile
	dig	dug	4.7	a hole
	swing	swung	4.4	my bat
	wring	wrung	0.0	my towel
	grind	ground	2.9	the corn
	bend	bent	4.0	a spoon
	bite	bit	4.2	my tongue
	feed	fed	4.5	her cat
Mean			3.7	
SD			1.9	
Range			0–5.0	

APPENDIX B2

Individual novel verb stems and expected regularised and plausible irregularised past tense forms, together with the complements/adjuncts used in sentences for their presentation.

	Verb stem	Expected regularised past tense form	Plausible irregularised past tense form	Verb complement/ adjunct
Novel regulars				
	spuff	spuffed	spaff	for TV
	dotch	dotched	doach	your car
	stoff	stoffed	stoaf	my room
	cug	cugged	cogue	more furniture
	trab	trabbed	trub	a paper
	crog	crogged	crug	with John
	vask	vasked	vosk	a ring
	brop	bropped	brap	his jacket
	satch	satched	sotch	around water
	grush	grushed	grash	near Eric
	plam	plammed	plome	my leg
	scur	scurred	skeer	a bean
Novel irregulars				
	strink	strinked	strunk	a horse
	frink	frinked	frunk	over dinner
	strise	strised	strose	for them
	crive	crived	crove	a lot
	shrell	shrelled	shrelt	with Chris
	vurn	vurned	vurnt	about London
	steeze	steezed	stoze	my watch
	shrim	shrimmed	shram	at home
	cleed	cleeded	cled	very well
	scrit	scritted	scrat	for Steve
	ret	retted	rit	around here
	sheel	sheeled	shelt	among them
	blide	blided	blid	with her
	prend	prended	prent	a mouse
	shreep	shreeped	shrept	my friend
	drite	drited	drit	a field

APPENDIX C

Stem Familiarity Rating Task

Procedure: The subjects were tested individually in a quiet room, and were seated opposite the examiner. A card with five bars of increasing size was placed on the table in front of the child. A card with codes (0–4) corresponding to the bars was placed parallel to the bars in front of the examiner. The experimenter spoke the following instructions: "I am going to read you some words and ask you to tell me how many people you think might say each word. The word is going to be in a sentence. I will read each sentence out loud, and then ask you to show me on this picture how many people you think might say the word." The experimenter then pointed to the appropriate bar while saying "This one means almost nobody says the word; this one means very few people; this one means some people here is quite a lot of people; and this one means lots and lots of people." Three demonstrations were given: "So, for example, 'Every day I **go** to school.' The verb was stressed and repeated after the first one or two practice sentences was repeated in isolation to ensure that the child judged the verb and not the whole sentence. "**Go**, I think lots and lots of people might say that word. I've heard it a lot of times before. Have you?" The experimenter then pointed to bar 4, the tallest bar. "What about 'Every day I **weep** over her'? **Weep**, I think quite a lot of people might say that word." The experimenter then pointed to tower 3. "What about 'Every day I **prame** quite well'? Oh, I haven't heard that word much at all. I'd say only very few people might say that one." The experimenter then pointed to bar 1, the shortest bar. Two practice items were then administered: The experimenter said " 'Every day I **scrig** over there.' How many people might say that word? 'Every day I **play** in the park.' How many people might say that word?" When the experimenter was reasonably confident that the child understood the task indicated by him/her pointing to appropriate bars for two practice items, the test sentences were administered. The set of 60 verbs was pseudo-randomised using the same criteria as were used in the production task. All subjects received the same item presentation order.

LANGUAGE AND COGNITIVE PROCESSES, 2001, *16* (2/3), 219–239

What atypical populations can reveal about language development: The contrast between deafness and Williams syndrome

Virginia Volterra, Olga Capirci, and M. Cristina Caselli

Institute of Psychology, C.N.R., Rome, Italy

Two distinct lines of investigation are presented: the study of linguistic competence in the written language of deaf children and adults, and the study of linguistic development in children and adolescents with Williams syndrome (WS). Qualitative data focusing on spoken and written Italian and coming from cross-sectional and longitudinal studies conducted over the last 10 years are briefly reviewed and discussed. Italian people who are deaf demonstrate selective difficulties with aspects of grammatical morphology that play a syntactic rather than a semantic function. Italian people with WS display a particular asymmetric fragmentation within linguistic abilities: a profile of strength in phonological abilities but serious deficits in semantic and morphosyntactic aspects of language. The case of these two very different populations can offer us important clues for investigating which aspects of language and specifically of grammar are influenced by modality of perception.

INTRODUCTION

Language acquisition is a multi-faceted task involving the mastery of many different abilities: communicative, phonological, semantic, syntactic, morphological, and pragmatic. The study of language acquisition in special populations can offer particular insight into the relationship between linguistic, perceptual, and cognitive abilities. Through a close comparison of data on language development and use in individuals displaying atypical profiles, we can better explore the role played by external factors such as

Requests for reprints should be sent to Virginia Volterra, Istituto di Psicologia CNR, V. le Marx, 15-00137 Rome, Italy. E-mail: direz@ip.rm.cnr.it.

A preliminary version of this paper has been presented at the *Eighteenth Annual Symposium on Research in Child Language Disorders*, May 30–31, 1997, University of Wisconsin-Madison.

http://www.tandf.co.uk/journals/pp/01690965.html   DOI: 10.1080/01690960042000067

modality of perception. In the present paper we will review and integrate research findings from two distinct lines of investigation: the study of linguistic competence in the spoken and written language of deaf children and adults, and the study of linguistic development in children and adolescents with Williams syndrome (WS). These two populations show opposite, contrasting characteristics:

> Children born deaf or those who lose their hearing in the first two years of life display intact cognitive capabilities but because of their hearing loss, they can not spontaneously learn the language spoken around them.
> WS children can hear language perfectly well (often displaying a form of hyperacusia), but they show mental retardation and display special difficulties in visuo-spatial abilities.

We will compare studies conducted by our laboratory over the last 10 years on both these populations, including cross-sectional and longitudinal studies of the acquisition of spoken and written Italian. Many of the results reported here have been already published separately elsewhere, but this is the first publication in which results for WS and deaf speakers of Italian have been discussed side by side. We cannot conduct direct comparisons between these two populations, given the fact that the type of linguistic material examined in the two cases was completely different: written language for the deaf population, spoken language for WS syndrome population. But the case of these two very different groups can offer useful insights into those aspects of language and specifically of grammar that are or are not influenced by perceptual modality. Furthermore, because Italian is a language with a rich and complex grammatical morphology, these data offer the opportunity to investigate specific patterns of morphological sparing and/or impairment that would be difficult to detect in English.

DEAF PEOPLE AND THE ITALIAN LANGUAGE

Children born deaf or those who became deaf early in life, usually have many problems in acquiring spoken and written Italian (for studies regarding English see Mogford, 1993). These difficulties do not depend on an impairment in language processing per se, because, as we know, a deaf child can acquire perfectly well a Sign Language in the same time period required for the acquisition of a spoken language (Abrahamsen, 2000; van den Bogaerde, 2000). But deaf children can not learn spontaneously the auditory-vocal language spoken around them. Instead, they are often forced to learn through the visual modality (i.e., through reading) a language that evolved to meet the problems and opportunities provided by the acoustic-vocal modality. Thus there are many reasons why we might expect to find linguistic difficulties in a deaf speaker of an auditory-vocal language.

The most obvious reason for these difficulties is, of course, the fact that deaf children receive auditory stimuli in a degraded and incomplete form (if at all). Although some individuals are able to exploit the visual cues that accompany speech (i.e., lip-reading), these cues greatly underspecify the phonetic distinctions required for normal speech. In addition, the deaf child's acquisition of a spoken and written code always takes place under "abnormal" conditions, i.e., under conditions that differ markedly from the informal contexts of first language acquisition by a hearing child. Most deaf children in oral or bimodal language programmes are exposed to auditory-vocal language under intense formal training by an adult, with the aid of various devices, for a limited number of hours per day. In most cases, children are also considerably older than they would be if they were to acquire the same spoken language under natural conditions. Furthermore, for those deaf children who have acquired a signed language as their native language, both the spoken and written versions of a spoken language constitute a case of second language learning. All of these conditions could contribute in some fashion to delays or arrests in language learning, and/or to specific patterns of deviation in the final state reached by the deaf speaker. However, the results of our studies show that we can exclude many of these possible factors as direct causes of specific difficulties exhibited by deaf people in the spoken and written language.

Through our research we are trying to answer the following questions:

Do deaf children adopt different strategies in the acquisition of Italian in respect to hearing children?
Do they attain native levels of competence at least in the written form of a vocal language?
Is it possible to detect in written Italian used by deaf people specific linguistic difficulties in particular aspects of the language?

Over the last 10 years we have conducted a series of systematic studies in order to explore this topic and answer these questions, analysing both performance on specific linguistic tasks and spontaneous written production by deaf children, adolescents, and adults (see also Caselli & Volterra, 1993).

In one study, 25 profoundly deaf children between the ages of 11 and 15 were compared with hearing controls ranging in age from 6 to 15 years (Taeschner, Devescovi, & Volterra, 1988). The children were tested in the written modality, in a series of production and comprehension items designed to explore aspects of bound morphology and free-standing grammatical morphemes. In particular we will report here the results of this comparison on three morphosyntactic aspects of Italian which involve

TABLE 1
Pluralisation of the four classes of Italian nouns

	Singular	*Plural*
Major patterns		
masculine singular		
with *-o* ending	telefon**o** (telephone)	telefon**i** (telephons)
feminine singular		
with *-a* ending	tavol**a** (table)	tavol**e** (tables)
Minor patterns		
masculine singular		
with *-e* ending	can**e** (dog)	can**i** (dogs)
feminine singular		
with *-e* ending	tigr**e** (tiger)	tigr**i** (tigers)

different types of linguistic problems: pluralisation of nouns, use of definite articles, and position of the clitic pronoun. Details regarding these three aspects of Italian morphology are summarised in Tables 1–3.

Summarising briefly, pluralisation of nouns in Italian requires a modification of the noun ending and involves bound morphology. Articles are free-standing morphemes, which have to agree in gender and number with the noun to which they refer. The clitic pronoun may be placed before the verb as a freestanding morpheme or after the verb as a bound morpheme, thus providing a problem of morpheme ordering. In complex sentences with infinitive clauses the position of the clitic pronoun varies

TABLE 2
Italian system of definite articles

Major patterns		
	masculine singular: **il**	masculine plural: **i**
	feminine singular: **la**	feminine plural: **le**
	Singular	*Plural*
masculine	**il** telefono (**the** telephone)	**i** telefoni (**the** telephones)
	il cane (**the** dog)	**i** cani (**the** dogs)
feminine	**la** tavola (**the** table)	**le** tavole (**the** tables)
	la tigre (**the** tiger)	**le** tigri (**the** tigers)
Minor masculine patterns		
	masculine singular: **lo**	masculine plural: **gli**
	Singular	*Plural*
	lo sgabello (*the* stool)	**gli** sgabelli (*the* stools)
	lo stile (**the** style)	**gli** stili (**the** styles)

TABLE 3
Clitic pronoun ordering in Italian

With some verbs, the clitic may be used in either preverbal or postverbal position:

I bambini vanno a comprare il gelato
'The children are going to buy the ice cream'.
*I bambini **lo** vanno a comprare.*
'The children **it** are going to buy'.
*I bambini vanno a comprar**lo**.*
'The children are going to buy-**it**'.

With other types of verb, only one of the two positions is allowed:

Preverbal position
La bambina fa cadere il piatto.
'The girl drops the plate'.

Correct form with pronoun:
*La bambina **lo** fa cadere.*
'The girl **it** causes to fall'.

Wrong form:
*La bambina fa cader**lo***.*
'The girl causes to fall-**it**'*.

Postverbal position
La nonna cerca di acchiappare il gatto.
'The grandmother tries to catch the cat'.

Correct form with pronoun:
*La nonna cerca di acchiappar**lo**.*
'The grandmother is trying to catch-**it**'.

Wrong form:
*La nonna **lo*** cerca di acchiappare.*
'The grandmother **it*** is trying to catch'.

---

according to the verb used in the main clause. These three quite complex and contrasting grammatical features permit us to examine the competence of deaf people in written Italian under different linguistic constraints.

All participants, deaf and hearing, were given written tasks designed to test several morphosyntactic aspects of Italian, including the three we have just mentioned. Results showed that on the plural task (both with real and nonsense words), deaf children performed like age-matched controls. On the morpheme ordering (clitic) task, deaf participants showed a strong preference for the post-verbal position, and their performance was, in terms of both quality and quantity, similar to that of young hearing children, suggesting a pattern of delay. However, on the article task, deaf performance was markedly deviant from hearing controls at any age. Not only did deaf participants make a greater number of errors than age-matched controls, but they also relied on an idiosyncratic and incorrect agreement strategy. Table 4 reports some examples of errors observed in both hearing and deaf children, and of incorrect agreement produced uniquely by deaf children.

This study suggests that deaf children take a qualitatively different approach to the acquisition of grammatical morphology, at least for some aspects of the language, in a written form. Because the deaf sample included children with and without sign language experience, and because all these children showed the same error profile, the results cannot be attributed to interference between signed and spoken language.

The research we have just summarised does not address the question of a possible dissociation between grammatical morphology and other aspects of language (e.g., syntax), but we addressed this specific issue in a case study of a deaf woman who has achieved a remarkably good control over written and spoken Italian. In particular we examined just how far a profoundly deaf learner can go under ideal conditions in acquiring the complex Italian system of grammatical morphology, by examining patterns of dissociation that occur at the highest level of acquisition (Volterra & Bates, 1989).

The subject of this study, Z, was a native signer with deaf parents who also acquired spoken Italian early in life. Z produces complex and well-formed syntactic constructions comparable to those of highly educated, hearing native speakers of the language. Nevertheless she produced a large number of systematic errors in her spontaneous speech and writing. In Table 5 we report some examples of Z's errors in spontaneous writing.

TABLE 4
Examples of errors

Kind of errors observed in deaf and hearing children

Correct Form	Wrong Form	Type of Error
lo zaino	*il* zaino	article substitution
gli zaini	*i* zaini	article substition

Kind of errors observed in deaf children but not observed in hearing children

Correct Form	Wrong Form	Type of Error
il fucile	*le fucile*	agreement between
le notti	*i notti*	final vowels
la notte	*le notte*	of articles and nouns

TABLE 5
Errors from Z's corpus

Z's letter 1:

Correct form *Potresti rispondere a queste mie domande*
Z's version *Potresti rispondermi*** *queste mie domande* ...
Could you respond me* these my questions
(pronoun "mi" added; preposition "a" omitted)

Correct form *... per dirmi belle parole*
Z's version *... ha faticato soltanto per dirmi di* belle parole.*
... he struggled only to tell me of* beautiful words
(preposition "di" added)

Z's letter 2:

Correct form *... pensa bene che nessuno mi ha insegnato a fare questo lavoro*
Z's version *... pensi* bene che nessuno mi ha insegnato di* fare questo lavoro.*
... imagine* that no one has taught me of to do this job
(verb conjugation wrong; preposition "di" instead of "a")

We compared examples of Z's spoken and written language with equivalent samples for a bilingual hearing speaker (BC) who acquired Italian as a second language after 16 years of age. Analysing the errors produced by Z and BC we observed interesting similarities and differences. BC produced a large number of lexical errors that did not occur in Z's corpus, and she produced invented lexical forms and/or inappropriate phrase structures that were rarely produced by Z. Furthermore, whereas Z's morphological errors were restricted primarily to free-standing function words and agreement, BC committed roughly equal numbers of bound and free morpheme violations and she produced a very high proportion of gender errors that were rare in Z's corpus. In the spoken corpora for these two adults we found the same morphological errors that occurred in the written corpora, with a similar distribution within and across categories.

We can conclude that, while BC's morphological deficit is part of a much more general lexical problem, Z's problems constitute a more narrowly defined impairment of grammatical morphology. Furthermore, because her morphological errors do not include errors of position, nor the production of illegal/impossible forms in the language, we can conclude that the individual morphological items themselves have been perceived and stored properly, in their appropriate phrase structure and word frames. Z seems to "know" the rules of Italian in a metalinguistic sense; but apparently she experiences some kind of interference or failure to access some of this knowledge in spontaneous speaking and writing.

In particular the different error profiles of the two bilinguals suggest that the specific morphological difficulties found in the corpora of the deaf bilingual, Z, can not be attributed solely to her late and second language learning of Italian.

The results of this case study have been recently confirmed by more extensive research with a larger number of adults. Fabbretti, Volterra and Pontecorvo (1998) have examined four different writing tasks produced by three groups of adults. The first group was composed of 10 Italian profoundly deaf native signers with deaf parents (DD) from middle social-cultural class. The mean age of this group was 29 years and their mean age of schooling was 12 years. The second group included 10 hearing adults with deaf parents (HD) with early exposure to Italian sign language (LIS). The mean age of this group was 30 years and the mean educational level was 12 years. The third group included 10 hearing adults with hearing parents (HH) from low social-cultural status who had no contact with deaf

TABLE 6
Omissions, additions and substitutions of grammatical morphological and lexical elements

	Grammatical-Morphological	Lexical
Omissions	Stalio ha chiesto ø (a) Olio Stan asked (to) Oliver	perché non aveva potuto ø (seguire) l'ordine numerico because she could not (follow) the order of numbers
	che ø (è) successo what (is) happened	
Additions	Poi la sua moglie disse Then the his wife said	per cui non sanno dove erano quel posto so they do not know where they are that place
	il marito desiderava di uscire con gli amici the husband wanted of go out with friends	
Substitutions	Olio gli ha risposto male con (a) quel uomo Oliver answered rudely with (to) that man	in quel momento quella ragazza voleva rubare il collare (la collana) d'oro in that moment the girl wanted to steal the gold collar (necklace)
	prima cosa succedere (succede) first what to happen ('s happened)	

Omissions are indicated by a ø, non-standard forms are underlined and standardised forms are reported in parentheses. A different version of this table appeared in Fabbretti et al. (1998).

people or sign language. The mean age of this group was 27 years and the mean educational level was 9 years.

The results show that deaf participants produced more linguistic nonstandard forms than hearing participants. However the pattern of difficulties exhibited was interestingly different: deaf adults produced more linguistic than orthographic nonstandard forms, while hearing adults showed the opposite pattern. In particular, results of this study replicate previous findings already described: the 10 deaf native signers studied here displayed a pattern of selective difficulty with Italian grammatical morphology, especially with free-standing function words. Examples of omissions, additions and substitutions of grammatical, morphological, and lexical elements, are reported in Table 6. Even though the Italian language provides many opportunities for errors of bound morphology on nouns and verbs, such errors were infrequent in deaf participants (see examples reported in Table 7).

A comparison of the texts written by deaf native signers (DD) with those of the hearing native signers (HD) confirms the view that difficulties in the acquisition of written Italian are best explained by deafness itself rather than by the influence of an early acquired sign language.

The comparison between the deaf native signers (DD) and the hearing

TABLE 7
Examples of non-standard forms referring to bound morphology

---

comincia* io → comincio io
I starts* (**wrong verb inflection for person**: 3rd person "comincia" instead of 1st person "comincio")

come era* i capelli? → come erano i capelli?
how was* the hair? (**wrong verb inflection for number**: singular form "era" instead of plural form "erano". It sounds correct in English because only the singular form of "hair" is used)

allora lei è uscita con la macchina e andrà* in giro → allora lei è uscita con la macchina e è andata in giro
then she went out with the car and she will* go around (**wrong verb inflection for tense in the second coordinate sentence**: future "andrà" instead of compound past tense "è andata" as in the first sentence)

gli* armi → le armi
the* weapons (**wrong gender agreement between article and noun**: plural masculine article "gli" instead of plural feminine article "le")

circa 2 milione* → circa 2 milioni
about 2 million* (**wrong number agreement between noun and modifier**: singular noun "milione" instead of plural noun "milioni"

A different version of this table appeared in Fabbretti et al. (1998)

individuals who had no exposure to sign language (HH) but shared with our deaf adults a relatively low familiarity with written texts, showed that the specific difficulties with grammatical morphology displayed by the deaf adults cannot be attributed solely to their limited experience with written Italian.

The three studies reported here suggest that we can exclude many possible factors previously described as direct causes of specific difficulties exhibited by deaf people in Italian, in particular Sign language interference, second language learning, and limited experience with the written text. Our findings are compatible with the claim that acoustic perception (and consequently phonetic/phonological factors) plays a special role in the acquisition and use of grammatical morphology. In particular, deaf people have specific problems with those parts of speech that are identifiable only through the acoustic channel and for which no other channel can play a similarly reliable role.

This hypothesis can be supported by the following observations. Free-standing function words tend to convey relatively little semantic content in their own right. To the extent that semantic content plays a role in lexical retrieval, morphological items suffer a marked disadvantage. This disadvantage is offset in part by their high frequency of occurrence—at least for hearing speakers. But in the case of the deaf, the frequency of these items looks very different: many Italian morphological forms tend to be short items that are produced rapidly and with low stress in fluent language. It is possible to pick up many or most of these forms in skilled lip-reading, but it is far from easy. This state of affairs may mean that deaf speakers of Italian are often failing to receive and encode morphological markers; their input may thus consist much of the time of "islands" of content words in properly sequenced syntactic frames. This degraded input in turn may mean that the deaf speaker literally has less "practice", i.e., fewer opportunities to observe the application of morphological processes. In addition, however, hearing speakers/listeners of a spoken language may have evolved some kind of auditory and/or articulatory code that aids in item retrieval—a mode of retrieval in which sensorimotor cues related to the "shape" of that item play a major role. Presumably such a code could be used for all lexical items, but it might come to play a larger role for grammatical morphemes by default, because other modes of retrieval and rehearsal (for example based on meaning) are less effective for these items. Deaf listeners would have a marked disadvantage in the development and application of such an acoustic/articulatory code, although it may not be altogether absent.

Many studies have shown that it is possible to access phonological information despite profound prelinguistic deafness and that the use of phonological information is not necessarily dependent upon the auditory modality. Different hypotheses about how deaf people can store phonological information on the form of words have been put forward. Conrad (1979) suggested that a phonological code can be built through silent articulation and Dodd (1987) has found that deaf people can and do generate a phonological code by using visual information derived from lip-reading. All authors, even from different perspectives, agree that deaf children develop a phonological code in different ways from hearing children. We can infer that in order to learn some specific rules on free-standing morphemes, the acoustic channel is necessary and can hardly be substituted or integrated by the visual channel especially when other means are not effective (Mogford & Bishop, 1993). From a theoretical perspective this implies that it is possible to receive phonological, lexical, syntactic and, for the most, morphological information through the visual channel. The morphological rules of Italian clearly can be learned through the visual modality, because they are quite clearly marked in the written form of the language. However information derived from lip-reading and written information are not sufficient in order to achieve a correct and fluent production of grammatical morphemes (Mogford, 1993).

"In short, any language learning device needs adequate auditory input if oral language is to be learned successfully. If it is not, then written language problems will ensue" (Bishop, 1997, p. 150). The specific difficulties deaf children and adolescents have in using particular aspects of grammatical morphology (for example Italian free morphemes such as articles and prepositions) show that some aspects of codification and access of free morphemes can be related to acoustic features and frequency of use in the language.

Another possible factor could be that deaf children acquire spoken and written Italian under different conditions and at a later age than hearing children. Many authors have suggested that grammatical morphology is particularly difficult to acquire after the putative critical period for language (Goldowsky & Newport, 1993; Johnson & Newport, 1989). Indeed, a number of studies have shown that grammatical morphology presents a particularly serious problem for second language learners, including deaf people who are acquiring the visual-spatial morphology of ASL at a later than normal age (Johnson & Newport, 1989; Mayberry, 1993; McDonald, 1997).

We may find that a critical period account and an account based on phonetic/phonological mechanisms are not mutually exclusive. In both cases, spoken languages and signed languages, those aspects of grammatical morphology more related to code of transmission (the acoustic for spoken and the visual for sign) have to be learned earlier in life. People who acquire Signed Languages later in life have specific problems with those aspects of grammars more dependent on the visual code, while people (born deaf) who acquire a vocal language later in life seem to have specific problems with those aspects of grammar more dependent on the acoustic code.

To summarise and answer our previous questions, deaf people appear to use partially different strategies in the acquisition of Italian. They can attain a high level of competence in the written language, but in these cases, although lexical and syntactic abilities are comparable to those of hearing people with the same school level, they can demonstrate specific difficulties partially different from those found in hearing controls. These specific difficulties among the deaf concern especially free-standing grammatical morphemes such as articles and prepositions, and as the various examples provided in the tables demonstrate, these problems are especially sever when function words carry out a syntactic rather than a semantic function.

CHILDREN AND ADOLESCENTS WITH WILLIAMS SYNDROME AND THE ITALIAN LANGUAGE

In this part of the paper we present and discuss recent data on linguistic abilities of children and adolescents with Williams syndrome (WS), focusing on specific difficulties they exhibit in some aspects of the Italian language.

Williams syndrome (WS) is a rare genetic condition that involves a range of symptoms including a characteristic facial structure, post-natal growth deficiency, and renal and cardiovascular anomalies (supra-valvular aortic stenosis and peripheral pulmonary artery stenosis). Williams syndrome children are also mildly to severely mentally retarded (Beuren, Apitz, & Harmjanz, 1962; Williams, Barratt-Boyes, & Lowe, 1961; Morris, Thomas, & Greenberg, 1993).

Previous studies which focused on adolescents with WS found that the syndrome results in major dissociations in cognitive function, both within and across domains: severe cognitive deficits co-occurring with relatively spared language; and severe difficulties in spatial construction but not in facial recognition (Bellugi, Bihrle, Jernigan, Trauner, & Doherty, 1990; Bellugi, Marks, Bihrle, & Sabo, 1993; Reilly, Klima, & Bellugi, 1990). More recently it has been argued that individuals with Williams syndrome show a characteristic cognitive profile: relative strengths in auditory rote memory and in language, accompanied by extreme weakness in visual-spatial constructive cognition (Mervis, Morris, Bertrand, & Robinson, 1999).

The apparent language/cognition dissociation is further complicated by recent findings indicating that children with WS display a complex pattern of strengths and weaknesses within the "spared" linguistic domain. These studies have been conducted in Great Britain and France as well as in the United States (Arnold, Yule, & Martin, 1985; Karmiloff-Smith, 1992; Rubba & Klima, 1991; Wang & Bellugi, 1993). Our group has contributed to this revised perspective with several studies of linguistic abilities of Italian children with WS (Capirci, Sabbadini, & Volterra, 1996; Pezzini, Vicari, Volterra, Milani, & Ossella, 1999; Volterra, Capirci, Pezzini, Sabbadini, & Vicari, 1996; Volterra, Longobardi, Pezzini, Vicari, & Antenore, 1999), in order to answer the following questions:

Are children with WS ahead/behind/equal to normally developing children of the same mental age on linguistic measures?

Is it possible to detect specific difficulties in particular aspects of the language?

Do children with WS adopt different strategies in the acquisition of Italian?

One of our studies focused on lexical and morphosyntactic abilities in 17 individuals with WS between 4.10 and 15.3 years of age (Volterra et al., 1996). The mean mental age of these children calculated with the Leiter Scale (Leiter, 1980) was 5.2 years (range 3.8 to 6.8 years), reflecting a mean IQ of 56 (range 38–90). In all of the relevant language measures children with WS were compared with a sample of 116 normally developing children whose chronological age corresponds to the mental age range of our WS children. The language measures that were used included both lexical and grammatical measures. Comprehension was evaluated by the Peabody Picture Vocabulary test (Dunn & Dunn, 1981), an Italian version of the Test for Reception of Grammar (TROG; Bishop, 1979).[1] Production was evaluated by the Boston Naming test (Nicholas et al., 1989), by the Category Test for Semantic Fluency and by the Phonological Fluency Test (Semel, Wiig, & Secord, 1980), by the Sentence Repetition Test (Vender et al., 1981), and by three Story Description tasks (Borel-Maisonny, 1968; Karmiloff-Smith, 1985)

Results of the comparison showed that the two groups did not differ in the Peabody test for lexical comprehension, in the Category Test for Semantic Fluency and in the Mean Length of Utterance calculated on the story descriptions. However, children with WS did obtain significantly poorer results than controls in the TROG, in the Boston Naming Test, and in the Sentence Repetition Test. In contrast, the children with WS performed significantly better than controls in the Phonological fluency test.

---

[1] The Italian version of the TROG does not correspond exactly to the English version, for some details and data on children with WS and normally developing children, see Volterra et al., 1996.

We can answer our first question by saying that the language produced by children with WS in this age range is for the most part not ahead of their mental age (for similar findings see Gosch, Stading, & Pankau, 1994). The only evidence in favour of a linguistic advantage comes from the Phonological fluency task. However our children with WS were older than the control group of normally developing children (whose chronological age corresponded to the mental age range of WS children). Therefore we do not know whether the apparent advantage of WS was an effect of many years of school experience that the normal controls simply did not have.

In order to answer our second question, on specific difficulties exhibited by WS in particular linguistic aspects, we now consider in more detail the errors produced. In the TROG, the overall pattern of lexical and morphosyntactic errors made by children with WS was equivalent to that of normally developing younger children and the percentage of errors is similarly distributed across different grammatical structures. Examples of typology of errors across different grammatical structure, is reported in Table 8.

TABLE 8
Examples of errors produced by WS subjects across different grammatical structures in the Test for Reception of Grammar

Noun e.g., target sentence "La *gonna* a fiori è appesa al filo" (The flowered *skirt* is hanging on the washing line); the child points to the picture where the flowered *trousers** are hanging on the washing line.

Adjective e.g., target sentence "Il gatto *nero* sta seduto sotto l'albero" (The *black* cat is sitting under the tree); the child points to the picture where the *white** cat is sitting under the tree.

Verb e.g., target sentence "L'elefante lo *trasporta*" (The elephant *carries* it); the child points to the picture where the elephant *is carrying nothing**.

Preposition e.g., target sentence "La matita sta sopra il fazzoletto" (The pencil is *on* the handkerchief); the child points to the picture where the pencil is *near** the handkerchief.

Reversible sentences e.g., target sentence "*La bambina spinge* la mucca" (The *child pushes* the cow); the child points to the picture where *the cow** pushes* the child.

Gender e.g., target sentence "L'elefante *lo* trasporta" (The elephant carries *it*); the child points to the picture where the elephant carries *her**.

Singular/plural e.g., target sentence "*L'orsacchiotto* sta nel cesto" (*The teddy bear* is in the basket); the child points to the picture where the teddy *bears** are in the basket.

Relation between elements of the sentence e.g., target sentence "La *gallina* che sta sopra la *palla* è *nera*" (The *hen* that is on the *ball* is *black*); the child points to the picture where the *hen* is on the *black ball**.

In the Boston Naming Test, we note two types of errors: lexical substitutions (from the same semantic category, for example "airplane" or "boat" labelling the picture of a helicopter) and semantic paraphrases (for example "to hang up clothes" describing the picture of a coat hanger).

In the Sentence Repetition Test and in the transcribed tapes of the three Story Descriptions children with WS produced morphological errors in addition to lexical substitutions. Examples are reported in Table 9.

As to our second question, the language produced by children with WS was unusual from several points of view. Their speech was fluent and they appeared to be good conversationalists, but the content of their speech was often odd or out of place in a particular social context. We noted informally that the children often had a difficult time following the questions the experimenters asked them. Moreover some of the grammatical errors produced were qualitatively different from those that

TABLE 9

Examples of morphological errors, produced by WS subjects during the Sentence Repetition Test and the Story Description

Sentence Repetition Test

Target sentence	Child's production	Type of error
I nipotini colgono i fiori con la nonna the grandchildren gather flowers with their grandmother	*I bambini acco* i fiori sulla** nonna* the children (ga)ther* the flowers on the top* of the grandmother	*incomplete verb form **substitution of preposition
la bambina non legge il libro the little girl is not reading the book	*la bambina non leggere* il libro* the little girl not to read* the book	*wrong verb inflection

Story Description

Target Picture	Child's Production	Type of error
una bambina con sua madre a girl with her mother	*la befana* fairy godmother	lexical substitution
il palloncino vola via col vento the balloon goes away with the wind	*niente pallone è volata** no more balloon (masc) it's gone* (fem)	*wrong past participle agreement
una bambina con sua madre a girl with her mother	*una bambina e una mamma che stava* passeggiando* a girl and a mother who was* walking	*singular instead of plural verb inflection

are usually reported for normally developing children acquiring Italian: errors of gender agreement and verb conjugation, and substitutions of prepositions and other function words. These findings show that children with Williams syndrome have specific semantic and morphological difficulties, and could suggest that they acquire language with a qualitatively different mix of processing mechanisms.

In order to address the third question on language acquisition strategies, we can consider the main results of a longitudinal study we conducted on the linguistic development of a girl with WS (Elisa), followed from the age of 2.0 until 4.10 years of age (Capirci et al., 1996).

Despite an initial delay which appeared less marked than is usually reported for children with WS, Elisa's rate and sequence of development seemed to be similar to those observed in typically developing children. However, unlike typically developing children, Elisa did not seem to attain a good mastery of the rules governing some aspects of morphology, such as article/noun agreement, use of preposition, use of clitics, and verb conjugations. Sometime, she produced both correct and incorrect agreement in the course of the same session.

Elisa also displayed an uneven pattern of within-domain dissociations. She exhibited good vocabulary and proficient use of syntax, at least in some contexts, but failed with simple grammatical agreement: she made several kinds of grammatical errors (gender agreement between article and noun and in pronominalisation) that are rarely produced by children at the same syntactic level. The limitation in Elisa's linguistic abilities appeared in tasks such as the Sentence Repetition Test but were even more evident in the context of spontaneous narration. When Elisa tried to report something that had happened to her, the sentence structure appeared reduced and she produced many morphological errors. Examples are reported in Table 10.

Some of the errors reported here, in particular incorrect agreement between article and noun, show that grammar is not intact in this child.

Results of the longitudinal study confirm a delayed but also complex and partially atypical profile of linguistic development in children with WS but other detailed longitudinal studies are needed to explore if the qualitative deviations reported in Elisa's case are determined by a different rate and/ or strategies in the language acquisition process.

Taken together, the results reported here are consistent with other recent studies on French, German, and English speaking children and adolescents with WS. According to these studies children with WS show a characteristic profile in that some linguistic abilities are more preserved than others. Children and adolescents with WS perform well on some language tasks but they rarely, if ever, perform at their chronological age level (Karmiloff-Smith et al., 1995, 1997).

TABLE 10
Examples of errors produced by a girl with WS

Age 3.1	Correct form
● *ce l'*ho due* *pronoun "l" instead of "ne"*	(ce ne ho due, referring to two coins) I have two of these
● *io pettini* *second person instead of first person*	(io pettino) I comb
● *è uno* gioco bello* *article "uno" instead of "un"*	(è un gioco bello) it is a nice game

Age 3.6–3.8	Correct form
● *oh s'è* versata due* *singular instead of plural auxiliary and past participle inflections*	(si sono versate due) oh two spilled
● *due le* preso* *auxiliary omitted and singular instead of plural participle*	(due le ho prese) (I) took two of these
● *le * tavolini* ● *le * spazzolini* *incorrect agreement between article and noun*	(i tavolini or le tavoline) the little tables (le spazzoline or gli spazzolini) the little brushes

Age 4.2–4.5	Correct form
● *alle * montagne* *incorrect preposition and plural form of the name instead of the singular one*	(in montagna) (to go) to the mountains
● *mi fa* vederlo* *incorrect position of the clitic "lo" and third person instead of second person of the verb*	(me lo fai vedere) me let see it
● *noi ce lo* abbiamo* mangiati*, mangiati* perchè era fredda* *singular clitic instead of plural and auxiliary "to have" instead of "to be"*	(noi ce la siamo mangiata, mangiata perchè era fredda – la neve-) we have eaten it, eaten it because it was cold (the snow)

Age 4.8–4.10	Correct form
● *il * stivalo* *article "il" instead of "lo" and error of termination of the name ("-o" instead of "-e")*	(lo stivale) the boot
● *Sonia vieni* co te a giocare* *second person instead of first person verb*	(… vengo con te a giocare) I come with you to play

The same authors have emphasised that the language of WS is not intact, and that individuals with WS can show serious deficits in semantic and morphosyntactic aspects of language. In particular French speaking children with WS showed clear-cut problems with grammatical gender and English-speaking adolescents with WS often make errors in prepositions (Karmiloff-Smith et al., 1997; Rubba & Klima, 1991). Neither prepositions nor grammatical gender are particularly difficult for very young normal children.

CONCLUSIONS

To summarise our results on both the deaf and the WS groups, we would first like to suggest that it is important to study children who are acquiring morphologically complex languages like Italian. This can lead us to uncover specific difficulties these children may have, which cannot be easily identified in languages such as English.

Which aspects of language are influenced by modality of perception and/ or cognitive abilities? Deaf children acquire Italian without hearing it. WS children acquire Italian despite serious cognitive difficulties particularly in visuo-spatial constructive abilities.

Deaf people learning Italian demonstrate selective difficulties with grammatical morphology and in particular with free standing function words that carry out a syntactic rather than a semantic function. The particular pattern of errors observed in our data is different from the more general problem with Italian morphology demonstrated by hearing bilinguals.

Italian people with WS display a particular asymmetric fragmentation within both linguistic and visuo-spatial domains. They show a linguistic profile of strength in phonological fluency but moderate to severe impairment in some aspects of lexical production and in grammatical comprehension and production. In particular these problems are especially evident with those aspects of morphology carrying out a semantic function.

There is clear evidence of a remarkable separability (and potential variability) of different components within the linguistic domain itself and at the same time a complex relationship between language, cognitive, and perceptual abilities. The acquisition of some specific aspects of Italian morphology (e.g., gender agreement, semantic function of prepositions) seem to be dependent on more general cognitive abilities, while the acquisition of other aspects (e.g., syntactic function of prepositions) appear to be at least partially dependent on perceptual abilities. Our findings agree with a recent suggestion by Bishop "... one important factor determining language proficiency in different clinical groups could be the capacity for auditory short-term memory" (1999, p. 14). In the case of children with WS, their spared ability to hear and store speech sounds may permit them to acquire those aspects of grammar that are especially difficult for deaf children. But their spared auditory and phonological abilities do not assure a correct acquisition of grammar: some morpho-syntactic errors shown by children with WS (e.g., noun-article agreement) indicate that their grammar does not appear so intact, contrary to the hypothesis recently suggested by Clahsen and Almazan-Hamilton (1998).

Clearly, the data from the two populations discussed here involve different types of linguistic material (written vs. spoken language) and thus are not directly comparable with one another. In addition, more specific tasks have to be designed to test for morphosyntactic properties and separately for lexical aspects of Italian language. Nevertheless, the pattern of findings described above suggests that in the future, direct comparisons of morphological production in deaf children and children with WS may be particularly fruitful for identifying aspects of morphology that are resilient and those that are more sensitive to variations in modality of perception.

REFERENCES

Abrahamsen, A.A. (2000). Exploration of enhanced gestural input to children in the bimodal period. In K. Emmorey & H. Lane (Eds), *The signs of language revisited. An anthology to honor Ursula Bellugi and Edward Klima*, pp. 358–399. Mahwah, NJ: Lawrence Erlbaum Associates Inc.

Arnold, R., Yule, W., & Martin, N. (1985). The psychological characteristics of infantile hypercalcaemia: a preliminary investigation. *Developmental Medicine and Child Neurology, 30*, 315–328.

Bellugi, U., Marks, S., Bihrle, A., & Sabo, H. (1993). Dissociation between language and cognitive functions in Williams syndrome, in D. Bishop & K. Mogford (Eds), *Language development in exceptional circumstances*, pp. 177–189. Hove, UK: Lawrence Erlbaum Associates Ltd.

Bellugi, U., Bihrle, A., Jernigan, T.L., Trauner, D., & Doherty, S. (1990). Neuropsychological neurological and neuroanatomical profile of Williams Syndrome. *American Journal of Medical Genetics, 6*, 115–125.

Beuren, A.J., Apitz, J., & Harmjanz, D. (1962). Supravalvular aortic stenosis in association with mental retardation and a certain facial appearance. *Circulation, 26*, 1235–1240.

Bishop, D.V.M. (1979). Comprehension in developmental disorders. *Develomental Medicine and Child Neurology, 21*, 225–238.

Bishop, D.V.M. (1997). *Uncommon understanding.* Hove, UK: Psychology Press.

Bishop, D.V.M. (1999). An innate basis for language? *Science, 286*, 228–229.

Bishop, D., & Mogford, K. (1993). *Language development in exceptional circumstances.* Hove, UK: Lawrence Erlbaum Associates Ltd.

Borel-Maisonny, S. (1968). *Percezione ed educazione.* Roma: Armando.

Capirci, O., Sabbadini, L., & Volterra, V. (1996). Language development in Williams Syndrome: A case study. *Cognitive Neuropsychology, 13*, 1017–1039.

Caselli, M.C., & Volterra, V. (1993). "Vedere" l'italiano: il caso dei sordi. In E. Cresti, & M. Moneglia (Eds), *Ricerche sull'acquisizione dell'Italiano*, pp. 247–271. Roma: Bulzoni.

Clahsen, H., & Almazan-Hamilton, M. (1998). Syntax and morphology in Williams Syndrome. *Cognition, 68*, 167–198.

Conrad, R. (1979). *The deaf schoolchild: language and cognitive function*. London: Harper and Row.

Dodd, B. (1987). Lip-reading, phonological coding and deafness. In B. Dodd, & R. Campbell (Eds), *Hearing by eye: The psychology of lip-reading*. Hove, UK: Lawrence Erlbaum Associates Ltd.

Dunn, L.M., & Dunn, L.M. (1981). *Peabody Picture Vocabulary Test*. Wilmington, DE: Guidance Associates.

Fabbretti, D., Volterra, V., & Pontecorvo, C. (1998). Written language abilities in Deaf Italian. *Journal of Deaf Studies and Deaf Education, 3*, 231–244.

Goldowsky, B.N., & Newport, E.L. (1993). Modeling the effects of processing limitations on the acquisition of morphology: the less is more hypothesis. In E. Clark (Ed.), *Proceedings of the 24h Annual Child Language Forum*, pp. 124–138. Stanford, CA: CSLI.

Gosch, A., Stading, G., & Pankau, R. (1994). Linguistic abilities in children with Williams-Beuren Syndrome. *American Journal of Medical Genetics, 52*, 291–296.

Johnson, J.S., & Newport, E.L. (1989). Critical period effects in second language learning: the influence of maturational state on the acquisition of English as a second language. *Cognitive Psychology, 21*, 60–99.

Karmiloff-Smith, A. (1985). Language and cognitive processes from a developmental perspective. *Language and Cognitive Processes, 1*, 61–85.

Karmiloff-Smith, A. (1992). *Abnormal phenotypes and the challenges they pose to connectionist models of development*. Technical Reports in Parallel Distributed Processing and Cognitive Neuroscience, TR.PDP. CNS. 92.7, Carnegie Mellon University.

Karmiloff-Smith, A., Klima, E., Bellugi, U., Grant, J., & Baron-Cohen, S. (1995). Is there a social module? Language, face processing, and theory of mind in individuals with Williams syndrome. *Journal of Cognitive Neuroscience, 7*, 196–208.

Karmiloff-Smith, A., Grant, J., Berthoud, I., Davies, M., Howlin, P., & Udwin, O. (1997). Language and Williams syndrome: How intact is "intact"? *Child Development, 68*, 246–262.

Leiter, R.G. (1980). *Leiter International Performance Scale*. Illinois: Stoelting Co.

Mayberry, R.I. (1993). First-language acquisition after childhood differs from second-language acquisition: the case of American Sign Language. *Journal of Speech and Hearing Research, 36*, 1258–1270.

McDonald, J.L. (1997). Language acquisition: the acquistion of linguistic structure in normal and special populations. *Annual Review of Psychology, 48*, 215–241.

Mervis, C., Morris, C.A., Bertrand, J., & Robinson, F.R. (1999). Williams Syndrome: findings from an integrated program of research. In H. Tager-Flusberg (Ed.), *Neurodevelopmental disorders: contribution to a new framework from the cognitive neurosciences*. Cambridge, MA: MIT Press.

Mogford, K. (1993). Oral language acquisition in the prelinguistically deaf. In D. Bishop & K. Mogford (Eds), *Language development in exceptional circumstances*, pp. 110–131. Hove, UK: Lawrence Erlbaum Associates Ltd.

Mogford, K. & Bishop, D. (1993). Five questions about language acquisition considered in the light of exceptional circumstances. In D. Bishop & K. Mogford, *Language development in exceptional circumstances*, pp. 239–260. Hove, UK: Lawrence Erlbaum Associates Ltd.

Morris, C.A., Thomas, I.T., & Greenberg, F. (1993). Williams syndrome: autosomal dominant inheritance. *American Journal of Medical Genetics Supplements, 47*, 478–481.

Nicholas, L., Brookshire, R., McLennan, D., Shummacher, J., & Porrazzo, S. (1989). Revised administration and scoring procedures for the Boston Naming Test and norms for non-brain damaged adults. *Aphasiology, 3,* 569–580.

Pezzini, G., Vicari, S., Volterra, V., Milani, L., & Ossella, M.T. (1999). Children with Williams Syndrome: Is there a single neuropsychological profile? *Developmental Neuropsychology, 15,* 141–155.

Reilly, J., Klima, E., & Bellugi, U. (1990). Once more with feeling: affect and language in atypical populations. *Development and Psychopathology, 2,* 637–391.

Rubba, J. & Klima, E.S. (1991). Preposition use in a speaker with Williams Syndrome: some cognitive grammar proposals. *Center for Research in Language Newsletter, 3,* 3–12.

Semel, E., Wiig, E.H., & Secord, W. (1980). *CELF-R: Clinical evaluation of language fundamentals—Revised.* San Antonio: The Psychological Corporation.

Taeschner, T., Devescovi, A., & Volterra, V. (1988). Affixes and function words in the written language of deaf children. *Applied Psycholinguistics, 9,* 385–401.

van den Bogaerde, B. (2000). *Input and interaction in deaf families.* Utrecht, The Netherlands: Landelijk Onderzoekschoole Taalwetenschap.

Vender, C., Borgia, R., Cumer Bruno, S., Freo, P., & Zardini, G. (1981). Un test di repetizione frasi. Analisi delle performances di bambini normali. *Neuropsichiatria Infantile, 243–244,* 819–831.

Volterra, V. & Bates, E. (1989). Selective impairment of Italian grammatical morphology in the congenitally deaf: A case study. *Cognitive Neuropsychology, 6,* 273–308.

Volterra, V., Capirci, O., Pezzini, G., Sabbadini, L., & Vicari, S. (1996). Linguistic abilities in Italian children with Williams Syndrome. *Cortex, 32,* 663–677.

Volterra, V., Longobardi, E., Pezzini, G., Vicari, S., & Antenore, C. (1999). Visuo-spatial and linguistic abilities in a twin with Williams Syndrome. *Journal of Intellectual Disability Research, 43,* 294–305.

Wang, P.P. & Bellugi, U. (1993). Williams Syndrome, Down Syndrome and cognitive neuroscience. *American Journal of Diseases of Children, 147,* 1246–1251.

Williams, J., Barratt-Boyes, B., & Lowe, J. (1961). Supravalvular aortic stenosis. *Circulation, 24,* 1311–1318.

LANGUAGE AND COGNITIVE PROCESSES, 2001, *16* (2/3), 241–259

Phonological and semantic contributions to children's picture naming skill: Evidence from children with developmental reading disorders

Kate Nation, Catherine M. Marshall, and
Margaret J. Snowling

University of York, York, UK

This experiment investigated the picture naming skills of dyslexic children, poor comprehenders and children with normally developing reading skills, using pictures whose names varied in word length and word frequency. Relative to young children reading at the same level, dyslexic children were less accurate at naming pictures that have long names, and they made a disproportionate number of phonological errors. In contrast, poor comprehenders showed normal effects of length but were slower and less accurate at naming pictures than control children, and in particular, they were poor at naming pictures that have low frequency names. These findings are discussed within a framework in which picture naming efficiency is related to underlying language skills in both the phonological and semantic domains.

A substantial body of research documents the picture naming difficulties that many language or reading-impaired children experience (for example, Catts, 1991; Constable, Stackhouse, & Wells, 1997; German, 1982; Katz, 1986; Kail, Hale, Leonard, & Nippold, 1984; Leonard, Nippold, Kail, & Hale, 1983; Snowling, Van Wagtendonk, & Stafford, 1988; Swan & Goswami, 1997; Wolf & Goodglass, 1986; Wolf & Obregon, 1992). However, what is less clear is where the picture naming deficits of children

---

Requests for reprints should be addressed to Kate Nation, Department of Psychology, University of York, Heslington, York, YO10 5DD, UK. E-mail: k.nation@psych.york.ac.uk.

This work was supported by Wellcome Trust Grant 048147 to Margaret Snowling and Kate Nation, and by a studentship from the British Dyslexia Association to Catherine Marshall. We would like to thank Jeff Bowers, Steven Frisson and Martin Pickering for helpful discussions. We are most grateful to the staff and pupils at Westfield Junior School, Fulford St. Oswald's Primary School and Kinloss School for their help and co-operation.

---

http://www.tandf.co.uk/journals/pp/01690965.html   DOI: 10.1080/01690960042000003

with developmental disorders originate with respect to cognitive models of naming. In addition to the perceptual processes used to identify a picture, semantic processing is needed in order to recognise and select the appropriate name whereas phonological processes are needed so that the picture name can be retrieved or assembled (for review, see Johnson, Paivio, & Clark, 1996). Plausibly, deficits in any of these processes may result in impaired picture naming.

For dyslexic children who have difficulty learning to decode print, there is strong evidence that their reading difficulties are underpinned by weak phonological skills (Brady & Shankweiler, 1991; Snowling, 1991; Stanovich & Siegel, 1994). The difficulty that dyslexic children experience when naming pictures has also been interpreted as a symptom of weak phonological skills. On this view, dyslexic children are able to recognise the pictures but are poor at retrieving their names from long-term memory (Katz, 1986; Snowling et al., 1988). Swan and Goswami (1997) showed that dyslexic children were particularly poor at naming pictures that have long, phonologically complex and unusual names (e.g. *protractor*, *harmonica*, *binoculars*), even when compared with young children matched for reading age. Indeed, the dyslexic readers were only as accurate as poor readers with below average general intelligence, so called garden-variety poor readers. Unlike garden-variety poor readers however, the dyslexic children often demonstrated good vocabulary knowledge for many of the pictures they failed to name. Swan and Goswami also found that the dyslexic children produced far more phonological errors (for example, naming *clog* as "cog" or "shog") than control children. Taken together, these findings provide strong support for the view that dyslexic children's difficulties with picture naming are related to their phonological processing deficits.

As the relationship between a picture and its phonological label is arbitrary, picture naming must rely on some form of semantic mediation between the perception and recognition of the object. In dyslexic readers, this is unlikely to be a source of difficulty as their semantic skills are generally thought to be intact (Frith, Landerl, & Frith, 1995). Nonetheless, individual differences in semantic ability should be related to picture naming ability. Consistent with this, aphasic patients with semantic impairments also tend to be anomic (Butterworth, Howard, & McLoughlin, 1984; Humphreys, Riddoch, & Quinlan, 1988; Lambon Ralph, Graham, Ellis, & Hodges, 1998). While children's performance on standardised tests of picture naming correlates well with measures of vocabulary and comprehension (with coefficients varying from 0.46 to 0.80; Johnson et al., 1996), there is relatively little evidence linking picture naming performance directly with semantic skills in populations of children with developmental disorders. Although children with specific language impairment are slow and inaccurate at naming pictures (Kail et al., 1984;

Leonard et al., 1983; Wiig & Becker-Caplan, 1984), such difficulties may be a consequence of phonological processing weaknesses rather than being mediated by semantic skills.

In order to tease apart the role of phonological and semantic skills in children's picture naming, we used a between-groups comparison of children with selective impairments of either phonological or semantic skills. In contrast to dyslexic children, poor comprehenders are defined as those children who decode print well: they have age-appropriate reading accuracy but poor reading comprehension (Nation & Snowling, 1997; Yuill & Oakhill, 1991). In line with their reading profile, studies have found poor comprehenders to have normal phonological processing skills (Cain, Oakhill & Bryant, in press; Nation & Snowling, 1998; Nation, Adams, Bowyer-Crane, & Snowling, 1999; Stothard & Hulme, 1995); however, they have poor word knowledge and are slow and inaccurate at accessing and retrieving semantic knowledge (Nation & Snowling, 1998, 1999).

To investigate the role of phonological factors in naming skill, we compared dyslexic children with younger children, matched for reading level. On the basis of previous work, we expected dyslexic children to perform less well than reading-level controls (Swan & Goswami, 1997). To test the hypothesis that semantic impairments may impede children's picture naming, we compared poor comprehenders with normal readers, matched for chronological age and decoding ability. As poor comprehenders have normal phonological skills (Nation & Snowling, 1998; Stothard & Hulme, 1995), any naming difficulties they experience are unlikely to be the consequence of underlying phonological deficits. Instead, it is reasonable to predict that poor comprehenders' naming will be compromised by weaknesses in semantic processing.

According to models of skilled speech production (e.g. Dell, 1986; Levelt, 1989), following object identification two lexical steps or stages can be distinguished. The first is concerned with name selection and it is at this stage that abstract lexical representations specify semantic and syntactic information. Following this, phonological information becomes involved at a second stage of processing as pronunciations are retrieved and assembled. Despite broad agreement that lexical selection and name retrieval are functionally distinct, debate continues as to whether the stages interact during processing (Dell & O'Seaghdha, 1992; Griffin & Bock, 1998; Humphreys et al., 1988) or whether the two stages are separate and temporally distinct (Levelt, 1989; Roelofs, 1992).

As Johnson et al. (1996) noted in their review of the picture naming literature, this issue has not been a matter of concern or debate in developmental research where studies have tended to document *overall* naming performance rather than to specify how different naming stages are influenced by developmental factors. Similarly, studies investigating children with poor picture naming have not attempted to pinpoint at what stage in the naming process the deficits originate. In the present study, we investigated this by first asking how individual differences in both phonological and semantic skills are related to picture naming and by comparing the children's naming for pictures whose names varied in word length and word frequency.

Longer names require more phonological information to be specified in, and retrieved from, long-term memory. Thus, children's naming tends to be slower and less accurate as word length increases (e.g. Katz, 1986; Swan & Goswami, 1997). The other item characteristic we manipulated was word frequency. Both children (Leonard et al., 1983) and adults (Humphreys et al., 1988; Oldfield & Wingfield, 1965) are better at naming pictures that have high frequency names. From a developmental perspective, it is reasonable to suggest that common words develop semantic representations more readily than less common words and that highly familiar words may have "stronger" semantic representations. It is likely that any retrieval difficulties will be exacerbated for low frequency words that are not well-learned and therefore, in addition to predicting main effects of length and frequency, we also anticipated that the two factors would interact with children being particularly slow and inaccurate at naming pictures that have long, low frequency names.

In addition, interactions between children's underlying language skills and their sensitivity to manipulations of word length and frequency may shed light on where their deficits originate, with respect to cognitive models of naming. To the extent that word length influences the ease of phonological output processes, sensitivity to length can be considered a marker of phonological skill. Thus, if children's naming problems are associated with phonological deficits, they should experience particular difficulty naming pictures that have longer names. We anticipated, therefore, that dyslexic children's naming performance would be adversely influenced by word length. In contrast, if children's naming problems are associated with semantic weaknesses, performance should not be adversely influenced by word length; poor comprehenders, therefore, should show normal word length effects when naming pictures. However, as these children have weak semantic skills, we predicted that they would be impaired at naming pictures that have low frequency names.

METHOD

Participants

To provide stringent tests of our hypotheses, dyslexic children and poor comprehenders were individually matched to children in separate control groups. Dyslexic children were matched with reading-age controls while poor comprehenders were matched with normal readers.

Dyslexics and reading-age controls. Fifteen dyslexic children and fifteen reading age (RA) control children participated in this study (Table 1). The dyslexic children attended a special residential school for dyslexic children and all had been diagnosed on the basis of a discrepancy between their expected and actual reading attainment, taking account of IQ. At the time of the study, all had a reading age at least 18 months below their chronological age. RA control children were drawn from local primary schools and all were reading within 6 months of the level expected for their chronological age. They were individually matched to the dyslexic children for single word reading level using raw scores from the Wechsler Objective Reading Dimensions (Basic Reading Scale; Rust, Golombok, & Trickey, 1993). Although the two groups did not differ in reading age, the dyslexic children were significantly older than the RA control children ($F = 46.39, p < .001$).

Poor comprehenders and normal readers. We selected 10 normal readers and 10 poor comprehenders, matched for decoding skill and chronological age. Decoding ability was assessed using the Graded Nonword Reading Test (Snowling, Stothard, & McLean, 1996) which provides norms for children aged between 6 and 11 years. Text reading accuracy and reading comprehension were assessed using the Neale Analysis of Reading Ability-Revised (Neale, 1989). In this test, children read aloud short passages of text and are then asked questions to assess literal and inferential understanding.

Children were recruited into these groups according to the following criteria. All of the normal readers had a least average-for-age nonword reading, reading accuracy and reading comprehension. Children in the poor comprehender group were matched with the normal readers as

TABLE 1
Mean (SD) chronolocal age and reading age of dyslexic children and RA controls

	Dyslexic children $n = 15$	RA controls $n = 15$
Chronological age[a]	13.12 (1.9)	8.91 (1.02)
Reading age[a]	8.92 (1.33)	8.75 (1.04)
Reading accuracy[b]	77.73 (10.76)	98.13 (2.61)

[a] In years. [b] Standard scores, M = 100, SD = 15.

closely as possible for nonword reading. However, their reading comprehension was at least one year below the expected level. The performance of the two groups on the selection tasks is summarised in Table 2. The two groups did not differ in terms of chronological age or decoding but the poor comprehenders' reading comprehension was substantially lower than the control children's, $F(1, 18) = 80.41$, $MSE = 53.04$, $p < .001$.

Materials

Fifty-six picturable objects, selected from the Morrison, Chappell, and Ellis (1997) corpus, were used in this experiment (see Appendix). Half of the picture names were short and half were long. Short names were all monosyllables three or four phonemes in length. The long items consisted of three or four syllables and varied between six and ten phonemes in length. The picture names also varied in frequency with half being high frequency and half low frequency. Frequency estimates were taken from Morrison et al.'s norms of rated frequency (in their studies, adult raters estimated the frequency with which they encountered a word, in either spoken or written format, on a scale of 1 to 5 where 1 represents low and 5 represents high). The high frequency items varied in rated frequency from 2.5 to 4.35 whereas the low frequency items varied in rated frequency from 1.45 to 2.05 on a scale of 1 to 5.

Thus, four groups of pictures were formed: high frequency short (e.g. *glove*, *nurse*), high frequency long (e.g. *umbrella*, *television*), low frequency short (e.g. *harp*, *axe*) and low frequency long (e.g. *gorilla*, *parachute*). Fourteen items were included in each group and the four groups of items were matched for imageability, age of acquisition and name agreement (Table 3).

TABLE 2
Mean (SD) performance of poor comprehenders and normal readers on selection tests

	Poor comprehenders n = 10	Normal readers n = 10
Chronological age[a]	8.86 (0.31)	8.75 (0.29)
Reading comprehension[b]	86.44 (1.94)	106.20 (4.10)
Reading accuracy[b]	106.70 (6.00)	110.50 (6.38)
Non-word reading[c]	17.90 (1.85)	17.70 (2.00)

[a] In years. [b] Standard scores, M = 100, SD = 15. [c] Maximum score is 20.

TABLE 3
Details of stimulus characteristics

| | High frequency | | | | Low frequency | | | |
| | Short | | Long | | Short | | Long | |
	M	SD	M	SD	M	SD	M	SD
Length (in phonemes)	3.57	0.51	7.29	1.20	3.21	0.43	7.50	0.85
Frequency[a]	3.23	0.49	3.23	0.64	1.88	0.20	1.87	0.13
Age of acquisition[a]	2.61	0.38	2.84	0.95	2.93	0.66	3.53	0.69
Name agreement[a]	97.21	3.07	88.86	13.71	97.21	4.98	88.43	16.04
Imageability[a]	5.98	0.16	6.19	0.31	6.0	0.19	6.13	0.28

[a] Norms taken from Morrison et al. (1997).

Procedure

To allow computer-presentation of the stimuli, line drawings (taken from those used by Morrison et al., 1997) were scanned onto a Macintosh SE/30 computer. At the beginning of each trial, a fixation point appeared in the centre of the screen for 1000 ms and immediately at the offset of the fixation, a picture appeared on the screen where it remained until a response was initiated. A voice activated relay interfaced with the computer timed naming response latencies (in milliseconds) from the appearance of the stimulus to the onset of the child's response. The next trial began following a 2500 ms interval. The children were tested individually and were instructed to name each item as quickly as possible. The items were randomly split into two sets with the proviso that an equal number of pictures of each type appeared in each set. The children received a few minutes rest between each set and the order of presentation of the sets was counterbalanced across the four groups of children. All errors and equipment failures were noted.

RESULTS

Accuracy and speed of picture naming

We present separate analyses comparing the naming skills of the dyslexics with RA controls, and the poor comprehenders with the normal readers. Only the RTs to correctly named items were analysed and to better approximate a normal distribution, trimmed means were calculated from the RT data by eliminating the largest 5% and smallest 5% of data points for each child in each condition. Number of errors and trimmed mean RTs were analysed using 2 (frequency: high vs. low) × 2 (length (short vs. long)

× 2 (reader group) analyses of variance with repeated measures on the first two factors.

Dyslexics and reading-age controls.　The mean number of errors and RTs for the dyslexics and RA controls are shown in Table 4. Forty-nine observations (2.92%) were voice key errors and these were not included in the analyses. Five responses (0.37%) that abbreviated the picture name (e.g. TELEVISION → *telly* or *TV*; TELEPHONE → *phone*) were counted as correct but removed from the RT analysis.

In the accuracy analysis, the main effects of frequency, $F(1, 28) = 39.41$. MSE = 69.01, $p < .001$, and length, $F(1, 28) = 34.95$, MSE = 33.08, $p < .001$, were significant, as was the interaction between length and frequency, $F(1, 28) = 26.30$, MSE = 37.41, $p < .001$. Tests of simple main effects showed that the effect of frequency was significant for the long words only ($F(1, 28) = 49.09$, MSE = 104.02, $p < .001$; for short words, $F < 1.5$). Neither the main effect of group ($F < .01$), nor the interaction between group and frequency ($F < 1.0$) were significant. However, the interaction between group and length was significant, $F(1, 28) = 3.89$, MSE = 3.68, $p = .05$; tests of simple main effects indicated that although both groups made more errors on the long words (dyslexics: $F(1, 28) = 31.06$, MSE = 29.40, $p < .001$; controls: $F(1, 28) = 7.77$, MSE = 7.35, $p < .01$), control children made more errors than dyslexic children on the short words whereas the

TABLE 4

Mean RTs (ms) and error rates (maximum = 14) produced by the four groups of children

	High frequency				Low frequency			
	Short		Long		Short		Long	
	M	SD	M	SD	M	SD	M	SD
Dyslexics[a]								
RT	1236.87	261.78	1360.53	239.14	1241.27	257.22	1815.20	656.34
Errors	0.93	0.96	1.40	1.59	1.60	0.83	3.93	1.16
RA-Controls[b]								
RT	1260.40	187.92	1409.93	349.13	1353.60	281.66	1678.13	534.24
Errors	1.53	1.19	0.93	0.88	1.67	1.11	3.67	1.87
Poor comprehenders[a]								
RT	1388.20	370.81	1366.20	266.77	1408.20	396.21	1764.90	571.93
Errors	2.6	1.51	2.40	1.23	3.40	1.58	5.50	2.17
Normal readers[b]								
RT	1087.00	183.24	1214.70	259.05	1115.90	199.54	1496.90	379.54
Errors	1.60	0.70	1.30	0.68	1.50	0.85	2.70	0.95

[a] N = 15, [b] N = 10.

dyslexics made more errors than controls on the long words. The three-way interaction between group, length and frequency was not significant ($F < 1.0$).

The RT data were normally distributed (with skew and kurtosis close to zero) except for the long, low frequency items which were moderately positively skewed (skew = 1.32, SE = 0.43; kurtosis = 1.25, SE = 0.83). Consistent with the accuracy analysis, the main effects of frequency, F $(1, 28) = 10.47$, MSE = 120608.5, $p < .01$, and length, $F(1, 28) = 24.05$, MSE = 107048.4, $p < .001$, were significant, as was the interaction between frequency and length, $F(1, 28) = 6.63$, MSE = 110601.5, $p < .02$. Simple main effects confirmed that the effect of frequency was significant for the long words only ($F(1, 28) = 9.62$, MSE = 203731.6, $p < .001$; short words: $F < 1.4$). Neither the main effect of group, nor any of the interactions with group, were significant (all $Fs < 1.3$).

As the data were not normally distributed in the long, low frequency condition, an additional analysis was performed to compare the two groups of children after the data in this condition were square root transformed, as recommended by Tabachnick and Fidell (1989). The dyslexic children and the RA controls did not differ on this measure ($t = -0.59$).

Poor comprehenders and normal readers.   The mean number of errors and trimmed mean RTs for the poor comprehenders and normal readers are shown in Table 4. Thirty-two observations (2.89%) were voice key errors and these were not included in the analyses. Twelve responses (1.07%) that abbreviated the picture name were scored as correct but were not included in the RT analysis.

In the accuracy analysis, the main effects of frequency, $F(1, 18) = 18.86$, MSE = 33.80, $p < .001$, and length, $F(1, 18) = 10.72$, MSE = 9.80, $p < .01$, were significant. The interaction between length and frequency was also significant, $F(1, 18) = 22.18$, MSE = 18.05, $p < .001$, and tests of simple main effects confirmed that the effect of frequency was significant for the long ($F(1, 18) = 28.79$, MSE = 50.63, $p < .001$) but not the short items ($F(1, 18) = 1.45$, MSE = 1.22). This pattern is identical to that observed in the data from dyslexic and RA control children.

Turning to the group comparisons, the main effect of group was significant showing that poor comprehenders made more errors than the normal readers, $F(1, 18) = 17.50$, MSE = 57.80, $p < .01$. However, this was qualified by a significant interaction between group and frequency, $F(1, 18)$ $= 4.72$, MSE = 8.45, $p < .05$. Tests of simple main effects showed that the poor comprehenders were especially poor at naming low frequency pictures, $F(1, 18) = 21.22$, MSE = 28.03, $p < .001$. Neither the interaction between length and group ($F < 1.4$) nor the three-way interaction between frequency, length and group ($F < 1.0$) were significant.

The RT data were normally distributed in the high frequency conditions; however, both low frequency conditions had substantial kurtosis values and moderate skew (short: kurtosis = 4.32, SE = 0.99; skew = 1.82, SE = 0.51; long: kurtosis = 3.34, SE = 0.99; skew = 1.76, SE = 0.51). Thus, although we report an analysis of variance on these data, the results should be interpreted cautiously.

Consistent with the accuracy data, the children were faster at naming high frequency words, $F(1, 18) = 9.79$, MSE = 67996.7, $p < .01$, and short words, $F(1, 18) = 12.21$, MSE = 72844.9, $p < .01$. The interaction between frequency and length was also significant, $F(1, 18) = 5.92$, MSE = 84384.0, $p < .03$, and again, this was caused by a larger frequency effect for the long, $F(1, 18) = 9.65$, MSE = 120168.7, $p < .01$, than the short picture names, $F < 1.0$. The poor comprehenders were slower overall, $F(1, 18) = 4.87$, MSE = 263423.7, $p < .05$). None of the interactions involving length approached significance.

As the data were not normally distributed in the low frequency conditions, some additional analyses were conducted to check the robustness of these findings. Non-parametric Wilcoxon tests confirmed that there was a frequency effect for the long words ($z = -2.91, p < .001$) but not for the short words ($z = -1.1$). We also compared the two groups of children after the data in the two low frequency conditions were log transformed (Tabachnick & Fidell, 1989). Although the poor comprehenders were slower than the normal readers for the short words ($t = 2.23, p < .04$), the difference did not reach significance for the long words ($t = 1.3$).

In summary, all children were more accurate and faster at naming pictures with short, high frequency names. Although the dyslexic children performed similarly to the RA control children overall, they were less accurate at naming long words, regardless of word frequency. In contrast, the poor comprehenders were slower and less accurate at naming pictures than normal readers and although their performance was not differentially affected by length, they were adversely affected by frequency.

Analysis of errors

Dyslexics and RA controls. "Don't know" responses constituted 31.36% and 29.91% of the errors made across the four conditions by the dyslexic children and RA controls respectively. After removing these, it was clear that many of the children's errors were close approximations to the target either in terms of the visual appearance of the pictured item (e.g., POTATO → *rock*), in terms of meaning (e.g., NURSE → *doctor*) or were related both visually and semantically (e.g., GORILLA → *monkey* and SWORD → *knife*).

To provide more objective estimates of how closely related an error was to its target either visually or semantically, we obtained similarity ratings from independent raters, all of whom were members of the psychology department at the University of York. They were unaware of the nature of the experiment, and they were not told that they were rating children's naming errors. To assess visual similarity, we assembled booklets containing each target line drawing and a list of the errors made when naming each picture. Fifteen adults rated how visually similar errors were to targets on a scale of 1 to 5 (with 1 being visually dissimilar and 5 being visually very similar). To assess semantic similarity, booklets were assembled containing each picture name and a list of the errors made for each word. Fifteen different adults rated how similar the errors were to the targets on a scale of 1 to 5 (with 1 being unrelated in meaning and 5 being very closely related in meaning). Thus, for each error, we obtained an estimate of visual similarity (M = 2.44, SD = 0.98) and semantic similarity (M = 3.10, SD = 1.04).

An error was classified as semantically close if it obtained a semantic similarity score greater than 3.2 (this being the median score). Errors with semantic similarity scores below 3.2 were classified as semantically distant. Likewise, an error was classified as visually close if it scored above the median visual similarity score (2.4) and visually distant if it fell below the median. This procedure resulted in four error categories: (i) semantically close/visually close (e.g., SWORD → *knife*); (ii) semantically close/visually distant (e.g., HELICOPTER → *plane*); (iii) semantically distant/visually close (e.g., POTATO → *rock*) and (iv) semantically distant/visually distant (e.g., VOLCANO → *rain*). Table 5 shows the percentage of errors made by the dyslexic and RA controls for each of these four categories.

Following the methods recommended by Ferguson (1981, pp. 185–187), the significance of the difference between the two groups was calculated by dividing the observed difference between the proportions by the estimate of the standard error of the difference (separately for each error category).

TABLE 5
Percentage errors (after removing omissions) classified according to semantic and visual similarity for dyslexics and RA controls

	Semantically close		Semantically distant	
	Dyslexics	RA controls	Dyslexics	RA controls
Visually close	24.66[a]	42.17	8.22[a]	24.10
Visually distant	27.40[b]	13.25	36.99[b]	20.40

Superscripts show that dyslexics made significantly fewer errors [a] or more [b] errors of that type than RA controls, $p < .01$. See text for information.

The younger RA control children made significantly more errors that were visually related to the target. The dyslexic children produced more semantically related errors, suggesting that they were often able to recognise the picture but unable to retrieve the correct label, for example, naming HELICOPTER as PLANE. Similarly, the finding that the dyslexic children produced more errors that were neither semantically nor visually related to the target may also be consistent with difficulties in phonological retrieval; plausibly, these errors may be phonological errors and thus neither semantically or visually related to the targets.

To assess to what extent the children's naming errors were phonologically related to the target names, we calculated a score for each error according to the proportion of phonemes it shared with the target. For example, the response *stethoscope* shares five of the nine in the target *microscope* and therefore the proportion of phonemes common to both is 0.56. *Babybird* in response to a picture of a *ladybird* also included a high proportion of common phones (0.75). In contrast, the error *bat* contained only 0.33 of the phonemes of the target name *banana*, and the response *violin* did not share any phonemes with the target *harp*. Consistent with our predictions, the errors of the dyslexic children contained a greater proportion of the target phonemes than those of the younger control children ($M = 0.22$ and 0.12 respectively), a statistically reliable difference, $F(1, 174) = 9.58$, $MSE = 0.04$, $p < .01$.

Poor comprehenders and normal readers. "Don't know" responses constituted 33.3% and 25% of the errors made across the four conditions by the poor comprehenders and normal readers respectively. To provide estimates of how closely related an error was to its target either visually or semantically, we obtained similarity ratings, as described above. Twenty-four different adults rated the errors; 12 adults rated for visual similarity ($M = 2.57$, $SD = 1.09$) and 12 rated for semantic similarity ($M = 3.15$, $SD = 1.15$). Errors falling above the median were classified as close whereas those that scored below the median were regarded as distant (median scores were visual 2.8, semantic 3.8). Table 6 shows the percentage of errors made by the poor comprehenders and normal readers for each of these four categories.

Both groups made a similar number of errors that were classified as semantically distant/visually close. This suggests that all of the children were equally likely to produce the name of a visually similar alternative. However, the normal readers made far more errors that were both semantically and visually close to the target than the poor comprehenders. Like the dyslexic children, there was a tendency for the poor comprehenders to make more errors that were neither semantically nor visually related. In contrast to the dyslexics however, it was not the case that these

TABLE 6

Percentage errors (after removing omissions) classified according to semantic and visual similarity for poor comprehenders and normal readers

	Semantically close		Semantically distant	
	Poor comprehenders	*Normal readers*	*Poor comprehenders*	*Normal readers*
Visually close	28.39[a]	48.83	14.8	13.95
Visually distant	17.28	9.30	39.51[b]	27.90

Superscripts show that poor comprehenders made significantly fewer errors [a] ($p < .01$) or more errors [b] ($p < .09$) of that type than normal readers. See text for information.

errors were phonological in nature. Using the same phonological coding system described earlier, the poor comprehenders and normal readers obtained similar phonological error scores (M = 0.17 and 0.19 respectively; $F < 1.0$). Thus, poor comprehenders' tendency to produce visually and semantically unrelated errors cannot be attributed to them making more phonological errors. Instead, the poor comprehenders' errors that were classified into the "visually and semantically unrelated" category tended to be semantically related to the target, but unlike the control children's errors, they were not rated highly enough to fall into the semantically close category (for example, *butterfly* for *ladybird*, *boat* for *submarine*, *balloon* for *parachute*, *priest* for *nun*).

DISCUSSION

This experiment investigated the picture naming skills of dyslexic children, poor comprehenders and children with normally developing reading skills. Relative to younger children reading at the same level, dyslexic children were less accurate at naming pictures that have long names, and they made a disproportionate number of phonological errors. In contrast, poor comprehenders showed normal effects of length and they made no more phonological errors than control children. However, they were slower and less accurate at naming pictures than control children and in particular, they were poor at naming pictures that have low frequency names.

Our finding that dyslexic children were worse than RA controls at naming pictures that have long names replicates earlier findings by Swan and Goswami (1997) and is consistent with the language profile of underlying phonological processing deficits characterising dyslexic children (Snowling, 1991; Stanovich & Siegel, 1994). Word length may influence the ease with which phonological forms are activated in long-term memory. Alternatively (or additionally), length effects could emerge at a later stage in processing when vocal outputs are assembled prior to responses being generated. On the basis of existing data, it is not possible to distinguish between these two alternatives. However, if dyslexic children's difficulties lie at a stage in processing when names are activated, they should also show length-related deficits on tasks which require name activation, but not vocal output (for example, picture-word matching). In contrast, if their length-related difficulties arise at a later stage in processing, perhaps when speech-motor programmes are assembled, deficits will only emerge in those tasks requiring spoken output. An additional possibility is that part of dyslexic children's difficulties with retrieval stem from underlying difficulties with encoding: if they fail to encode phonological forms in a well-specified manner, slow and inefficient retrieval may ensue (Katz, 1986; Swan & Goswami, 1997). Although it is difficult to see how encoding and subsequent processing can be distinguished empirically, both views are entirely consistent with the conclusion that phonological processing deficits are at the core of picture naming difficulties in children with developmental dyslexia.[1]

Like dyslexic children, poor comprehenders were also worse at picture naming than normally developing children. In contrast to dyslexic children however, poor comprehenders were not adversely affected by word length, nor did they produce a disproportionate number of phonological errors. To the extent that sensitivity to word length is a marker of phonological skill, these data converge with the results of a number of different studies using different paradigms which failed to find evidence of phonological processing weaknesses in this group (Cain et al., in press; Nation & Snowling, 1998; Nation et al., 1999; Stothard & Hulme, 1995). In contrast to their competence in the phonological domain, poor comprehenders are slow and inaccurate at accessing and retrieving semantic information (Nation & Snowling, 1998, 1999). We suggest that poor comprehenders' generally slower and less accurate picture naming, especially for pictures with low frequency forms, and their tendency to produce fewer semantically related errors, are consequences of underlying semantic weaknesses that restrict their ability to access and utilise semantic information efficiently.

Poor comprehenders were especially poor at naming low frequency words. Word frequency is a variable which, according to models of speech production (e.g. Levelt, 1989) exerts an influence at a stage in processing when phonological information is retrieved and assembled. However, it is

---

[1] An alternative explanation could be that the dyslexics did not have the correct name within their vocabulary stores. At post-test we asked each child to define those picture names that they were unable to produce in the experiment. The dyslexics were unable to define only 6.78% of the words whereas the younger RA controls were unable to define 12.7%. Thus the dyslexic children's failure to name pictures accurately can not be attributed to lack of vocabulary knowledge.

not necessary to posit that poor comprehenders have an impairment that originates at this level of processing. Within a more interactive framework with bi-directional flow of activation (e.g., Dell & O'Seaghdha, 1992), representations used early in processing may affect—and themselves be influenced by—the state of later representations. As poor comprehenders have semantic deficits, it is likely that the amount of activation flowing from semantics to phonology will be generally reduced. It we assume that the phonological forms of high frequency words are easier to activate (due to their lower thresholds), it follows that high frequency forms are more likely to be activated by impoverished semantic input than low frequency forms. On this view, even though poor comprehenders have no difficulty with name retrieval per se, reduced semantic activation has a knock-on effect which particularly disadvantages the production of low frequency words.

This account provides an explanation of why children with semantic processing weaknesses have particular difficulty with low frequency words while maintaining the locus of the frequency effect at the level of phonological retrieval, in line with models of skilled speech production. An alternative explanation, however, is that the actual meanings of low frequency words are less well represented in poor comprehenders. In other words, frequency exerts an influence not only at phonological retrieval, but at a stage in processing when names are selected. Within distributed models of semantic memory (e.g., Farah & McClelland, 1991; McRae, de Sa, & Seidenberg, 1997; Plaut & Shallice, 1993), individual concepts are represented by a unique pattern of activation across a set of semantic units. By manipulating the number of semantic features associated with a concept as well as the degree of semantic overlap between words, a number of semantic effects in lexical processing have been simulated (e.g., semantic and associative priming, Booth & Plaut, in press; imageability effects, Plaut & Shallice, 1993; prototypicality effects, McRae et al., 1997; category-specific impairments of semantic memory, Farah & McClelland, 1991). By extending this approach and adopting a developmental perspective, it is reasonable to suggest that common words develop semantic representations more readily than less common words and that highly familiar words will have "stronger" semantic representations as they consist of a greater number of attributes or features.[2] Thus, children who have developed a poorly specified semantic system are likely to be

---

[2] In our experiment we used rated frequency (from the norms provided by Morrison et al., 1997) as a measure of frequency. Our high and low frequency words also differed in familiarity, $F(1, 54) = 71.68$, MSE $= 0.33$, $p < .001$. This suggests that rated frequency reflects individuals' stored knowledge about concepts (although we note that rated frequency also correlates strongly with objective frequency measures taken from printed and spoken word counts, see Morrison et al., for details).

particularly disadvantaged when it comes to the processing of less familiar words. The consequences of this for picture naming is that less activation for uncommon words will propagate to the phonological forms. This would lead to the observed pattern of results, namely, that poor comprehenders are especially poor at naming pictures that have low frequency names. From our experiment, it is not possible to distinguish between this account and the one described above. Central to both accounts, however, is the notion that poor comprehenders' semantic weaknesses impinge on their naming performance.

Notwithstanding the separate contributions that phonological and semantic processing skills make to picture naming, it is important to remember that individual differences in naming will arise from interactions between strengths and weaknesses in both phonological and semantic processing. This can be illustrated by considering why the dyslexic children experienced no greater difficulty dealing with low frequency words than the RA control children. Experiments with adults (e.g., Jescheniak & Levelt, 1994) have shown that word frequency influences the ease of phonological retrieval. As dyslexic children have phonological difficulties, it would be reasonable to predict them to have particular problems producing low frequency forms. However, the dyslexic children in this experiment were neither slower nor less accurate on such words, relative to control children. Importantly however, as the control children were matched to the dyslexic children for reading age, they were four years *younger* in chronological age than the dyslexics. As such, their semantic skills, as indexed by spoken vocabulary knowledge and experience, were less well-developed than those of the dyslexic children. Given this, it is likely that the dyslexic children received more of a "boost" from increased semantic activation than the RA control children (especially for less common words), thereby preventing a Group × Frequency interaction from emerging. Relative to their chronological age-matched peers of course, we would anticipate that dyslexic children would be particularly disadvantaged when naming low frequency pictures. Indeed, Swan and Goswami (1997) found precisely this. In fact, the dyslexic children in their study were also less accurate than RA controls at naming low frequency pictures. However, our dyslexic children were older than those who took part in Swan and Goswami's study (age 13 years vs. 11 years) and moreover, the age gap between our dyslexic participants and the RA controls was greater (4 years vs. 2 years in the two studies respectively). Arguably therefore, the dyslexic children in our study were more likely to benefit more from semantic-level contributions, relative to the RA control children, than would have been the case in Swan and Goswami's study.

In conclusion, by investigating cases of developmental disorder where different component language skills are developing out of step, and by manipulating the characteristics of the items to be named, we have begun to tease apart the contribution to picture naming of individual differences in underlying phonological and semantic skills. Our experiment found that both dyslexic children and poor comprehenders were poor at picture naming but importantly, we suggest that the source of children's difficulties varies according to the nature of their underlying language strengths and weaknesses. For dyslexic children, our findings are consistent with previous studies which see their naming impairments as a symptom of poor phonological processing. Poor comprehenders also have naming impairments but we argue that their difficulties are not related to phonological deficits. Instead, we propose that relatively weak semantic skills constrain picture naming performance in this group. Thus, our results show that picture naming performance is sensitive not only to individual differences in phonological skills, but also to individual differences in underlying semantic skills. In our view, these findings are well-accommodated by a framework in which an important determiner of picture naming is the efficiency of an individual's underlying language skills in both the phonological and semantic domains.

REFERENCES

Booth, J.R., & Plaut, D.C. (in press). Individual and developmental differences in semantic priming: empirical and computational support for a single-mechanism account of lexical processing. *Psychological Review*.

Brady, S., & Shankweiler, D. (Eds.) (1991). *Phonological processes in literacy*. Hillsdale, NJ: Lawrence Erlbaum Associates, Inc.

Butterworth, B., Howard, D., & McLoughlin, P. (1984). The semantic deficit in aphasia: The relationship between semantic errors in auditory comprehension and picture naming. *Neuropsychologia, 22*, 409–426.

Cain, K., Oakhill, J., & Bryant, P. (in press). Phonological skills and comprehension failure: A test of the phonological processing deficit hypothesis. *Reading and Writing*.

Catts, H.W. (1991). Early identification of reading disabilities. *Topics in Language Disorders, 12*, 1–16.

Constable, A., Stackhouse, J., & Wells, B. (1997). Developmental word-finding difficulties and phonological processing: The case of the missing handcuffs. *Applied Psycholinguistics, 18*, 507–536.

Dell, G.S. (1986). A spreading-activation theory of retrieval in sentence production. *Psychological Review, 93*, 283–321.

Dell, G.S., & O'Seaghda, P.G. (1992). Stages of lexical access in language production. *Cognition, 42*, 287–314.

Farah, M.J., & McClelland, J.L. (1991). A computational model of semantic memory impairment: Modality specificity and emergent category specificity. *Journal of Experimental Psychology: General, 120*, 339–357.

Ferguson, G.A. (1981). *Statistical analysis in psychology and education* (5th edition). NY: McGraw-Hill.

Frith, U., Landerl, K., & Frith, C. (1995). Dyslexia and verbal fluency: More evidence for a phonological deficit. *Dyslexia, 1*, 2–11.

German, D. (1982). Word-finding substitutions in children with learning disabilities. *Language, Speech and Hearing Services in Schools, 13*, 223–230.

Griffin, Z.M., & Bock, K. (1998). Constraint, word frequency, and the relationship between lexical processing levels in spoken word production. *Journal of Memory and Language, 38*, 313–338.

Humphreys, G.W., Riddoch, M.J., & Quinlan, P.T. (1988). Cascade processes in picture identification. *Cognitive Neuropsychology, 5*, 67–103.

Jescheniak, J.D., & Levelt, W.J.M. (1994). Word frequency effects in speech production: Retrieval of syntactic information and of phonological form. *Journal of Experimental Psychology: Learning, Memory and Cognition, 20*, 824–843.

Johnson, C.J., Paivio, A., & Clark, J.M. (1996). Cognitive components of picture naming. *Psychological Bulletin, 120*, 113–139.

Kail, R., Hale, C.A., Leonard, L.B., & Nippold, M.A. (1984). Lexical storage and retrieval in language impaired children. *Applied Psycholinguistics, 5*, 37–49.

Katz, R. (1986). Phonological deficiencies in children with reading disability: Evidence from an object naming task. *Cognition, 22*, 225–257.

Lambon Ralph, M.A., Graham, K.S., Ellis, A.W., & Hodges, J.R. (1998). Naming in semantic dementia—what matters? *Neuropsychologia, 36*, 775–784.

Leonard, L.B., Nippold, M.A., Kail, R., & Hale, C. (1983). Picture naming in language impaired children. *Journal of Speech and Hearing Research, 26*, 609–615.

Levelt, W.J.M. (1989). *Speaking: From intention to articulation.* Cambridge, MA: MIT Press.

McRae, K., Sa, V.R.de, & Seidenberg, M.S. (1997). On the nature and scope of featural representations of word recognition. *Journal of Experimental Psychology: General, 126*, 99–130.

Morrison, C.M., Chappell, T.D., & Ellis, A.W. (1997). Age of acquisition norms for a large set of object names and their relation to adult estimates and other variables. *Quarterly Journal of Experimental Psychology, 50A*, 528–559.

Nation, K., Adams, J.W., Bowyer-Crane, C.A., & Snowling, M.J. (1999). Working memory deficits in poor comprehenders reflect underlying language impairments. *Journal of Experimental Child Psychology, 73*, 139–158.

Nation, K., & Snowling, M.J. (1997). Assessing reading difficulties: The validity and utility of current measures of reading skill. *British Journal of Educational Psychology, 67*, 359–370.

Nation, K., & Snowling, M.J. (1998). Semantic processing and the development of word recognition skills: Evidence from children with reading comprehension difficulties. *Journal of Memory and Language, 39*, 85–101.

Nation, K., & Snowling, M.J. (1999). Developmental differences in sensitivity to semantic relations among good and poor comprehenders: Evidence from semantic priming. *Cognition, 70*, B1–13.

Neale, M.D. (1989). *The Neale Analysis of Reading Ability-Revised.* Windsor, UK: NFER.

Oldfield, R.C., & Wingfield, A. (1965). Response latencies in naming objects. *Quarterly Journal of Experimental Psychology, 17*, 257–273.

Plaut, D.C., & Shallice, T. (1993). Deep dyslexia: A case study of connectionist neuropsychology. *Cognitive Neuropsychology, 10*, 377–500.

Roelofs, A. (1992). A spreading-activation theory of lemma retrieval in speaking. *Cognition, 42*, 107–142.

Rust, J., Golombok, S., & Trickey, G. (1993). *Wechsler Objective Reading Dimensions.* London: The Psychological Corporation.

Snowling, M.J. (1991). Developmental reading disorders. *Journal of Child Psychology & Psychiatry, 32*, 49–78.

Snowling, M.J., Stothard, S.E., & McLean, J. (1996). *The Graded Nonword Reading Test.* Reading: Thames Valley Test Company.

Snowling, M.J., Wagtendonk, B.V., & Stafford, C. (1988). Object-naming deficits in developmental dyslexia. *Journal of Research in Reading, 11*, 67–85.

Stanovich, K.E., & Siegel, L.S. (1994). The phenotypic performance profile of reading-disabled children: A regression-based test of the phonological-core variable-difference model. *Journal of Educational Psychology, 86*, 24–53.

Stothard, S.E., & Hulme, C. (1995). A comparison of phonological skills in children with reading comprehension difficulties and children with decoding difficulties. *Journal of Child Psychology and Psychiatry, 36*, 399–408.

Swan, D., & Goswami, U. (1997). Picture naming deficits in developmental dyslexia: The phonological representations hypothesis. *Brain and Language, 56*, 334–353.

Tabachnick, B.G., & Fidell, L.S. (1989). *Using multivariate statistics.* New York: Harper Collins.

Wiig, E.H., & Becker-Caplan, L. (1984). Linguistic retrieval strategies and word-finding difficulties among children with language disabilities. *Topics in Language Disorders, 4*, 1–18.

Wolf, M., & Goodglass, H. (1986). Dyslexia, dysnomia, and lexical retrieval: A longitudinal investigation. *Brain and Language, 28*, 154–168.

Wolf, M., & Obregon, M. (1992). Early naming deficits, developmental dyslexia, and a specific deficit hypothesis. *Brain and Language, 42*, 219–247.

Yuill, N., & Oakhill, J.V. (1991). *Children's problems in text comprehension.* Cambridge, UK: Cambridge University Press.

APPENDIX

Short		Long	
High Frequency	*Low Frequency*	*High Frequency*	*Low Frequency*
bell	harp	umbrella	kangaroo
screw	shawl	screwdriver	cockerel
torch	kite	butterfly	volcano
glove	crown	pineapple	microscope
nurse	axe	strawberry	submarine
train	nun	motorbike	telescope
tent	crab	envelope	scarecrow
cloud	dice	microwave	gorilla
ring	goat	cigarette	ladybird
lamp	clown	banana	astronaut
purse	king	tomato	diamond
shirt	cap	potato	helicopter
cheese	pipe	television	microphone
toast	sword	telephone	parachute

LANGUAGE AND COGNITIVE PROCESSES, 2001, *16* (2/3), 261–286

Patterns of naming objects and actions in children with word finding difficulties

Julie E. Dockrell

Psychology and Special Needs, Institute of Education,
London, UK

David Messer

Psychology Division, University of Hertfordshire, Hatfield, UK

Rachel George

Division of Psychology, University of Central Lancashire,
Preston, UK

Children who experience difficulties in naming are described as having word finding difficulties (WFDs). In the present study 31 children with WFDs were identified through a wider survey of educational provision for those with language and communication difficulties. The children were included if they were between 6;4–7;10 years, had normal non-verbal intelligence, no major articulation difficulties, and had WFDs as diagnosed by the Test of Word Finding Difficulties. Three control groups were identified who were matched on: chronological age ($N = 31$), naming age ($N = 31$), and level of receptive grammar ($N = 31$). Children's comprehension of words, accuracy of naming, and latency to name were assessed for numerals, letters, and pictures of

Requests for reprints should be sent to Julie E. Dockrell, Psychology and Special Needs, Institute of Education, 20 Bedford Way, London WC1H 0AL, UK.

The work reported here was funded by a Wellcome Trust grant to Julie Dockrell and David Messer. We are grateful to Gillie Wilson for collecting part of the data presented here and all the children who participated. Two anonymous reviewers and the editor have provided detailed and constructive criticisms.

A proportion of the data on naming objects was presented at the Child Language seminar 1997 and published in the conference proceedings and a proportion of the comparative data between objects and actions was presented at the International Congress for the Study of Child Language 1999.

http://www.tandf.co.uk/journals/pp/01690965.html   DOI: 10.1080/01690960042000030

objects and actions. Half the pictures presented were high frequency items and half were low frequency items. The children with WFDs formed a heterogeneous group with respect to other language measures with the primary defining feature being their poor performance in word retrieval and their poor performance on a semantic fluency test. No differences were found between the children with WFDs and their age-matched peers when naming letters and numerals or in the comprehension of objects and actions. In contrast, the accuracy and latency of naming were significantly worse than that of age-matched peers. Accuracy of naming was equivalent to that of the language-matched peers and error patterns also were similar. However, the children with WFDs were the slowest to provide responses and for naming high frequency objects this difference approached significance in comparison to language-matched peers ($p = .052$). The findings point to the importance of using appropriate control groups, and are discussed in relation to the idea that WFDs are caused by impoverished semantic representations.

INTRODUCTION

There is increasing appreciation of the important role of the lexicon in language development and the acquisition of literacy abilities (Catts & Kamhi, 1999). Difficulties in accessing the lexicon are likely to compromise children's communication and their ability to acquire academic skills (Snyder & Godley, 1992), and these problems are especially likely to be experienced by children who are described as having Word Finding Difficulties (WFDs). These children are characterised as having long delays in word retrieval, a high occurrence of circumlocutions and word substitutions (German & Simon, 1991). However, the causes of WFDs remain uncertain because of the variety of samples studied and the limited types of comparison groups that are employed. Therefore, this investigation has been designed to address two key issues, (1) the selection of an objectively identified sample of children with WFDs who are compared with an appropriate set of matched comparison groups to determine the nature of WFDs, and (2) the use of a range of systematically identified targets to extend our understanding of WFDs across a larger range of lexical items.

Rationale for the choice of groups

There have been a number of approaches to the study of WFDs. Some researchers have focused on a clinical population of language-impaired children and have investigated WFDs in that population. Indeed it has been argued that WFDs do not occur in isolation from language disabilities (Kail, Hale, Leonard, & Nippold, 1984; Wiig, Semel, & Nystrom, 1982) or other learning disabilities (Kail & Leonard, 1986). Studies within this tradition have found that children who have specific problems with their expressive language have associated WFDs both in tests and in spontaneous discourse. Findings also indicate that WFDs are not exclusively identified in populations with specific language impairments. WFDs have also been identified in children with learning difficulties (German, 1975, 1985; Wiig & Semel, 1975) and with dyslexia (Rudel, Denckla, & Broman, 1981; Swan & Goswami, 1997; Wolf & Segal, 1992).

Investigations that are concerned with WFDs in special populations usually do not identify whether or not children have WFDs with the use of objective standardised tests. As a result, there often is uncertainty about the proportion of children with or without WFDs in such samples and there are, therefore, difficulties in drawing conclusions about the nature of WFDs per se. If one is interested, as we were, in the general characteristics of a group of children who all have objectively defined WFDs then an alternative method of selection is needed. For these reasons two selection procedures were instituted. First, speech and language therapists and teachers identified children in language support services who had marked WFDs. Then the children were assessed using the Test of Word Finding Difficulties (TWF; German, 1989) to confirm the therapists' diagnosis. This test allows both the identification of word finding difficulties in relation to age-matched peers and where necessary a procedure to prorate performance in relation to the child's level of lexical comprehension. Additional entry criteria were average non-verbal intelligence, no major articulation problems that could have affected word production, and no other hearing or neurological disabilities. These selection criteria resulted in the identification of a clearly delineated sample of children with WFDs who possessed average non-verbal abilities and no articulation problems.

The performance of children with WFDs has been, in almost all previous studies, either examined in isolation or compared to chronological age matches. This provides a basis for establishing whether certain of the abilities of children with WFDs are below what would be expected based on their age. However, such comparisons fail to take into account the level of language in the samples. Since children with language difficulties will often have a smaller vocabulary than their peers (Leonard, 1988; Rescorla & Schwartz, 1990; Rice, 1991), it is important to consider their word-finding skills in relation to this and other indicators of language capacity. If children with WFDs perform slightly worse than language-matched controls on a task this will identify an area of performance where they experience difficulties beyond that expected for their language level (Dockrell, Messer, & George, 2000). Such comparisons should help to identify the essential characteristics of WFDs and help understand the causes of WFDs by, for example, allowing differentiation between 'developmental immaturities' in word-finding and alternative explanations in terms of phonological or semantic factors (McGregor, 1997). Thus, in this study we chose the following matches: (i) a chronological age comparison group (CA) that was controlled for non-verbal ability, (ii) a naming age comparison group (NA) who were at a similar level of picture naming ability as the children with WFDs, and (iii) a group matched for syntactic comprehension who were at a similar level of receptive grammar (RG) as the children with WFDs. In all cases, reliable and valid measures standardised on the local population were chosen to identify controls. By employing an objective measure of WFDs and a greater range of comparison groups, we aimed to identify the language difficulties of a well defined population of children with WFDs. In addition information about the phonological skills of the WFDs group were collected to provide descriptive information about these skills. Our particular interest was the identification of differential performance across tasks with the aim of elucidating patterns of delay and difference in the performance of children with WFDs.

Rationale for the choice of test items

There are few developmental models of WFDs (but see Constable, Stackhouse, & Wells, 1997) and discussions about the causes of WFDs have tended to focus on either phonological or semantic deficits (see also Menyuk, 1975; Nippold, 1992 for ideas about retrieval problems). The view that WFDs are caused by semantic deficits has involved the suggestion that the lack of elaborate semantic representations makes it more difficult for children to retrieve words (Kail & Leonard, 1986; Lahey & Edwards, 1996, 1999; McGregor & Leonard, 1989; McGregor & Windsor, 1996). In contrast, other accounts suggest that phonological representations are more difficult to access and/or that the transfer of information between the semantic and phonological systems is impaired (Chiat & Hunt, 1993; Constable et al., 1997). To address these issues and to extend the range of lexical items employed in the study of WFDs we presented children with tasks that involve: (i) naming objects (as in most previous studies); (ii) naming actions; (iii) naming single-numerals and letters, and (iv) naming both high and low frequency items. The rationale for these choices is set out below.

Studies of WFDs have rarely considered children's naming of actions even though there are indications that naming actions involves different processes to the naming of objects. Gentner (1981) suggests that the naming of actions is delayed relative to that of objects, although the differential advantage for naming objects above actions has been called into question by Davidoff and Masterson (1995/6). McGregor (1997), in one of the few studies of the naming of actions in children with WFDs, compared their performance with age-matched peers using the sub-tests from the TWF. The performance of children with WFDs appeared delayed across both word classes, with some evidence for a differential pattern of responses. Interestingly, in adults, clearer differences in error patterns have been found for nouns and verbs (Davidoff & Masterson, 1995/6). There also appears to be evidence for differences in performance according to the types of verb studied. Davidoff and Masterson (1995/6) found that actions involving intransitive verbs were more difficult to name than those involving transitive verbs. The authors argue that the unavailability of associated representations might make retrieval of intransitive verbs more difficult than transitive verbs. As there is evidence that the semantics of verbs differ from those of nouns, and that verbs may be a particular problem area for children with general language problems, these items may pose greater problems for children with WFDs. Given these concerns and findings it was decided to investigate the naming of actions and employ both transitive and intransitive items.

The nature of semantic representations is likely to vary across conceptual domains (Braisby & Dockrell, 1999; Markman, 1989; Soja, 1994) and by corollary across lexical items. Actions and objects denote complex concepts, whereas single numerals and alphabetic letters involve concepts with low semantic complexity. We, therefore, also investigated the naming of letters and single numerals, as well as the naming of objects and actions. By selecting these different types of lexical items, we aimed to investigate whether children with WFDs, in comparison to language age matches, find certain types of lexical items especially difficult to produce. Furthermore, the presence of differences between world class could provide support for the idea that the impoverished nature of children's representations contributes to WFDs. Difficulties in naming objects and actions and not letters and numerals would suggest that the semantic complexity of the items were critical.

When investigating naming it also is important to consider word frequency. Word frequency is associated with quicker and more accurate responses when picture naming and these effects are typically described as a consequence of changes to lexical representations that affect the access process. Consequently, if children with WFDs experience a similar word frequency effect to typically developing peers this would suggest that their representations are influenced, in a similar manner to typical children, by the amount of exposure to words. In contrast, a lack of a frequency effect would implicate more general problems with access irrespective of the nature of the representations.

A similar argument can be developed that the age when a lexical item is acquired has an influence on children's naming. Earlier acquired lexical items are likely to be better established than later acquired ones. Unfortunately there are insufficient data about the age of acquisition of lexical items to construct the appropriate stimuli sets. However, data about the age of acquisition of the lexical items used in the current study are presented where available in the methods section.

Studies of word frequency that involve children with naming difficulties have produced contradictory findings. On a picture naming task, Denckla and Rudel (1976) reported that with low-frequency words, children with dyslexia produce more errors and longer response times than children with language difficulties. German (1979, 1984) published similar findings for children with language difficulties and children with learning difficulties. In contrast, Wiig et al. (1982) reported that the picture naming of high frequency words differentiated normal and language-disordered children but Wolf (1980) found no frequency effects. All these findings point to the importance of considering this dimension in relation to WFDs. However, estimating word frequency for children's oral language is complex. Studies with adults tend to use estimates of printed word frequency; such a measure would be inappropriate for young children who cannot read, children who are at the early stages of literacy acquisition or children whose language may be delayed. Consequently, several methods of selecting high and low frequency words were employed in this study.

To summarise, one of the aims of the present study was to identify a clearly delineated group of children with objectively defined WFDs using the TWF. The performance of these children was compared with a group of typical children matched for chronological age (CA), a group who have similar productive language (NA), and a group matched for grammatical comprehension (RG). As a result, it should be possible to identify language delays in children with WFDs that are below those expected for their chronological age, and identify specific language delays which go beyond those expected for the children's level of language. These comparisons can give a more detailed picture of the strengths and weaknesses of children with WFDs. In addition, the comparisons should contribute to under-standing the underlying cause of the difficulties of these children.

METHOD

Participants

The total sample consisted of 124 children attending schools, language support services, and nurseries in the south east of England. Thirty-one children who experienced word-finding difficulties participated in the study, mean age 7;1 [range 6;4–7;10]. The lower age-band was determined by the standardisation of the TWF and the upper age band was used to minimise the variability in the sample in terms of educational opportu-nities (such as access to the National Curriculum) and other developmental experiences. The children were identified following a wider survey of educational provision for children with word-finding difficulties (Dockrell, Messer, George, & Wilson, 1998). Schools were sampled where professionals had reported that they had children with primary word-finding difficulties. Children were drawn from 11 different language support services, nine of these were attached to mainstream schools. Once identified by the professional (teacher or speech and language therapist), children were required to meet the following criteria for inclusion in the WFDs sample: (1) to fall within an 18-month age band (6;4–7;10); (2) demonstrate word-finding difficulties relative to their comprehension skills as identified by the Test of Word Finding Difficulties; (3) have age appropriate (at or above the 25th centile) non-verbal abilities as measured by Raven's matrices (1983) and, (4) have no marked difficulties in articulation as measured by the Edinburgh Articulation Test (EAT; Anthony, Bogle, Ingram, & McIsaac, 1971). The articulation criterion was operationalised as not scoring below −1 SD for the age group 5;5–6;0 (the test ceiling). The minimum EAT raw score was 49, the mode and median for the sample was 60. A raw score of 60 is equivalent to a standard score of 106 for the age range 5;9–6;0.

The children in the control groups were drawn from similar geographical areas to the children with WFDs and where possible were attending the same school. All the control children attended state mainstream educational provision. None of the children had identified special educational needs or English as an additional language. Children in the language age control groups were required to achieve a typical score on the matched language measure (see below) within a 3-month band of their chronological age.

The 31 children in each of the three control groups were individually matched to the children in the WFDs group. Each child in the chronological age (CA) control group had a birthday within 3 months of a matched child in the target sample and their Matrices score was in the same centile band. A naming age-matched group (NA) was identified using the British Abilities naming scale (BAS; Elliot, Smith, & McCulloch, 1997). Each child in this control group had an ability score that was (1) age appropriate and (2) exactly matched to a child in the WFDs group. The children's mean naming age was 4;10. A Reception of Grammar matched group (RG) was identified using scores from Test of Reception of Grammar scores (TROG; Bishop, 1989). Each child in this control group had a TROG score that was (1) age appropriate and (2) the raw score was matched exactly to a child in the WFDs group. The age equivalent score of each child in this control group was exactly matched to those of the children with WFDs. The children's mean reception of grammar age was 5;9. Table 1 presents the group scores on the relevant matched measures.

TABLE 1
Results of standardised tests used for matching

	N	Mean age	Mean Ravens centile	British Abilities Naming Scale		Test of Reception of Grammar	
				Mean ability score	Mean age equivalent	Mean raw score	Mean age equivalent
WFDs	31	7;1 (range, 6;4-7;10)	61 (range, 25–95)	77.6 (range, 53–98)	4;10	11.3 (range, 7–17)	5;9
NA matches	31	5;8 (range, 3;4–7;3)		77.6 (range, 53–98)	4;10		
RG matches	31	5;9 (range; 4;3–10)				11.3 (range, 7–17)	5;9
CA matches	31	7;2 (range, 6;5–7;9)	58 (range, 25–90)				

Description of language skills of the children with WFDs

The children with WFDs were not a homogeneous group with respect to language measures. Although all had word-finding problems as defined by clinicians and the TWF, other language skills showed a marked variation. Assessment of their phonological skills on the Phonological Assessment Battery (PhAB; Fredrickson, Frith, & Reason, 1997) revealed that the majority of the children had low scores on the Fluency measures on the PhAB (for these tasks children are required to generate as many words as possible according to phonological or semantic criteria) and notably low scores for semantic fluency (for this measure all children had scores at least 1 SD below the mean with 77% of the children scoring 2 SD below the mean). These fluency results corroborate clinical descriptions of this population. In contrast mean scores on the other phonological measures (rhyme and alliteration) did not fall below 1 SD of the mean, with an average standardised score of 85 for both (range 69–101 for alliteration and 69–112 for rhyme). Statistical analyses were conducted to investigate whether subgroups could be identified based on the other language scores, such as the TROG. No homogeneous subgroups were identified. This failure to identify prominent subgroups, together with the careful matching of the control groups on key language measures, helps to justify the decision to carry out analyses on the whole of the sample of children with WFDs.

Materials

The complete set of naming stimuli consisted of 40 coloured drawings of objects and 20 coloured drawings of actions, together with 5 single digit numerals and 5 letters. The items that were used are presented in Appendix 1. The drawings chosen were ones commonly used successfully in a pre-school speech and language unit and were therefore deemed appropriate for the population. The pictures were scanned into a specially designed computer program. In the comprehension tests four pictures were presented on the screen. The location of the correct picture on the computer screen varied randomly across trial items. Three foil pictures were chosen to allow different error patterns to be investigated: a semantic foil (an item from the same semantic domain), a phonological foil (an item starting with the same sound pattern), and finally an irrelevant foil. Frequency was controlled across foil items.

The main task of the participants was to name this set of pictures as quickly as possible. To provide a controlled stimulus set we restricted, as far as possible, the domains, frequencies, picturability, and length of the items chosen. Object names were selected from the domains of animals, body parts, clothes, and household items. These domains were chosen to: span natural kinds and artifacts; provide sufficient differentiation in frequency ranges; be familiar and interesting to children, and contain a sufficient number to fulfil the additional criteria for the items. A set of 'actions' was selected to include both transitive and intransitive verbs. For each of these six domains an equal number of high and low frequency words were selected. The frequency selection was from Francis and Kucera (1982) as a best approximation, and items were only included if they also were contained in at least one of three primary grade sources books (Burroughs, 1957; Edwards & Gibbon, 1973; Gates, 1935). It was not possible to match for frequencies across categories. However, frequency ranges did not overlap, thus the lowest frequency count for a high frequency item was 46 and the highest frequency count for a low frequency item was 17. In addition low frequency items were excluded if they were contained in the top 1000 words of Burroughs (1957), as were items of low picturability.

The age of acquisition could be identified for 32 of the 40 object names using a combination of databases (Gilhooly & Logie, 1980; Morrison, Chappell, & Ellis, 1997), but no data could be found about the age of acquisition for any of the verbs. Data were available for all high frequency objects with a mean age of acquisition of 25.4 months (range 15.3–47.6) and 12 low frequency items with a mean age of acquisition of 38.6 (range 17.7–74.1). From these figures it would appear that all high frequency items and most low frequency items had an age of acquisition of below 4 years (see Appendix 1).

Procedure

Each child was tested individually. Children's naming and comprehension of the test stimuli were assessed in a single session. All children completed the naming task before the comprehension task. Items were randomly presented to each child for naming and there were five preset random orders for the comprehension items. Object naming occurred before action naming.

The stimuli for both naming and comprehension were presented on a portable computer that recorded accuracy and latency. In parallel, a tape recorder was used to capture oral responses for later error analysis and an ongoing written record was kept. Children were provided with five practice items for each condition. No feedback was provided on the test items. Children appeared to enjoy the task. Naming and comprehension tasks were always completed in a single session.

Error analysis

Errors were coded to capture the full range of responses made by the children. These included semantic errors, phonological errors, 'don't know' and 'other errors'. Semantic errors were deemed to be substitutions that preserved the general features of the meaning of the word and were nearly always members of the same grammatical form class e.g., 'mug' for 'cup' or 'knitting' for 'sewing'. In contrast phonological errors were those which preserved either the initial or end pattern of the target item e.g., 'bog' for 'dog' or 'strong' for 'stroke'. A 'don't know' response was recorded if the child either said they did not know or indicated non-verbally that they did not know. 'Other errors' included circumlocutions, nonsense words, descriptions of the items in the picture, or naming responses where links between target and answer were indirect or thematic e.g., 'desert' for 'camel' or 'drinking' for 'sweating'. It was, however, possible for children to provide answers that were deemed both phonological and semantic errors or 'other' and phonological. In such cases responses were coded in both error categories. Two investigators coded a subsample of each group's responses. Any disagreements in coding were scored by a moderator until agreement on codes was achieved. The two investigators then coded the remaining errors. Any errors that had not been discussed or identified in the initial coding were considered by the team again and then coded.

RESULTS

The results are presented in four sections. The first examines the children's performance with numerals and letters. These data are considered before the data concerning objects and actions, because interpretation of these findings is more straightforward. The second compares the performance of the four groups across the remaining naming domains. The initial analysis includes data for both objects and actions and allows a comparison of the two word classes. Because differing patterns in performance were identified for objects and actions, separate group comparisons were performed for these items. The between group differences for objects are described in the third section, and similar analyses for actions are presented in the fourth section. In all cases the ANOVA analyses use group as a between subject factor and the relevant stimulus dimensions as within subject factor.

There is a complex set of differences between groups, stimulus dimensions, and assessed response (comprehension, naming, and latency). To aid interpretation of the data Table 2 provides a summary of the main differences based on the post-hoc comparisons between groups presented in the third and fourth sections. For letters and numerals the performance of children with WFDs was not significantly different from the CA matches and was usually better than the LA matches (LA refer to the combined pattern for the NA and RG matches when no differences between the language matches occurred). In contrast, for objects and actions there was a marked difference in performance across the three different forms of assessment—comprehension, naming accuracy, and latency.

TABLE 2
Summary of significant differences between the groups

		Frequency	Comprehension	Naming	Latency
Letters and numerals	CA vs. WFDs		=	=	=
	WFDs vs. LA		WFDs > LA	WFDs > LA	=
	CA vs. LA		CA > LA	CA > LA	CA > = NA*
Objects	CA vs. WFDs	HF	=	CA > WFDs	CA > WFDs
		LF	=	CA > WFDs	=
	WFDs vs. LA	HF	=	=	LA ≠ WFDs
		LF	=	=	=
	CA vs. LA	HF	=	CA > LA	=
		LF	CA > LA	CA > LA	=
Actions	CA vs. WFDs	HF	=	= }	CA > WFDs }
		LF	=	= }	
	WFDs vs. LA	HF	=	= }	= }
		LF	WFDs > NA	= }	
	CA vs. LA	HA	=	CA > LA }	= }
		LF	CA > NA		
			CA ≠ RG		

Note: WFDs, word finding difficulties group; NA, naming age-matched group; RG, Reception of Grammar matched group; CA, chronological age control group.

LA (language age) matches refer to the combined pattern for the NA and RG matches when no differences between the language matches occur.

* CA > NA for letters, CA = LA for letters.

= No signifciant differences between groups.

> Performance of first named group significantly better either in terms of accuracy or speed.

≠ Trend for better performance by first named group.

} Analysis collapsed for high and low frequency items, see results section.

Comprehension and naming of letters and numerals

Table 3 presents the findings from the letters and numerals tasks. Separate ANOVAs (involving comprehension, naming accuracy, and latency) were conducted on letters and numerals. These revealed that there were significant differences between the groups in terms of comprehension (Letters $F(3, 120) = 8.094$, $p < .001$; Numerals $F(3, 120) = 5.337$, $p < .001$), accuracy (Letters $F(3, 120) = 10.07$, $p < .001$; Numerals $F(3, 120) = 6.98$, $p < .001$) and latency (Letters $F(3, 120) = 3.91$, $p < .001$; Numerals $F(3, 120) = 2.89$, $p < .05$). Post hoc tests revealed no significant differences between the children with WFDs and their CA matched peers in comprehension, naming accuracy, or latency. Children with WFDs in comparison to the NA matches were significantly more accurate in comprehension (for letters $p < .01$ and for numerals $p < .05$) and in naming (for letters $p < .05$ and for numerals $p < .001$). In terms of the mean latency for both letters and numerals, the groups were ordered as follows: CA, WFDs, and then the NA and RG groups. The only significant difference occurred between the NA and CA groups for letters ($p < .05$). Thus, when comprehending and naming letters and numerals, children with WFDs were neither less accurate nor slower than typical children of the same age.

Overall results, objects and actions

For objects and actions, the proportion scores for comprehension accuracy, naming accuracy and naming latency are presented in Table 4. In all cases, ANOVA reveal significant differences according to group and frequency.

TABLE 3
Correct responses for comprehension and naming of letters and numerals by group

Task		Letters (N = 5)				Numerals (N = 5)			
		WFDs	NA	RG	CA	WFDs	NA	RG	CA
Compre-	Mean	4.84	3.87	4.19	5	4.94	4.23	4.68	5
hension	Range	3–5	0–5	1–5	—	4–5	0–5	1–5	—
	SD	0.46	1.48	1.4	—	0.25	1.38	0.95	—
Naming	Mean	4.09	2.68	3.06	4.9	4.96	3.96	4.55	5
	Range	0–5	0–5	0–5	4–5	4–5	0–5	1–5	—
	SD	1.46	2.15	3.38	0.3	0.18	1.67	1.15	—
Latency	Mean	1.34	1.81	1.57	0.79	1.03	1.29	1.31	0.74
in seconds	Range	0.64–5.92	0.6–6.48	0.68–8.32	0.48–1.48	0.64–1.88	0.6–4.72	0.68–8.84	0.48–1.2
	SD	0.92	1.47	1.74	0.18	0.28	0.87	1.5	0.13

Note: WFDs, word finding difficulties group; NA, naming age-matched group; RG, Reception of Grammar-matched group; CA, chronological age control group.

TABLE 4
Proportion of correct responses for comprehension, naming, and latency for correct response by group and frequency

Task	Frequency		Objects				Actions			
			WFDs	NA	RG	CA	WFDs	NA	RG	CA
Compre-	High	Mean	0.97	0.96	0.97	0.99	0.99	0.96	0.97	0.99
hension		Range	0.75–1	0.9–1	0.9–1	0.9–1	0.9–1	0.8–1	0.7–1	0.9–1
		SD	0.05	0.03	0.04	0.03	0.03	0.07	0.06	0.02
	Low	Mean	0.91	0.88	0.90	0.97	0.89	0.83	0.88	0.95
		Range	0.65–1	0.6–1	0.7–1	0.75–1	0.7–1	0.6–1	0.7–1	0.8–1
		SD	0.09	0.09	0.08	0.06	0.08	0.11	0.1	0.07
Naming	High	Mean	0.88	0.86	0.87	0.93	0.87	0.78	0.85	0.92
when		Range	0.67–1	0.67–1	0.67–1	0.8–1	0.6–1	0.13–1	0.56–1	0.8–1
compre-		SD	0.08	0.11	0.08	0.07	0.12	0.2	0.14	0.07
hension	Low	Mean	0.47	0.49	0.52	0.64	0.54	0.47	0.5	0.61
correct		Range	0.18–0.75	0.18–0.8	0.07–0.85	0.2–0.95	0.11–0.89	0–0.88	0.13–0.9	0.4–0.8
		SD	0.15	0.15	0.18	0.2	0.21	0.23	0.2	0.12
Naming	High	Mean	1.96	1.65	1.69	1.56	2.02	1.92	1.93	1.57
latency		Range	1.22–3.99	1.16–2.32	1.21–3.59	1.14–2.12	1.31–3.43	1.46–3.2	1.20–4.06	1.27–2.12
when		SD	0.63	0.30	0.43	0.26	0.59	0.42	0.56	0.22
response	Low	Mean	1.83	1.73	1.96	1.94	2.25	2.09	2.07	1.90
correct		Range	0.88–2.94	1.2–2.73	1.56–4.06	1.93–4.72	1.37–3.30	1.43–3.15	1.05–3.88	1.23–3.07
in seconds		SD	0.51	0.36	0.74	0.78	0.53	0.39	0.59	0.50

Note: See Table 3 for classifications of groups.

As Table 4 shows, all children were highly accurate in their comprehension. The comprehension data were analysed with word class (objects or actions) and word frequency (high or low) as within subject factors and group (CA, NA, RG, and WFDs) as the between subject factors. There was a significant effect of both word frequency ($F(1, 120) = 158.19, p < .001$) and experimental group ($F(3, 120) = 14.86, p < .001$) for comprehension, but no main effect of word class. There were significant interactions between group and word frequency ($F(3, 120) = 6.78, p < .001$) and word class and word frequency ($F(1, 120) = 8.14, p < .001$). Thus despite the overall high levels of success, the groups were performing significantly differently and all children performing better with high frequency items.

In the analyses of naming accuracy and naming latency it was decided to eliminate any lexical items which children failed to identify in the comprehension tests in order to establish a set of 'known' items for each child, thus allowing a direct assessment of word finding difficulties. This resulted in different item sets for each child and therefore proportion scores are used in subsequent analyses. Latency scores were tabulated for correct responses only. Using the same design as had been employed for comprehension two further ANOVAs were conducted on accuracy of naming and latency of naming as the dependent variable. For naming accuracy, as with comprehension, there was a main effect for both word frequency ($F(1, 120) = 980.82, p < .001$) and group ($F(3, 120) = 10.34, p < .001$) with an interaction between word class and group ($F(3, 120) = 2.74, p < .05$). For latency measures there was a main effect of word frequency ($F(1, 117) = 23.41, p < .001$), group ($F(3, 117) = 4.09, p < .01$) and word class ($F(1, 117) = 34.30, p < .001$) and an interaction between group and word frequency ($F(3, 117) = 3.06, p < .05$). The differential effect of word class on latency suggests that naming objects and actions involve different processing demands. To explore these differences further post-hoc analyses to test for group and task effects were carried out separately for each word class. These are presented in the next sections, first for objects and then for actions. For each word class there is an examination of comprehension accuracy, naming accuracy, naming latency, and error responses.

Objects

Accuracy of object comprehension.   Analysis of the full data set for comprehension revealed a significant effect of group ($F(3, 120) = 6.296, p < .01$), word frequency ($F(1, 120) = 65.648, p < .001$) and an interaction between group and word frequency ($F(3, 120) = 3.284, p < .05$). Post hoc Scheffe's tests between the four groups of children revealed no differences in the accuracy of comprehension for high frequency items. However, for low frequency items there were differences between groups. The CA control group was significantly better than the two language match groups (NA: $p < .01$; RG: $p < .05$). The children with WFDs had intermediate scores and were not significantly different from their NA, RG, or CA peers.

Accuracy of object naming.   Although there was a significant correlation between naming accuracy and comprehension accuracy ($r = .473, N = 124, p < .001$) the children accurately named significantly fewer object words than they comprehended ($t = -25.27, df = 123, p < .001$). Analysis of the data set of 'known' items revealed that there were significant effects of group ($F(3, 120) = 9.04, p < .001$), word frequency ($F(1, 120) = 692.28, p < .001$) and an interaction between group and word frequency ($F(3, 120) = 3.20, p < .05$). Post hoc Scheffe's tests between groups revealed that the CA group was performing significantly better than the other three groups for high frequency (WFDs: $p < .05$; NA: $p < .01$; RG: $p < .01$) and low frequency items (WFDs: $p < .001$; NA: $p < .001$; RG: $p < .05$). No other significant differences between the groups were identified.

Latency of object naming.   Mean latencies for correct responses to high and low frequency items are presented in Table 4. There was a significant effect of word frequency ($F(1, 120) = 9.04$, $p < .01$) and an interaction between group and word frequency ($F(3, 120) = 5.05$, $p < .01$). Post hoc Scheffe's tests indicated that the children with WFDs were significantly slower than CA matches for high frequency items ($p < .01$) and there was a trend suggesting that they were also slower than their NA matches ($p < .052$). There were no significant differences between the NA or RG matches and the CA matched peers for high frequency items and no significant differences between any of the groups for low frequency items.

Error patterns in naming objects. The analysis of the children's naming accuracy indicated that the CA matched children were producing significantly fewer errors, however, such an analysis does not indicate whether the nature of errors differed across the groups. If the relative frequency of different types of naming errors (semantic, phonological, 'don't know' and 'other errors') were similar across the four groups this would suggest that the language of children with WFDs was developing in a similar manner to typical children. To conduct these analyses the errors for low and high frequency items were combined and a calculation was made of the distribution of error types across total errors. Proportions were calculated to allow comparisons between groups and word classes. Object naming errors are presented in Table 5.

As Table 5 shows the overall distribution of error type across the groups was similar, and that semantic errors were the most common of the four types. Comparisons between the groups using a Kruskial–Wallis test revealed no significant differences in the proportion of semantic errors ($\chi^2 = 1.10$, $df = 3$, NS), 'don't know' responses ($\chi^2 = 1.88$, $df = 3$, NS) or

TABLE 5
Proportion of error types for naming objects

Error type		WFDs	NA	RG	CA
Semantic	Mean	0.60	0.62	0.59	0.62
	Range	0.25–0.91	0.29–0.90	0.13–0.83	0.00–1.0
	SD	0.17	0.16	0.16	0.24
Phonological	Mean	0.18	0.13	0.11	0.11
	Range	0.0–0.71	0.0–0.36	0.0–0.40	0.0–0.50
	SD	0.15	0.11	0.11	0.13
'Don't Know'	Mean	0.21	0.25	0.24	0.25
	Range	0.0–0.67	0.0–0.71	0.0–0.63	0.0–1.00
	SD	0.2	0.2	0.16	0.27
'Other errors'	Mean	0.22	0.19	0.20	0.21
	Range	0.0–0.75	0.0–0.64	0.0–0.63	0.0–0.75
	SD	0.18	0.14	0.17	0.19

Note: The sum of all proportions can total more than 1 since children's errors could be classed as both phonological and semantic. See Table 3 for classifications of groups.

'other errors' produced ($\chi^2 = 0.11$, $df = 3$, NS). In contrast the proportion of phonological errors varied significantly across the groups ($\chi^2 = 8.79$, $p <$ .05). The WFDs children produced significantly more phonological errors than their CA peers (U = 293, $p <$ .01) and their RG matches (U = 329, $p <$ .05) but not their NA matches. The distribution of phonological errors within the WFDs group was examined to establish whether individual children were accounting for these responses. This was not the case: phonological errors were distributed across the sample of children with WFDs. Thus, these analyses indicate that children with WFDs made proportionally more phonological errors than their CA matched peers and RG matched peers, but not proportionally more than their NA matched peers did. Overall semantic errors dominate all children's erroneous responses for the object pictures.

Actions

Accuracy of comprehension for actions.   For the accuracy of compre-hending actions, an ANOVA of the full data set identified a significant effect of group ($F(3, 120) = 12.29$, $p <$ .001), of word frequency ($F(1, 120) = 93.54$, $p <$ .001) and an interaction between group and word frequency ($F(3, 120) = 3.79$, $p <$ .05). Post hoc Scheffe's tests between groups revealed no differences for high frequency actions. However for low frequency actions both the CA control ($p <$ .001) and the children with WFDs ($p <$ .05) were significantly better than the NA group and there was a trend identified suggesting a difference between RG matches and CA matches ($p =$ .058). Thus, there was no evidence for a difficulty with the comprehension of verbs for children with WFDs.

Accuracy of naming actions.   There was a significant correlation between accurate naming and accurate comprehension ($r =$ .353, $N =$ 124, $p <$ .001) of actions, but children were less accurate in producing than in comprehending these items ($t = -20.57$, $df = 123$, $p <$ .001). Analysis of the full data set shows that there is a significant group effect ($F(3, 120) = 8.21$, $p <$ .001), word frequency effect ($F(1, 120) = 496.29$, $p <$ .001), but no significant interactions. All groups were more accurate on high frequency words. Since there were no significant interactions between group and frequency, high and low frequency results were collapsed and post hoc Scheffe's tests were conducted between groups. There were no differences between the WFDs group and their chronological and language age matches. In contrast both the NA matches ($p <$ .001) and the RG matches ($p <$ .05) were performing significantly poorer than the CA matches.

Latency to name actions.   Mean latencies for correct responses to high and low frequency items are presented in Table 4. There was a significant effect of group ($F(3, 117) = 5.98, p < .001$) and word frequency ($F(1, 117) = 17.22, p < .001$) but no interaction. All groups produced high frequency items more quickly than low frequency ones. Since there were no significant interactions between group and frequency, high and low frequency results were collapsed and post hoc Scheffe's tests were conducted between groups. The WFDs group were significantly slower than their CA matches ($p < .05$). No other significant differences existed between the groups. Nevertheless as shown in Table 4 the children with WFDs were the slowest group to respond for both low frequency and high frequency actions.

Error patterns in naming actions.   Action errors were initially subjected to the same analyses as object errors. Errors were classified as semantic, phonological, 'don't know' responses and 'other errors'. These are presented in Table 6.

As Table 6 shows the overall distribution of error types across the groups was similar, and 'other errors' were the most common of the four types. As with the object errors there were few phonological errors overall. In contrast to the object errors, for actions children were producing more errors that were categorised as 'other errors'. Since the error data did not meet the requirements of parametric tests the data were analysed with non-parametric tests. Comparisons between the groups using a Kruskal–Wallis test revealed no significant differences in the proportion of semantic errors ($\chi^2 = 3.22, df = 3$, NS), 'don't know' responses ($\chi^2 = 1.83, df = 3$,

TABLE 6
Proportion of error types for naming actions

Error type		WFDs	NA	RG	CA
Semantic	Mean	0.24	0.25	0.25	0.29
	Range	0.0–0.75	0.0–0.67	0.0–1.00	0.0–0.67
	SD	0.21	0.18	0.26	0.16
Phonological	Mean	0.14	0.09	0.11	0.13
	Range	0.0–0.40	0.0–0.50	0.0–0.33	0.0–0.40
	SD	0.13	0.12	0.11	0.14
'Don't Know'	Mean	0.15	0.12	0.10	0.07
	Range	0.0–1.0	0.0–0.61	0.0–0.60	0.0–0.50
	SD	0.24	0.18	0.16	0.14
'Other errors'	Mean	0.61	0.63	0.65	0.64
	Range	0.0–1.00	0.33–1.00	0.0–1.00	0.0–1.00
	SD	0.25	0.19	0.25	0.22

Note: The sum of all proportions can total more than 1 since children's errors could be classed as both phonological and semantic. See Table 3 for classifications of groups.

NS), phonological errors ($\chi^2 = 2.38$, df 3, NS), or 'other errors' produced ($\chi^2 = 1.18$, $df = 3$, NS).

The high proportion of 'other errors' suggested that an important dimension in the children's responses had been missed. When the 'other errors' were further analysed a number of non-target verbs were identified. These included general all purpose verbs such as 'doing' or 'moving', verbs that were similar to the target but incorrect e.g., 'knitting' for 'sewing', and non-target verbs that were inappropriate e.g., 'swimming' for 'fishing'. These non-target verbs accounted for over 50% of each group's non-target responses. The proportions of non-target verbs categorised as 'other errors' are presented in Table 7.

The children with WFDs produced *fewer* similar but incorrect verbs than their CA matched peers (U = 293.5, p < .05), NA matched peers (U = 327.5, p < .05) and RG matched peers (U = 296, p < .05). Instead the children with WFDs used more non-specific verbs (U = 372, p < .05) and more verbs that were inappropriate (U = 312, p < .05) than CA matched peers. These responses did not differ significantly from their language age matches. All these differences in error patterns suggest that, despite their equivalent naming accuracy with CA peers, the semantic domains for children with WFDs were less clearly delineated than their CA peers.

DISCUSSION

Comparing the performance of children with WFDs with that of chronological and language age controls across a number of measures can extend our understanding of the problems experienced by this group of children. If children with WFDs have a general delay with the lexicon then they would be expected to perform worse than children of the same chronological age but equivalent to children of the same language age. If, however, the children are experiencing a different pattern of development (see Leonard, 1998) we would predict differences between the WFDs and language-matched samples.

TABLE 7
Proportion of non-target verbs categorised as 'other errors'

Error type	WFDs	NA	RG	CA
Same domain but different meaning	0.31	0.44	0.47	0.45
Inappropriate	0.22	0.18	0.15	0.08
General all purpose verbs	0.08	0.02	0.01	0.01

Note: See Table 3 for classifications of groups.

Although children with WFDs performed as well as CA controls on comprehension tasks, they did not perform as well as these children in terms of the accuracy of naming. For the naming of low and high frequency objects, the CA group was significantly better than all the other three groups. In other words, for accuracy of object naming the children with WFDs did not differ significantly from their language-matched controls. In the case of actions, the pattern of differences was slightly more complicated. The CA group was significantly better than the language-matched groups but the performance of children with WFDs was between the highest and lowest scoring groups and their performance was not significantly different from any of the other groups. Thus, the naming accuracy of children with WFDs was equivalent to language-matched children for objects and intermediate between CA and LA controls for actions.

The examination of latency of naming reveals yet a third pattern of relations between the performance of children with WFDs and the control groups. Children with WFDs had the slowest responses of all four groups on latencies for high frequency objects and for low and high frequency action words. Furthermore, they were significantly slower than CA matches for high frequency objects and for all action words (see Table 2). The difference between children with WFDs and NA matches approached significance for high frequency objects suggesting that there may be a reliable difference between these groups. This trend deserves attention because it suggests that when children with WFDs are matched with typical children on the accuracy of naming (i.e., the BAS naming scale), then children with WFDs are slower than typical children in producing names. Consequently, the children appear to have a specific problem in accessing representations even when they accurately retrieve them.

In contrast to these findings, the latency of responses of children with WFDs to letters and numerals was found to be more similar to the CA group than both the language-matched groups. This suggests that the longer latencies identified for object words and actions were not simply a product of slower general processing, but this is an issue that needs to be considered in future investigations of the children's difficulties. Further investigations of the differential latencies between accurate, wrong and 'don't know' response have the potential to increase our understanding of the children's strategies for managing their difficulties.

Previous research on children with WFDs has identified high rates of semantic substitution errors (German, 1982; Lahey & Edwards, 1999; McGregor, 1997). Children with WFDs also appear to produce higher rates of 'don't know' responses than chronological age-matched peers in naming tasks (Fried-Oken, 1984; German, 1982; McGregor & Waxman, 1998). However, our analyses for object errors did not identify any significant differences across groups in the frequency of semantic, 'don't know' or 'other' responses. In contrast the children with WFDs were more likely to make phonological errors. However, this was not true for the action naming. In this case errors were suggestive of less differentiated semantic domains.

Previous studies also have found high levels of phonemic errors (Faust, Dimitrovsky, & Davidi, 1997). This finding is consistent with the argument that children with WFDs can access semantic information but have difficulty accessing phonological information (Constable, Stackhouse, & Wells, 1997). The nature of errors in children with language difficulties has been discussed by Lahey and Edwards (1999) who suggest that phonological errors are characteristic of expressive problems while semantic errors are characteristic of children who have additional receptive problems. In our data for naming objects, children with WFDs produced a higher proportion of phonological errors than the CA and RG groups, and this is consistent with the idea of a phonological deficit. Nonetheless only 18% of the errors were phonological and this proportion did not differ significantly from NA matches.

We argued in the introduction that it is of little practical or theoretical interest to apply the term WFDs to children who have general language delays and that it can be useful to compare the performance of these children with a carefully chosen set of matches. The findings from this study provide support for this argument. The analyses that have been conducted suggest that children with WFDs have lexical comprehension skills that are similar to those of typical children of the same age. However, the accuracy of naming of children with WFDs was similar to that of typical children who have the same language level, suggesting that the children are delayed in their naming accuracy. Finally, there was an important trend indicating that speed of naming of children with WFDs for high frequency objects was below that of naming of age-matched typical children and similar non-significant patterns were evidence for the naming of actions. It is important to note that neither of the language-matched groups differed significantly from the CA group in latency to respond. Thus, in the naming of objects and actions there appears to be a marked decline in the relative performance for children with WFDs across these three different forms of assessment. Any one set of these comparisons could give a very limited and possibly distorted picture of the abilities of children with WFDs, and so these findings reinforce our view that a better understanding of this condition requires a more extensive and careful use of comparison groups.

The comparisons made in this study also have implications for the hypothesis that the semantic representations of children with WFDs are less complex than those of other children and that this results in their having word retrieval problems. In relation to this issue, it is interesting to consider the pattern of performance on items such as letters and numerals with items that are more semantically complex such as objects and actions. The crucial comparisons involve determining whether, for a particular set of words, the performance of children with WFDs is similar to that of the comparison groups. In the case of numerals and letters, there were no significant differences between children with WFDs and typical CA-matched children in terms of speed and accuracy of naming. Furthermore, children with WFDs were significantly more accurate than typical LA-matched peers on numerals and letters. Thus, for the domains of numerals and letters, where it is argued complex semantic representations are not required, the children with WFDs were performing similarly to children of the same age. In contrast, for objects and actions, children with WFDs performed less well than their CA-matched controls. Given the low age of acquisition of many of the lexical items employed in this study, it is unlikely that time of exposure can explain the WFDs children's high levels of performance with numerals and letters. Therefore these differences between the set of words are unlikely to be simply due to the amount of time that the children have had to learn the items, and the pattern of differences is consistent with the idea of children with WFDs having impoverished semantic representations.

Comparisons of children's performance on object words and action words, as well as high frequency words and low frequency words, also has a relevance to evaluating the semantic elaboration hypothesis. These comparisons suggest that frequency rather than word type is more influential in determining accuracy. There was, for example, no main effect of word class for accurate naming but there was a main effect of word frequency. Children with WFDs performed significantly less well than chronological age-matched children in naming high frequency objects (see Table 2) and were slower to respond. However, there were no significant differences in corresponding comparisons involving low frequency items. Taken together these findings suggest that children with WFDs may experience more problems with lexical items that are relatively well established, rather than items that are likely to be less familiar. Such a pattern of findings is consistent with the idea that the children with WFDs have more problems in building up a complex set of representations than in initially forming these representations, and that as a result they have more problems than matched peers in retrieving these words.

The comparisons also show that across groups, word frequency effects produced similar patterns of results, thereby providing support for the view that the complexity of children's semantic representations influence word retrieval. These results stand in contrast to current research that has highlighted the difficulties with verbs for the language-impaired population

(Conti-Ramsden & Jones, 1997; Fletcher & Peters, 1984; Tomasello, 1992; Watkins, Rice, & Moltz, 1993). However, an examination of the children's errors and latency suggest that there are subtle problems in naming actions for this population. Firstly, there was the greater preponderance of non-verb responses, secondly when verbs were used they were often semantically inappropriate and finally general verbs were used more by the children with WFDs. The latter result is consistent with a reliance on general all purpose verbs that has been reported in the literature about children with language difficulties. Thus, the type of children's errors provide further support to the view that part of the difficulties is caused by impoverished semantic representations.

There are, however, two different sources of data that might serve to question the semantic interpretation. The children with WFDs generally had the longest latencies to name objects and actions. Moreover, when we consider their profiles on standardised measures they have particularly low scores on the semantic fluency task in the PhAB, a test that is time limited. This raises the question of whether these children's longer latency to respond can be explained by generalised limitations in processing capacity (Kail, 1994; Kail & Salthouse, 1994; Windsor & Hwang, 1999). Our present analyses do not directly address this question. Nonetheless, the data indicate that processing limitations per se are not a sufficient explanation of their naming patterns. This is because although children with WFDs had poorer accuracy of naming objects and actions than CA matches, they were not significantly different from CA matches in their latency to name numerals and letters.

Secondly, it is important to consider the comprehension data in more detail. Why was it that children with WFDs were no different from CA matches on comprehension tasks, but slower than CA matches when retrieving the very same words? It often has been argued that retrieval is a more demanding activity than comprehension and Ralli (1999) has provided evidence that children can succeed in comprehension tasks when they either fail to produce a word or provide additional evidence about the word's meaning. Successful comprehension only requires there to be available a partial representation about the relation between the word and the picture. Although our foils were carefully chosen to allow for either phonological or semantic errors, the choices were highly constrained. As a result, we cannot be sure that the children's knowledge about the word's meaning was comparable to that of their CA peers. Even so, it is not unreasonable to suppose that comprehension might be possible with limited representations and consequently, children with WFDs are able to perform almost as well as CA peers on this type of task. Future investigations of these children's representations could be especially valuable (see McGregor, 1999 as an example).

In sum the present data set supports the view that there is a specific group of children who have difficulties in both accuracy and speed of naming relative to their chronological age peers (Wiig, Semel, & Nystrom, 1982) and in certain conditions, relative to their language-matched peers. Further, these difficulties span different word classes and different word frequencies. There was little direct evidence that the children's difficulties are caused by problems with phonological representations. Both the entry criteria for the study and the nature of the lexical items may have reduced the presence of such effects in the present data set. In contrast, a number of different sources of evidence point of specific problems with the semantic representations for children with WFDs.

REFERENCES

Anthony, A., Bogle, D., Ingram, T.T.S., & McIsaac, M. (1971). *Edinburgh Articulation Test.* Edinburgh: Livingston.

Bishop, D.V.M. (1989). *Test of Reception of Grammar, 2nd edition.* Manchester: Age & Cognitive Performance Research Centre, University of Manchester.

Bishop, D.V.M. (1997). *Uncommon understanding: Development and disorders of language comprehension in children.* Hove, UK: Psychology Press.

Braisby, N., & Dockrell, J.E. (1999). Why is colour naming difficult? *Journal of Child Language, 26,* 23–27.

Burroughs, G.E.R. (1957). *A study of vocabulary of young children.* Birmingham: Oliver Boyd.

Catts, H.W., & Kamhi, A. (1999). *Language and reading disabilities.* Boston: Allyn and Bacon.

Chiat, S., & Hunt, J. (1993). Connections between phonology and semantics: an exploration of lexical processing in a language impaired child. *Child Language Teaching and Therapy, 9,* 201–213.

Constable, A., Stackhouse, J., & Wells, B. (1997). Development word-finding difficulties and phonological processing: The case of the missing handcuffs. *Applied Psycholinguistics, 18,* 507–536.

Conti-Ramsden, G., & Jones, M. (1997). Verb use in specific language impairment. *Journal of Speech Language and Hearing Research, 40,* 1298–1313.

Davidoff, J., & Masterson, J. (1995/6). The development of picture naming: Differences between nouns and verbs. *Journal of Neurolinguistics, 9,* 69–93.

Denckla, M.B., & Rudel, R. (1976). Naming of object drawings by dyslexic and other learning disabled children. *Brain and Language, 3,* 1–16.

Dockrell, J.E., Messer, D., & George, R. (2000). Accuracy and errors in naming objects in children with word finding difficulties. In M. Beers, B. v.d. Bogaerde, G. Bol, J. de Jong, & C. Rooijmans (Eds), *From sound to sentence—studies on first language acquisition.* Groningen: Centre for Language and Cognition.

Dockrell, J.E., Messer, D., George, R., & Wilson, G. (1998). Children with word-finding difficulties—prevalence, presentation and naming problems. *International Journal of Language and Communication Disorders, 33,* 445–454.

Edwards, R.P.A., & Gibbon, V. (1973). *Words your children use.* London: Burke Press.

Elliott, C.D., Smith, P., & McCulloch, K. (1997). *The British Ability Scales II*. Windsor: NFER-Nelson.

Faust, M., Dimitrovsky, L., & Davidi, S. (1997). Naming difficulties in language disabled children: Preliminary findings with the application of the Tip-of-the-Tongue paradigm. *Journal of Speech, Language and Hearing Research, 40*, 1026–1036.

Fletcher, P., & Peters, J. (1984). Characterizing language impairment in children: An exploratory study. *Language Testing, 1*, 33–49.

Francis, W.N., & Kucera, H. (1982). *Frequency analysis of English usage: Lexicon and grammar*. Boston: Houghton Mifflin.

Fredrickson, N., Frith, U., & Reason, R. (1997). *Phonological Assessment Battery*. Windsor: NFER-Nelson.

Fried-Oken, M. (1984). The development of naming skills in normal and language deficient children. Doctoral dissertation, Boston University.

Gates, A.I. (1935). *A reading vocabulary for the primary grades*. New York: Bureau of publications, Teacher College, Columbia University.

Gentner, D. (1981). Some interesting differences between verbs and nouns. *Cognition and Brain Theory, 4*, 161–178.

German, D.J. (1979). Word finding skills in children with learning disabilities. *Journal of Learning Disabilities, 12*, 43–48.

German, D.J. (1982). Word-finding substitutions in children with learning disabilities. *Language, speech and hearing services in schools, 13*, 223–230.

German D.J. (1984). Diagnosis of word-finding disorders in children with learning disabilities. *Journal of Learning Disabilities, 17*, 353–358.

German, D.J. (1985). The use of specific semantic word categories in the diagnosis of dysnomic learning-disabled children. *British Journal of Disorders of Communication, 20*, 143–154.

German, D.J. (1989). *Test of Word Finding TWF*. Chicago IL: Riverside Publishing Company.

German, D.J., & Simon, E. (1991). Analysis of children's word-finding skills in discourse. *Journal of Speech and Hearing Research, 34*, 309–316.

Gilhooly, K.J., & Logie, R.H. (1980). Age of acquisition, imagery, concreteness, familiarity and ambiguity measures for 1,944 words. *Behavior Research Methods and Instrumentation, 12*, 395–427.

Kail, R. (1994). A method of studying the generalized slowing hypothesis in children with specific language impairment. *Journal of Speech and Hearing Research, 37*, 418–421.

Kail, R., Hale, C., Leonard, L., & Nippold, M. (1984). Lexical storage and retrieval in language-impaired children. *Applied Psycholinguistics, 5*, 37–49.

Kail, R., & Leonard, L.B. (1986). Word-finding abilities in language-impaired children. *ASHA Monographs, 25*.

Kail, R., & Salthouse, T. (1994). Processing speed as mental capacity. *Acta Psychologica, 86*, 199–225.

Lahey, M., & Edwards, J. (1996). Why do children with specific language impairments name pictures more slowly than their peers. *Journal of Speech and Hearing Research, 39*, 1081–1098.

Lahey, M., & Edwards, J. (1999). Naming errors of children with SLI. *Journal of Speech Language and Hearing Research, 42*, 195–205.

Leonard, L.B. (1988). Lexical development and processing in specific language impairment. In R. Schiefelbusch & L. Lloyd (Eds), *Language perspectives: Acquisition, retardation and intervention*, pp. 69–87. Austin, TX: Pro-Ed.

Leonard, L.B. (1998). *Children with Specific Language Impairment*. Cambridge, MA: MIT Press.

Markman, E.M. (1989). *Categorisation and naming in children*. Cambridge, MA: MIT Press.

McGregor, K.K. (1999). Semantic representation and developmental word finding deficits. Paper presented at the VIII International Congress for the study of Child Language. San Sebastian, Spain.

McGregor, K.K. (1997). The nature of word-finding errors in preschoolers with and without word-finding deficits. *Journal of Speech, Language and Hearing Research, 40,* 1232–1244.

McGregor, K.K., & Leonard, L.B. (1989). Facilitating the word-finding skills of language-impaired children. *Journal of Speech and Hearing Disorders, 54,* 141–147.

McGregor, K.K., & Waxman, S. (1998). Object naming at multiple hierarchical levels: a comparison of preschoolers with and without word-finding deficits. *Journal of Child Language, 25,* 419–430.

McGregor, K.K., & Windsor, J. (1996). Effects of priming accuracy of preschoolers with word-finding deficits. *Journal of Speech, Language and Hearing Research, 39,* 1048–1057.

Menyuk, P. (1975). The language-impaired child: Linguistic or cognitive impairment? *Annals of the New York Academy of Sciences, 263,* 59–69.

Morrison, C., Chappell, T., & Ellis, A. (1997). Age of Acquisition Norms for a large set of object names and their relation to adult estimates and other variables. *Quarterly Journal of Experimental Psychology, 50,* 528–559.

Nippold, M. (1992). The nature of normal and disordered word finding in children and adolescents. *Topics in Language Disorders, 13,* 1–14.

Ralli, A. (1999). Investigating lexical acquisition patterns: Context and cognition. Doctoral dissertation, University of London.

Raven, J.C. (1983). *Raven's Progressive Matrices.* London: H.K. Lewis & Co.

Rescorla, L., & Schwartz, E. (1990). Outcome of toddlers with expressive language delay. *Applied Psycholinguistics, 11,* 393–407.

Rice, M. (1991). Children with specific language impairment: Toward a model of teachability. In N. Krasnegor, D. Rumbaugh, R. Schielfelbusch, & M. Studdert-Kennedy (Eds), *Biological and behavioural determinants of language development,* pp. 447–480. Hillsdale, NJ: Lawrence Erlbaum, Associates Inc.

Rudel, R., Denckla, M., & Broman, M. (1981). The effect of varying stimulus context on word-finding ability: Dyslexia further differentiated from other learning disabilities. *Brain and Language, 13,* 130–144.

Soja, N.N. (1994). Young children's concept of colour and its relation to the acquisition of colour words. *Child Development, 65,* 918–937.

Synder, L.S., & Godley, D. (1992). Assessment of word-finding disorders in children and adolescents. *Topics in Language Disorders, 13,* 15–32.

Swan, D., & Goswami, U. (1997). Phonological awareness deficits in developmental dyslexia and the phonological representations hypothesis. *Journal of Experimental Child Psychology, 66,* 18–41.

Tomasello, M. (1992). *First verbs: A case study of early grammatical development.* New York: Cambridge University Press.

Watkins, R., Rice, M., & Moltz, C. (1993). Verb use by language-impaired and normally developing children. *First Language, 37,* 133–143.

Wiig, E.H., & Semel, E.M. (1975). Productive language abilities in learning disabled adolescents. *Journal of Learning Disabilities, 8,* 578–586.

Wiig, E., Semel, E., & Nystrom, L. (1982). Comparison of rapid naming abilities in language-learning disabled and academically achieving eight-year-olds. *Language, Speech and Hearing Services in Schools, 13,* 11–23.

Windsor, J., & Hwang, M. (1999). Testing the generalized slowing hypothesis in specific language impairment. *Journal of Speech, Language and Hearing Research, 42,* 1205–1218.

Wolf, M. (1980). The word-retrieval process and reading in children and aphasics. *Children's Language*, *3*, 437–490.

Wolf, M., & Segal, D. (1992). Word finding and reading in the developmental dyslexias. *Topics in Language Disorders*, *13*, 51–65.

APPENDIX 1

Stimuli for naming

(A) Objects

Animals		Body parts		Household items		Clothes	
High Frequency	Low Frequency	High Frequency	Low Frequency	High Frequency	Low Frequency	High Frequency	Low Frequency
Bear[a]	Camel[a]	Eye[a]	Ankle[a]	Bed[a]	Bowl[a]	Coat[a]	Apron
Cow[a]	Deer[ab]	Finger[a]	Elbow[a]	Cup[a]	Cushion	Dress[a]	Cloak
Dog[a]	Mole	Foot[a]	Knee[a]	Knife[a]	Stool[a]	Hat[a]	Pyjamas
Horse[a]	Tiger[a]	Hand[a]	Toe[a]	Table[a]	Vase[ab]	Shoes[a]	Vest
Sheep[a]	Zebra[a]	Leg[a]	Wrist	Television[a]	Wardrobe	Skirt[a]	Waistcoat[ab]

[a]Items where age of acquisition data was available.
[b]Items where age of acquisition was above 4 years.

(B) Actions

Transitive		Intransitive	
High frequency	Low frequency	High frequency	Low frequency
Cut	Sew	Run	Bark
Ride	Wrap	Dance	Hop
Pick	Stroke	Fly	Crawl
Pull	Mow	Swim	Wobble
Blow	Stir	Cry	Sweat

LANGUAGE AND COGNITIVE PROCESSES, 2001, 16 (2/3), 287–308

An investigation of language impairment in autism: Implications for genetic subgroups

Margaret M. Kjelgaard

Eunice Kennedy Shriver Center, Waltham, MA, USA

Helen Tager-Flusberg

University of Massachusetts, Medical School, and Eunice Kennedy Shriver Center, Waltham, MA, USA

Autism involves primary impairments in both language and communication, yet in recent years the main focus of research has been on the communicative deficits that define the population. The study reported in this paper investigated language functioning in a group of 89 children diagnosed with autism using the ADI–R, and meeting DSM–IV criteria. The children, who were between 4 and 14 years old, were administered a battery of standardised language tests tapping phonological, lexical, and higher-order language abilities. The main findings were that among the children with autism there was significant heterogeneity in their language skills, although across all the children, articulation skills were spared. Different subgroups of children with autism were identified on the basis of their performance on the language measures. Some children with autism have normal language skills; for other children, their language skills are significantly below age expectations. The profile of performance across the standardised measures for the language-impaired children with autism was similar to the profile that defines the disorder specific language impairment (or SLI). The implications of this language impaired subgroup in autism for understanding the genetics and definition of both autism and SLI are discussed.

Requests for reprints should be sent to Helen Tager-Flusberg, Ph.D., Center for Research on Developmental Disorders, Eunice Kennedy Shriver Center, 200 Trapelo Road, Waltham, MA 02452. Email: htagerf@shriver.org.

This research was supported by grants from NIDCD and NINDS to the second author (PO1 DC 03610; RO1 NS 38668) and from NICHD (F32 HD 08494) to the first author. We are extremely grateful to Susan Bacalman, Laura Becker, Courtney Hale, Robert Joseph, Echo Meyer, and Jenny Roberts for their help in collecting the data reported in this paper. We also thank Susan Folstein, Robert Joseph, Kate Sullivan, Dorothy Bishop, and Gina Conti-Ramsden for their advice during the preparation of this manuscript. We offer special thanks to the children and families who participated in this study.

http://www.tandf.co.uk/journals/pp/01690965.html   DOI: 10.1080/0169096004200058

Autism is diagnosed on the basis of abnormalities or impaired development in three areas: social interaction, communication, and a severely restricted repertoire of activity and interests, present before the age of 3 (American Psychiatric Association, 1994). In the domain of communication, one criterion that is used to document the presence of autistic disorder is the delay or absence of spoken language. Indeed, this feature is important in differentiating between autism and another related developmental disorder, Asperger's syndrome, which is only diagnosed when there is no clinical delay in language (APA, 1994; Szatmari, 1998; Volkmar & Klin, 1998). Problems in language are central to our understanding of autism: they are often the first presenting symptom (Kurita, 1985; Lord & Paul, 1997); they vary widely in the population; and are the most important feature for predicting the prognosis and developmental course of children with this disorder (Rutter, 1970; Ventner, Lord, & Schopler, 1992).

Despite the significance of language impairment in the diagnosis of autism, in recent years few studies have addressed this area of functioning. Instead, research on the nature of the language and communication deficits in autism has focused almost exclusively on those aspects that are universal and specific to this disorder (Tager-Flusberg, 1996). Beginning with Baltaxe (1977), studies have explored the pragmatic deficits that are apparent in conversations and other discourse contexts, identifying those features that distinguish communication problems in autism from those found in other clinical groups. This body of research has led to the consensus that children with autism are seriously limited in their communicative abilities (see Lord & Paul, 1997; Tager-Flusberg, 1999; Wilkinson, 1998; for recent reviews). These limitations are evident in their restricted range of speech acts (e.g., Loveland, Landry, Hughes, Hall, & McEvoy, 1988; Wetherby, 1986), and impaired conversational and narrative skills (Loveland & Tunali, 1993; Tager-Flusberg & Sullivan, 1995). At a theoretical level, these communicative impairments have been related to deficits in understanding other minds and to other features of the disorder, particularly in social functioning (Capps, Kehres, & Sigman, 1998; Tager-Flusberg, 1993, 1996, 1999).

In contrast to the universal nature of these communicative deficits, language functioning in autism is much more variable. At one end, there are children with autism whose vocabulary, grammatical knowledge, and articulation skills are within the normal range of functioning, while at the other end a significant proportion of the population remains essentially non-verbal (Lord & Paul, 1997). Two decades ago psycholinguistic studies did investigate these aspects of language by comparing verbal children with autism to other children with general developmental delays or other syndromes such as Down syndrome (e.g., Bartolucci & Pierce, 1977;

Bartolucci, Pierce, & Streiner, 1980; Bartolucci, Pierce, Streiner, & Eppel, 1976; Boucher, 1976, 1988; Pierce & Bartolucci, 1977; Tager-Flusberg, 1981, 1985; Tager-Flusberg et al., 1990). The conclusions drawn from these studies, which relied on natural language samples or experimental tasks, were that autism does not involve *specific* deficits in phonology, syntax or lexical knowledge, because the children with autism were comparable in their performance to the control groups matched on language and general cognitive ability. However, these studies included small, perhaps unrepresentative, samples of children with autism. Furthermore, they did not provide a systematic evaluation of the profile of abilities or deficits across the different domains of language, leaving much unknown about the language impairments that may be present in the majority of children with autism.

Only one set of studies during this period did provide a broader assessment of language abilities in a group of children with autism (Bartak, Rutter, & Cox, 1975, 1977). The autistic children in these studies were compared to a group of children with severe receptive language disorder matched on non-verbal IQ. All the children were selected on the basis of having a serious problem in language comprehension. Among the total sample of children about 10% were classified as "mixed", in that they showed atypical disorder with some autistic features. Language abilities were measured using the Reynell Scales, the Peabody Picture Vocabulary Test (PPVT—a measure of receptive vocabulary), and a natural language sample. Although the autistic children had significantly lower PPVT scores, and were lower on the Reynell comprehension scale, there were no differences between the groups in measures of production such as mean utterance length or grammatical complexity. This pattern suggests that comprehension may be more seriously impaired in autism than production. However, because the autistic sample for these studies was pre-selected for the presence of difficulties in language comprehension, it is not clear whether this pattern holds across the population. Furthermore, although there were some similarities in the language profiles of the autistic and language disordered groups, numerous features did distinguish between the populations (e.g., presence of echolalia and pronoun reversals in the autistic group). A follow-up study, conducted when the children were in middle childhood indicated that the autistic group made less progress in language acquisition than did the language disordered group, but now this latter group had more signs of social deficit, making them in some ways more similar to the children with autism (Cantwell, Baker, Rutter & Mawhood, 1989).

There has been one recent study that investigated the profile of language abilities in a group of 120 children all of whom had behaviours that met DSM-IV criteria for autism. However, only about half had received a formal diagnosis of autism (Jarrold, Boucher, & Russell, 1997), and 10 received a diagnosis of Asperger's syndrome. The remaining children received formal diagnoses of severe communication and language disorder, semantic–pragmatic disorder, or the presence of autistic features. The children, ranging in age from 5 to 19, had participated in other experimental studies and had been administered some standardised measures of vocabulary and grammar as part of the test protocol. The measures, which varied somewhat across the studies and children, included vocabulary comprehension (the British Picture Vocabulary Test; the Renfrew Word Finding Vocabulary Scale) and production (Action Picture Test Information) and grammatical comprehension (Test for Reception of Grammar) and production (Action Picture Test of Grammar). The main findings were that the children's performance was equivalent across all the measures. Unlike other reports in the literature (e.g., Bartak et al., 1975; Lord & Paul, 1997; Tsai & Beisler, 1984) this study found that receptive abilities were similar to expressive abilities, and vocabulary was no different from grammatical knowledge. The authors also concluded that there was no significant heterogeneity in the language profiles of the children in their study; however they acknowledge that this was only tested in an indirect way.

Although this is an important study because it is the first to investigate language profiles in a large sample of children with autism, it is limited in a number of ways. First, the diagnoses of most of the children in the study by Jarrold et al. (1997) were not well documented, and the criteria used for autism and Asperger's syndrome were not clearly defined, even for those children receiving a clinical diagnosis. Second, the standardised language data were collected under different testing conditions, and did not include the same tests across all the participants. Third, the main analysis of the data involved converting raw scores to mental age equivalents and conducting all the test pair-wise comparisons that were possible. There are several methodological problems with this approach. The comparisons were made across tests that were normed across different samples of children. Mervis and Robinson (1999) have recently pointed out the problems in comparing age equivalents in this way, because, they argue, one cannot assume that the expected rates of growth on each test will be the same. Instead, a more appropriate approach to profile analysis should be done on the basis of standard scores, where possible using tests that have been normed on the same sample of children.

The goal of our study was to re-examine the language profiles of a large well-defined sample of children with autism. We included a broader range of language measures, including measures of phonological representation and production, lexical knowledge, semantics, and grammar. We were especially interested in revisiting the provocative findings from the earlier studies by Bartak et al. (1975, 1977) which suggested some similarity between autism and developmental language disorder (nowadays referred to as specific language impairment—SLI). SLI is a developmental disorder that is diagnosed on the basis of language levels that fall significantly below age expectations, but in the absence of other conditions (e.g., hearing loss, mental retardation, or evidence of organic pathology). While there is considerable heterogeneity in the pattern of language skills found in children with SLI (e.g., Tomblin & Zhang, 1999), it is generally defined in children whose non-verbal IQ scores are within the normal range, but whose performance on language tests (on measures of vocabulary and/or grammatical ability) fall more than one standard deviation below the mean. We included in our test battery standardised measures that are used in defining SLI, including an omnibus test of receptive and expressive language, the Clinical Evaluation of Language Fundamentals, as well as measures of vocabulary (Tager-Flusberg & Cooper, 1999; Tomblin & Zhang, 1999). We also included a measure that is considered highly sensitive to the diagnosis of SLI—a non-word repetition test (cf. Bishop, North, & Donlan, 1996; Dollaghan & Campbell, 1998; Gathercole & Baddeley, 1990).

Our study was designed to address the following questions. First, what is the relationship between expressive and receptive abilities among children with autism? Second, what is the profile of language ability across measures of phonology, vocabulary and higher order language skills (including semantics and syntax)? Third, how can we best characterise the heterogeneity of language abilities among children with autism? And finally, do children with autism who have impaired language skills resemble the profile of language disability that is found among children with SLI?

METHOD

Participants

The total sample of participants included 89 children with autism who were part of a multi-project investigation. There were no a priori selection criteria set, however one aim was to recruit at least 70 children for a study that required some language skills, thus biasing our sample toward the inclusion of more verbal children. The children were between the ages of 4 and 14, and included 80 boys and 9 girls. All the children were administered the Autism Diagnostic Interview—Revised version (Lord, Rutter, & LeCouteur, 1994) and the Autism Diagnostic Observation Schedule—Generic (DiLavore, Lord & Rutter, 1995) to document the diagnosis of autism. In addition an expert clinician observed all the children to confirm that they met DSM–IV criteria for autistic disorder.

The children's IQ scores were assessed using the Differential Abilities Scales (either the Preschool or School Age version, depending on the child's age and ability level), by a clinical neuropsychologist or clinical psychology intern. Table 1 presents the main characteristics of all the participants in this study.

Procedures

The children were administered a standard battery of language tests testing their phonological, lexical, and higher order semantic and grammatical language abilities. Because of the wide variability in the language skills of the children, in many cases not all the tests were given.

Goldman-Fristoe Test of Articulation (Goldman & Fristoe, 1986).   The Goldman–Fristoe sounds-in-words subtest measures the accuracy of productive phonology for the consonant sounds of English. The test presents the child with a series of pictures, such that across the set of pictures, all the consonant sounds of English are tested in the word initial, medial, and final position. Norms are provided for children between the ages of 2;0 and 16;0 in percentile ranks.

Peabody Picture Vocabulary Test–III (PPVT) (Dunn & Dunn, 1997).   The PPVT–III tests lexical comprehension by presenting an auditory word and asking the participant to pick the correct picture from an array of four pictures. Norms are available for the children over the age of 2;6, through adulthood.

Expressive Vocabulary Test (EVT) (Williams, 1997).   The EVT measures expressive vocabulary by asking the child to name pictures. As the test advances to more difficult items, participants are asked to produce synonyms for words represented in pictures. The norms for this test were derived from the same representative sample as the PPVT–III, and are available from 2;6 through adulthood.

TABLE 1
Participant characteristics

	N	M	SD	*Range*
Chronological age (months)	89	88.07	28.55	48–167
Full-scale IQ	84	68.49	24.38	25–141
Verbal IQ[1]	63	76.29	19.05	51–133
Non-verbal IQ[1]	66	82.95	20.92	43–153

[1] Note that scores on subdomains of IQ are only available for children who tested in age level on the Differential Abilities Scales.

Clinical Evaluation of Language Fundamentals (CELF): Preschool (Wiig, Secord, & Semel, 1992) or III (Semel, Wiig, & Secord, 1995). The CELF is designed to measure morphology, syntax, semantics, and working memory for language and is comprised of six subtests that are used to calculate measures of receptive and expressive language skills. There are three subtests in each of the domains, receptive and expressive. The Preschool version is suitable for children between the ages of 3;0 and 6;11, while the CELF–III covers the age range of 6;0 to 21;11. Norms are provided for these ages for the total CELF scores and for receptive and expressive domain scores.

Repetition of Nonsense Words.   We used the sub-test from the NEPSY, which is a comprehensive developmental neuropsychological assessment battery (Korkman, Kirk, & Kemp, 1998). This test assesses the ability to analyse and reproduce phonological knowledge by asking the child to repeat nonsense words that are presented on an audiotape. This test is normed for children aged 5;0 to 12;11.

In most cases the tests were given in the following order: PPVT, EVT, Goldman–Fristoe, CELF, and Repetition of Nonsense Words. Testing was typically conducted on two different days, providing the children with numerous breaks. All the language tests were administered and scored by a certified speech-language pathologist. The test data were all checked by a second coder, under the supervision of a speech-language pathologist.

RESULTS

For each test, the child's standard score was computed. For the PPVT, EVT, and CELF, the procedures described in the test manuals were followed to obtain standard scores, which are based on a mean of 100 and a standard deviation of 15. The Goldman–Fristoe percentile ranks and the Repetition of Nonsense Words standard scores were converted to the standard score scale of the other tests in order to be able to compare means across the measures. We should note however, that the tests are not all equivalent in that they have different floor and ceiling scores.

Children completing language tests

Table 2 presents the numbers of children who were able to complete each of the language tests included in the battery above the basal level, and provides the means and standard deviations for each test. Across the tests more than 90% of the total sample of children were able to complete the PPVT, EVT, and Goldman–Fristoe. In contrast only about half the children were able to complete the CELF (49%) and the Repetition of

TABLE 2
Performance on language measures

Measure	N	M	SD
Goldman–Fristoe	79	90.17	17.03
PPVT	82	70.37	22.68
EVT	81	68.99	23.62
CELF	44	72.32	17.71
Repetition of Nonsense Words	40	81.88	13.89

PPVT, Peabody Picture Vocabulary Test; EVT, Expressive Vocabulary Test; CELF; Clinical Evaluation of Language Fundamentals.

Nonsense Words (45%). The latter test was not attempted with children below the age of 5, since norms are not available for younger children.

We compared the children who were able to complete the CELF to those who were not. While there were no significant differences in age ($t[87] = .91$), the children who did complete the CELF had significantly higher IQ scores ($M = 85$, SD = 17.3) than the children who did not ($M = 50$, SD = 16.8), $t(82) = 9.4$, $p < .0001$. We also found that the scores of the PPVT and EVT were significantly higher for the children completing the CELF compared to those not completing the CELF. On the PPVT the means for the two groups were: $M = 85.6$, SD = 17.8, and $M = 52.8$, SD = 12.9, $t(80) = 9.44$, $p < .0001$; and on the EVT the means were : $M = 84.9$, SD = 17.5, and $M = 50.1$, SD = 14.1, $t(79) = 9.7$, $p < .0001$.

Finally we checked whether there were differences in the numbers of children who completed each test who were younger (below age 7) or older (over age 7). These data are summarised in Table 3. The only test that fewer young children completed was the Repetition of Nonsense Words. As noted earlier, the norms for this test only begin at age 5, so 14 children in our sample who were 4 years old, were not given the test. For all the other language measures, there were no differences in the numbers of younger and older children completing the tests.

Receptive vs. expressive abilities

The first set of analyses investigated whether there were significant differences between receptive and expressive abilities, using the lexical measures and the CELF. The standard scores from the PPVT ($M = 71.13$, SD = 22.43) and EVT ($M = 69.35$, SD = 23.55) were compared for the sample of 80 children who completed both tests using a two-tailed t-test: $t(79) = 1.342$, $p = .18$. The vast majority of children, 64, representing 80% of the sample, did not show more than one standard deviation

TABLE 3
Comparison of children under age 7, and age 7 and older, completing the language tests

Measure	Under 7 N = 50		Over 7 N = 39	
	N	%	N	%
Goldman–Fristoe	44	88	35	90
PPVT	46	92	36	92
EVT	45	90	36	92
CELF	28	56	16	41
Repetition of Nonsense Words	19	38	21	54

PPVT, Peabody Picture Vocabulary Test; EVT, Expressive Vocabulary Test; CELF, Clinical Evaluation of Language Fundamentals.

difference between PPVT and EVT scores. Of the 20% who did have a discrepancy of more than one standard deviation, 13 (16%) had higher PPVT scores while three (4%) had higher EVT scores. Overall, these results do not suggest that there are significant differences between receptive and expressive abilities in lexical knowledge among children with autism.

For the smaller sample of 44 children able to complete the CELF (either Preschool or III), the standard scores on the receptive subtests ($M = 70.89$, SD $= 19.73$) and the expressive subtests ($M = 74.86$, SD $= 17.63$) were also compared using a two-tailed t-test. This analysis revealed a significant difference between the receptive and expressive standard scores $t(43) = 2.445$, $p = .019$, indicating that among this group of children, expressive abilities for higher order language use were higher than receptive abilities. This pattern of higher expressive than receptive ability on the CELF held for over half the sample (25 children; 57%). Table 4 presents the scores (now with a mean of 10 and standard deviation of 3) on each of the subtests of the CELF Preschool and III. On the preschool version, the Formulating Labels (a word naming task) expressive subtest stands out as the single subtest that is higher than the others, and this was confirmed in a post-hoc analysis. On the CELF III, Word Structure (tapping grammatical morphology) and Sentence Assembly (tapping word order knowledge in children who can read) were the expressive tests that were higher than the other subtests. Nevertheless, it is important to note that there was considerable variability among the children in their performance across the subtests, and there was no clear profile that characterised the children with autism in this study.

TABLE 4

Performance on Subtests of Clinical Evaluation of Language Fundamentals (CELF) Preschool and CELF III

	N	M	SD
CELF Preschool			
Expressive subtests			
Recalling Sentences	25	4.08[1]	2.12
Formulating Labels	25	6.76	2.55
Word Structure	25	5.00	3.10
Receptive subtests			
Linguistic Concepts	25	4.08	2.58
Basic Concepts	25	5.60	3.21
Sentence Structure	25	4.56	2.40
CELF III			
Expressive subtests			
Word Structure[2]	9	7.78	3.83
Formulated Sentences	19	6.11	2.79
Recalling Sentences	19	7.16	2.95
Sentence Assembly[3]	10	7.40	3.24
Receptive subtests			
Sentence Structure[2]	9	6.11	2.67
Concepts and Directions	19	6.74	3.77
Word Classes	19	6.95	3.84
Semantic Relationships[3]	10	6.20	2.70

[1] Note that for subtests on the CELF the mean score is 10 with a SD of 3.
[2] For children aged 6–8.
[3] For children aged 9 and older.

Subgroups of language abilities in autism

The scores on each of the language tests showed wide variability among the
sample of children in this study, as shown in Table 2. To explore this
variability further, we created three subgroups of children, based on their
PPVT scores. The 82 children who completed the PPVT were divided into
those who scored within the normal range (standard scores of 85 and above,
$N = 22$), those who were between one and two standard deviations below
the mean (standard scores between 70 and 84, $N = 10$), and those whose
scores were more than two standard deviations below the mean (standard
scores below 70, $N = 50$). We refer to these groups as the normal language
group, the borderline group, and the impaired group, respectively.

We examined for each of these groups the pattern of scores on the EVT,
the Goldman–Fristoe and full scale IQ. We limited this profile analysis to
these tests since they are the ones available on the largest number of
children in the sample. Figure 1 shows the profile for each of the language
groups. This profile showed that on average, children's vocabulary and IQ

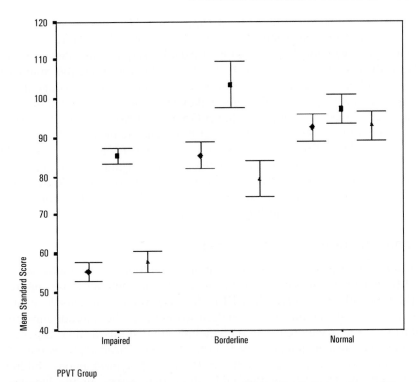

Figure 1. Profiles of Expressive Vocabulary Test (EVT) (◆), Goldman–Fristoe (■), and Full-Scale IQ (▲) in normal language ($N = 12$), borderline ($N = 10$), and impaired ($N = 50$) groups, based on Peabody Picture Vocabulary Test (PPVT) scores.

scores varied together and were lowest in the impaired group (EVT $M = 55$, SD $= 16.82$; IQ $M = 58$, SD 18.76), closer to normal in the borderline group (EVT $M = 85$, SD $= 13.86$; IQ $M = 79$, SD $= 14.6$) and highest in the normal group (EVT $M = 93$, SD $= 16.52$; IQ $M = 93$, SD 17.89). The correlations between IQ and both vocabulary measures were statistically significant (for PPVT, $r(77) = 0.83$, $p < .001$; for EVT, $r(77) = 0.77$, $p < .001$), confirming the relationship between vocabulary and full scale IQ across the sample in this study. At the same time, there were 14 children in the impaired language group whose full-scale IQ scores were above 70; and 9 children who were in the normal language group whose full-scale IQ scores were in the borderline to mentally retarded range. Within the normal language group, 12 children were under 7 (26%), and 10 were 7 or older (28%). Similarly in the impaired language group, 26 children were under 7 (57%), 24 were 7 or older (67%).

The profile shown in Figure 1 also illustrates that scores on the Goldman–Fristoe were in the normal range for all three groups (impaired group, $M = 85.3$, SD $= 13.86$; borderline group, $M = 103.55$, SD $= 18.76$; and normal language group $M = 97.23$, SD $= 17.2$). This pattern indicates that expressive phonology at the one word level is spared in autism overall. Nevertheless, a one-way ANOVA on the Goldman–Fristoe standard scores with language group as the between subjects variable was significant ($F (2, 74) = 8.11, p < .001$. Post-hoc Tukey HSD analyses revealed that the impaired group had significantly lower Goldman–Fristoe scores than either the borderline or normal language groups. The number of children for whom Goldman–Fristoe scores were greater than EVT scores was 60/79 (76% of the children). Thus, across the sample of children with autism in this study, articulation skills tend to be higher than vocabulary knowledge. The Goldman–Fristoe standard scores were only moderately correlated with age ($r(77) = .22$) and IQ ($r(74) = .38$).

Language profile using the CELF

In the second profile analysis we explored children's performance across all the language measures used in this study, including all those children who were able to complete the CELF ($N = 44$). Table 5 presents the means and standard deviations of the standard scores on all the tests administered for this group of children. The IQ data indicate that this group is generally within the normal range for non-verbal IQ. Not surprisingly, verbal IQ scores are lower than non-verbal; a pattern that is typical among children with autism. The data in this table show that across all the language measures, with the exception of the Goldman–Fristoe, scores are one standard deviation or more below the mean. Performance on the CELF is lower than on the measures of lexical knowledge (between 10 and 15 points), but again, there is significant variability on the language measures among this group of high functioning children with autism.

TABLE 5
Performance on the language tests for children who completed the CELF

Measure	M	SD	Range
Goldman–Fristoe	97.55	17.51	67–133
PPVT	85.57	17.77	55–134
EVT	84.89	17.51	40–136
CELF–Total	72.32	17.71	50–113
CELF–Receptive	70.89	19.73	50–116
CELF–Expressive	74.86	17.63	50–116
Repetition of nonsense words	85.32	11.23	65–110
Verbal IQ	83.57	18.04	53–133
Non-verbal IQ	90.07	19.63	49–153

PPVT, Peabody Picture Vocabulary Test; EVT, Expressive Vocabulary Test; CELF, Clinical Evaluation of Language Fundamentals.

The total language summary score on the CELF was used to divide this sample of children into three groups following the same approach used in the previous analysis. Thus, children were designated as normal language if their standard scores were 85 or higher ($N = 10$), borderline, if their standard scores were between 70 and 84 ($N = 13$), or impaired, if their standard scores were below 70, or more than two standard deviations below the mean ($N = 21$). The profiles for these groups is shown in Figure 2. For these profiles we created a combined vocabulary score (averaging the children's scores on the PPVT and EVT), and also included the Goldman–Fristoe, and the Repetition of Nonsense Words. As in the previous analysis, we compared the ages of the children in each language subgroup. The average ages of the children in the groups were 6;11 for the normal language group, 7;11 for the borderline group, and 6;11 for the impaired group. In the normal language subgroup, six children were younger than 7 (60% of this subgroup) and four (40%) were 7 or older; in the impaired language subgroup, 15 (71%) were younger than 7 and six (29%) were 7 or older.

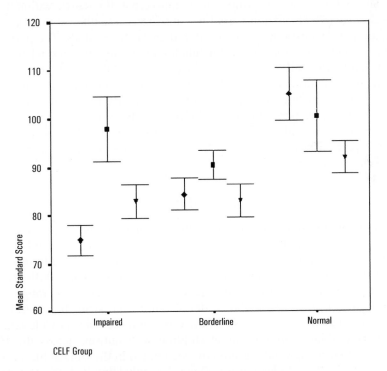

Figure 2.   Profiles of Vocabulary (◆), Goldman–Fristoe (■), and Repetition of Nonsense Words (▼) scores in normal language ($N = 10$), borderline ($N = 13$), and impaired ($N = 21$) groups, based on Clinical Evaluation of Language Fundamentals (CELF) scores.

We again found that the Goldman–Fristoe standard scores were in the normal range for all three groups (impaired, $M = 98.98$, SD $= 20.29$; borderline, $M = 92.58$, SD $= 9.63$; normal language, $M = 101.56$, SD $= 19.74$). A one-way ANOVA revealed no significant differences among the language groups on the Goldman–Fristoe ($F(2, 39) = 0.82$). Repetition of Nonsense Words fell lower than one standard deviation below the mean in the impaired ($M = 82.92$, SD $= 12.15$) and borderline groups ($M = 83$, SD $= 10.85$), but not in the normal language group ($M = 91.11$, SD $= 9.28$); the differences between the subgroups on the repetition of nonsense words was not significant ($F(2, 28) = 1.77$). Vocabulary varied as would be expected, with the impaired group falling more than one standard deviation below the mean ($M = 75.43$, SD $= 11.8$), the borderline group were about one standard deviation below the mean ($M = 86.65$, SD $= 10.24$), and normal group fell in the average range ($M = 103.95$, SD $= 14.16$). These differences were highly significant ($F(2, 41) = 19.45$, $p < .0001$).

Thus, even among the children able to complete a more comprehensive language battery, most of whom had non-verbal IQ scores within the normal range (31/44 had non-verbal IQs above 80), a significant proportion of children with autism were impaired in their language skills. The pattern of impairment found for this higher functioning group mirrored what was found across the full range of IQ: articulation skills remain relatively spared, but impairments are found in vocabulary, higher order use of semantic and syntactic knowledge, and in the ability to repeat nonsense words. At the same time, it is important to note that across the full sample of children in this study, there were five children, two of whom were aged below 7 years, whose language skills, across all the measures, were well within the normal range.

DISCUSSION

The goals of this study were to explore the range of language abilities among a large group of children with autism, varying in age and IQ level. Unlike previous research in this area, this study included a broad range of standardised measures of language, and profiles of language skills were derived from a comparison of standard scores across a range of phonological, lexical, and higher order semantic and syntactic measures. One of the main findings from this study was that there is a very wide range of language abilities found among children with autism, across the IQ spectrum, confirming what has already been noted in the clinical literature (Lord & Paul, 1997). Indeed, it is striking that only about half the children in this study were able to complete all the language measures that were included; a small number were not even able to reach a basal on the simplest measure of word naming or comprehension. We return to an analysis of this heterogeneity later in the discussion.

One question that we set out to address was whether expressive language abilities are relatively more spared among children with autism than receptive abilities, as has been reported in some other studies (e.g., Bartak et al., 1975; Tsai & Beisler, 1984). We were careful to make comparisons of standard scores on tests that had been normed on the same samples of children, to eliminate possible sources of differences due to test differences rather than domain differences in the children. Our main findings were that children with autism show no receptive-expressive differences in vocabulary knowledge, thus confirming the more recent findings of Jarrold et al. (1997). We did find that expressive abilities were higher on the CELF, but this was mostly due to the children's better performance on the Formulating Labels subtest, which is a single word-naming measure. Most other expressive and receptive subtests on the CELF tap higher order knowledge of semantics and syntactic knowledge that entail integration across language domains and have a significant working memory component. On these subtests there were no differences between receptive and expressive levels of performance, suggesting that in general, verbal children with autism do not show a major discrepancy between their receptive and expressive language skills.

Although we only compared receptive and expressive abilities within tests that were normed on the same sample, it is not clear whether this kind of comparison is especially useful because children's performance on structured tests reflects not only linguistic knowledge, but also a variety of other test-dependent variables. These include attentional factors, understanding the pragmatic demands of the task, and understanding the instructions. These kinds of variables are not equivalent across different tasks, so differences in performance on receptive and expressive tests may reflect test-related factors, rather than linguistic processing.

Across the full range of children in this study, we found a significant relationship between IQ and language abilities, especially as measured by vocabulary tests. Not surprisingly, only the children with higher IQ scores were able to complete the full range of language tests that were administered, and in general, the children with higher IQ scores had better language abilities overall. Thus, IQ itself accounts for some of the heterogeneity found in language among children with autism. At the same time it is important to note that among lower IQ children, some had language skills within the normal range, and among high IQ children, many had language skills in the impaired range. Thus, language skills can be independent of IQ in autism, and may in fact be more important in understanding both the current functioning and long-term prognosis for children with this disorder (Ventner et al., 1992).

There were some children, about 10% of the sample, who were unable to reach a basal on even the most basic language test (the vocabulary and articulation tests). Although it is not clear in each case why the children could not complete the test, in general it seemed that they had great difficulty understanding the task demands. These children tended to repeat the examiner's utterance, or perseverate across stimulus items. Some children would not attend to the examiner or the stimulus materials, and some exhibited severe behaviour problems that interfered with the testing. These difficulties highlight some of the limitations of using standardised tests to assess language in children with autism (Tager-Flusberg, 2000).

In order to understand the profiles of language skills across the range of children in this study, we looked at subgroups that were defined on the basis of those children whose performance on one of the major language measures (either the PPVT or CELF), was within the normal range, and those who fell more than one or two standard deviations below the mean. These divisions parallel the method taken in the SLI literature in defining children with this disorder. In general this approach indicated that there was a group of children representing about one quarter of the whole group participating in this study (22 children) with essentially normal language skills (see Figure 1). Thus deficits in language skills are not universal in autism, although they are found in the majority of children with this disorder. This contrasts with the universal impairments that are found in communication skills in this population, and which are among the defining features of autism (Tager-Flusberg, 1996). Because our participants were not selected on the basis of an unbiased population-based sample, we cannot provide exact estimates for the proportion of children with autism who have either normal language, as defined in this study, or have significant linguistic impairments. It is likely that we are underestimating the proportion of impaired children, given that our sample was biased in favour of children with some language skills.

Interestingly, we did not find significant differences between the younger (defined as below age 7) and older children in this study in the numbers of children unable to complete the tests (see Table 3). Thus, the kinds of test-related problems that interfered with obtaining a basal score on the standardised tests did not change as the children got older. On the other hand, this may reflect a bias in the sample, in that our recruitment for children at the younger ages may have stressed the need for some spontaneous language. For the subgroup analysis that was conducted on the children who did complete the CELF, the impaired group included relatively more younger than older children: 54% compared to 38%. Table 4 also shows that the scores on the Preschool CELF (given to the younger children) were lower than the CELF III. It is not clear whether these differences reflect genuine differences in language abilities of younger children with autism, or whether they reflect test differences. There were differences in the numbers of children who completed the CELF at the different age levels, 56% of the younger children, compared to 41% of the older children. So it is possible that the subtests on Preschool version of the test are simpler to understand than the subtests on the CELF III, thus allowing more children to complete them. The problems with interpreting the differences between the different age groups reflects some of the limitations inherent in using standardised tests, especially with autistic children who are likely to be more prone to test-taking variables than other populations, on whom these tests were normed.

Among the children whose language was defined as borderline (more than one standard deviation below the mean) or impaired (more than two standard deviations), systematic profiles were found across language domains. For the children who were able to complete the language battery, we found that vocabulary skills were higher than knowledge of syntax and semantics, as measured by the CELF (see Table 5). Although one must be cautious in comparing across these different tests, this finding does not replicate the results reported by Jarrold et al. (1997) who argued that vocabulary and grammatical skills (also measured on different tests, with different norms) were equivalent in children with autism. The differences between our studies may be related to a number of factors including the sample of children participating, the language tests used, and the methods for investigating language profiles. Because we created our profiles on the basis of standard scores, rather than age equivalents, our approach avoids the problems of comparing across non-equal growth rates in the language tests (cf. Mervis & Robinson, 1999). The profiles presented in Figure 2 do suggest that among children with normal language skills, vocabulary is equivalent to semantic and syntactic knowledge; it may be that Jarrold et al. (1997) included more of these children in their study. However, among children with autism with lower language abilities (either borderline or impaired), vocabulary tends to be relatively less impaired compared to higher order linguistic knowledge.

Our profile analysis confirmed earlier studies suggesting that articulation skills, as measured here by the Goldman–Fristoe, are almost always spared in this population (e.g., Boucher 1976), despite severe deficits in vocabulary, semantic, and grammatical knowledge. In contrast, however, we found that in children with low vocabulary and CELF scores, children with autism also were impaired on a nonsense word repetition test. This finding is somewhat surprising given what has been observed regarding the echolalic abilities in children with autism. However, unlike tests of articulation skill, and echolalic language, the Repetition of Nonsense Words test does not depend on rote memory skills. Instead, it requires the child to analyse the acoustic and phonetic properties of the speech stream to derive the phonological representation, and hold the representation of the segments in working memory in order to reproduce them in a motor programme. Our findings suggest that children with autism who have impaired language as measured on tests of vocabulary and higher order syntax and semantics, also have difficulty with this kind of phonological test.

The profile of language performance found among the children with autism who have borderline or impaired language abilities mirrors what has been reported in the literature on SLI. Thus, studies of children with SLI, who are defined on the basis of the PPVT and/or an omnibus test such as the CELF, suggest that this language disorder is characterised by poorer performance on tests of grammatical ability than vocabulary (e.g., Rice, 1999; Tomblin & Zhang, 1999). Furthermore, children with SLI, even when they have good articulation skills, show systematic difficulties on tests of non-word repetition (Bishop, North, & Donlan, 1996; Dollaghan & Campbell, 1998; Gathercole & Baddeley, 1990). This pattern of deficits has been viewed as defining the phenotype of SLI (Tager-Flusberg & Cooper, 1999).

What is the significance of this SLI profile of language impairment that characterises a subgroup of children with autism? On the one hand, the parallels in language deficits may simply be superficial—that is, the language deficits in autism are fundamentally different from those in SLI, despite the similarity in profiles we have found. On the other hand, it may be that these similarities suggest something deeper that may be in common in SLI and a subgroup of autism. We would like to claim that our profile analysis may be taken as evidence for theoretically significant overlap between these disorders. Although, by definition, SLI may not be diagnosed in children who meet criteria for autism, in fact, our data suggest that some children with autism may have a parallel or overlapping SLI disorder, as indicated by their pattern of impaired performance on diagnostic language measures. Support for this argument may be derived not simply for the language data we have presented here, but also from evidence in the literature on the genetics of autism and SLI.

Autism and SLI are complex genetic disorders that have very high heritability estimates, based on family and twin studies (for recent reviews, see Santangelo & Folstein, 1999; Tomblin & Zhang, 1999). Both disorders are thought to be caused by the interaction of several genes, and family studies have found that relatives of identified probands often have only parts of the syndrome (referred to as the 'broader phenotype'). Interestingly, among family members of probands with autism, there are significantly elevated rates of documented histories of language delay and language-based learning deficits (Bolton et al., 1994; Fombonne, Bolton, Prior, Jordan, & Rutter, 1997; Piven & Palmer 1997), and co-twins discordant for autism often have language deficits resembling what has been found in SLI children (Folstein & Rutter, 1977). Among family members of SLI probands, there are elevated rates of language disorder and reading difficulties (Tomblin, Freese, & Records, 1992). More recently, Hafeman and Tomblin (1999) found a significantly elevated risk of autism among siblings of SLI probands. Thus, these family studies of autism and SLI suggest that there is significant overlap between these disorders. Although no specific gene has yet been identified as the cause of either autism or SLI, genetic studies of both disorders have shown linkage to the *same* region on the long arm of chromosome 7 (Fisher, Vargha-Khadem, Watkins, Monaco, & Pembrey, 1998; The International Molecular Genetic Study of Autism Consortium, 1998).

The cumulative evidence from both family and genetic linkage studies suggests that autism and SLI may involve one or more shared genes, arguing strongly for biological overlap between these disorders. The findings presented in this paper, suggesting parallels between the language phenotype of SLI and the profile of language impairment found in a subgroup of children with autism, are complemented by the data from genetic studies. This hypothesis, of overlapping or shared genetics and phenotypic characteristics among families with SLI and autism, clearly requires further research. Genetic studies are needed to pinpoint the specific gene or genes on 7q associated with these disorders; and epidemiological studies are needed to identify what proportion of the autistic population in fact shares the SLI language profile.

Further research is needed to replicate and extend the findings reported here on the SLI profile found among a subgroup of children with autism. The next steps should include a wider range of language measures than those reported in this paper. In particular, we have highlighted numerous limitations in the use of standardised tests for assessing language profiles in children with autism, including the difficulties encountered by some children in understanding the demands of the tests, and difficulties comparing performance across different tests. Standardized tests also do not allow for fine-grained analyses of specific items that may cause problems for children with autism, or for separating out task demands and processing difficulty from deficits in linguistic knowledge. Future research should complement data collected from standardized tests with analyses of natural language samples, and experimental probes (Tager-Flusberg, 2000) in investigations of language impairment among children with autism.

Our findings suggest that some children with autism also show the pattern of language deficits that defines SLI, which can be independent of IQ. What are the implications of these findings for considering the *specificity* of SLI? Is it possible that other children with neurodevelop-mental disorders also show the same language profile as our language-impaired children with autism, and children with SLI? If so, this suggests that SLI may not be so specific, but can be found in different groups of language disordered individuals. To address these issues future studies will need to investigate the neurocognitive mechanisms underlying language processing in children with SLI, autism and perhaps other disorders, in much greater detail than we have done thus far. Such studies will help to advance our understanding of language disorder across a range of children, at both the clinical and theoretical level.

REFERENCES

American Psychiatric Association (1994). *Diagnostic and Statistical Manual of Mental Disorders* (Fourth Edition) (DSM–IV) Washington, DC: APA.

Baltaxe, C.A.M. (1977). Pragmatic deficits in the language of autistic adolescents. *Journal of Pediatric Psychology, 2,* 176–180.

Bartak, L., Rutter, M., & Cox, A. (1975). A comparative study of infantile autism and specific developmental receptive language disorder: I. The children. *British Journal of Psychiatry, 126,* 127–145.

Bartak, L., Rutter, M., & Cox, A. (1977). A comparative study of infantile autism and specific developmental receptive language disorders: II. Discriminant function analysis. *Journal of Autism and Childhood Schizophrenia, 7,* 383–396.

Bartolucci, G., & Pierce, S. (1977). A preliminary comparison of phonological development in autistic, normal, and mentally retarded subjects. *British Journal of Disorders of Communication, 12,* 137–147.

Bartolucci, G., Pierce, S., & Streiner, D. (1980). Cross-sectional studies of grammatical morphemes in autistic and mentally retarded children. *Journal of Autism and Developmental Disorders, 10,* 39–50.

Bartolucci, G., Pierce, S., Streiner, D., & Eppel, P. (1976). Phonological investigation of verbal autistic and mentally retarded subjects. *Journal of Autism and Childhood Schizophrenia, 6,* 303–315.

Bishop, D., North, T., & Donlan, C. (1996). Nonword repetition as a behavioural marker for inherited language impairment: Evidence from a twin study. *Journal of Child Psychology and Psychiatry, 36,* 1–13.

Bolton, P., Macdonald, H., Pickles, A., Rios, P., Goode, S., Crowson, M., Bailey, A., & Rutter, M.A. (1994). A case-control family history study of autism. *Journal of Child Psychology and Psychiatry, 35,* 877–900.

Boucher, J. (1976). Articulation in early childhood autism. *Journal of Autism and Childhood Schizophrenia, 6,* 297-302.

Boucher, J. (1988). Word fluency in high functioning autistic children. *Journal of autism and Developmental Disorders, 18,* 637–645.

Cantwell, D.P., Baker, L., Rutter, M., & Mawhood, L. (1989). Infantile autism and developmental receptive dysphasia: A comparative follow-up into middle childhood. *Journal of Autism and Developmental Disorders, 19,* 19–31.

Capps, L., Kehres, J., & Sigman, M. (1998). Conversational abilities among children with autism and children with developmental delays. *Autism, 2,* 325–344.

DiLavore, P.C., Lord, C., & Rutter, M. (1995). Pre-linguistic autism diagnostic observation schedule. *Journal of Autism and Developmental Disorders, 25,* 355–379.

Dollaghan, C., & Campbell, T. (1998). Nonword repetition and child language impairment. *Journal of Speech, Language, and Hearing Research, 41,* 1136–1146.

Dunn, L.M., & Dunn, L.M. (1997). *Peabody Picture Vocabulary Test, Third Edition.* Circle Pines, MN: American Guidance Service.

Fisher, S.E., Vargha-Khadem, F., Watkins, K.E., Monaco, A.P., & Pembrey, M.E. (1998). Localisation of a gene implicated in a severe speech and language. *Nature Genetics, 18,* 168–170.

Folstein, S., & Rutter, M. (1977). Infantile autism: A genetic study of 21 twin pairs. *Journal of Child Psychology & Psychiatry, 18,* 297–321.

Fombonne, E., Bolton, P., Prior, J., Jordan, H., & Rutter, M. (1997). A family study of autism: Cognitive patterns and levels in parents and siblings. *Journal of Child Psychology & Psychiatry, 38,* 667–683.

Gathercole, S., & Baddeley, A. (1990). Phonological memory deficits in language disordered children: Is there a causal connection? *Journal of Memory and Language, 29,* 336–360.

Goldman, R., & Fristoe, M. (1986). *Goldman–Fristoe Test of Articulation.* Circle Pines, MN: American Guidance Service.

Hafeman, L. & Tomblin, J.B. (1999). Autism behaviors in the siblings of children with specific language impairment. *Molecular Psychiatry, 4 (Supplement 1),* S14.

International Molecular Genetic Study of Autism Consortium, (1998). A full genome screen for autism with evidence for linkage to a region on chromosome 7q. *Human Molecular Genetics, 7,* 571–578.

Jarrold, C., Boucher, J., & Russell, J. (1997). Language profiles in children with autism: Theoretical and methodological implications. *Autism, 1,* 57–76.

Korkman, M., Kirk, U., & Kemp, S. (1998). *NEPSY: A Developmental Neuropsychological Assessment.* San Antonio: The Psychological Corporation, Harcourt Brace & Co.

Kurita, H. (1985). Infantile autism with speech loss before the age of 30 months. *Journal of the American Academy of Child Psychiatry, 24,* 191–196.

Lord, C., & Paul, R. (1997). Language and communication in autism. In D.J. Cohen & F.R. Volkmar (Eds.), *Handbook of autism and pervasive development disorders,* 2nd edition. New York: John Wiley & Sons.

Lord, C., Rutter, M., & Le Couteur, A. (1994). Autism Diagnostic Interview—Revised: A revised version of a diagnostic interview for caregivers of individuals with possible pervasive developmental disorders. *Journal of Autism and Developmental Disorders, 24,* 659–685.

Loveland, K., & Tunali, B. (1993). Narrative language in autism and the theory of mind hypothesis: A wider perspective. In S. Baron-Cohen, H. Tager-Flusberg, & D.J. Cohen (Eds.), *Understanding other minds: Perspectives from autism.* Oxford: Oxford University Press.

Loveland, K., Landry, S., Hughes, S., Hall, S., & McEvoy, R. (1988). Speech acts and the pragmatic deficits of autism. *Journal of Speech and Hearing Research, 31,* 593–604.

Mervis, C.B., & Robinson, B.F. (1999). Methodological issues in cross-syndrome comparisons: Matching procedures, sensitivity (Se) and specificity (Sp). *Monographs of the Society for Research in Child Development, 64,* 115–130.

Pierce, S., & Bartoclucci, G. (1977). A syntactic investigation of verbal autistic, mentally retarded and normal children. *Journal of Autism and Childhood Schizophrenia, 7,* 121–134.

Piven, J., & Palmer, P. (1997). Cognitive deficits in parents from multiple-incidence autism families. *Journal of Child Psychology and Psychiatry, 38,* 1011–1021.

Rice, M.L. (1999). Specific grammatical limitations in children with specific language impairment. In H. Tager-Flusberg (Ed.), *Neurodevelopmental disorders* (pp. 331–359). Cambridge, MA: MIT Press.

Rutter, M. (1970). Autistic children: Infancy to adulthood. *Seminars in Psychiatry, 2,* 435–450.

Santangelo, S.L., & Folstein, S.E. (1999). Autism: A genetic perspective. In H. Tager-Flusberg (Ed.), *Neurodevelopmental disorders* (pp. 431–447). Cambridge, MA: MIT Press.

Semel, E., Wiig, E.H., & Secord, W.A. (1995). *Clinical Evaluation of Language Fundamentals, Third Edition.* San Antonio: The Psychological Corporation, Harcourt Brace & Co.

Szatmari, P. (1998). Differential diagnosis of Asperger disorder. In E. Schopler, G.B. Mesibov, & L.J. Kunce (Eds.), *Asperger syndrome or high-functioning autism?* (pp. 61–76). New York: Plenum Press.

Tager-Flusberg, H. (1981). Sentence comprehension in autistic children. *Applied Psycholinguistics, 2,* 5–24.

Tager-Flusberg, H. (1985). Constraints on the representation of word meaning: Evidence from autistic and mentally retarded children. In S.A. Kuczaj & M. Barrett (Eds.), *The development of word meaning* (pp. 139–166). New York: Springer-Verlag.

Tager-Flusberg, H. (1993). What language reveals about the understanding of minds in children with autism. In S. Baron-Cohen, H. Tager-Flusberg, & D.J. Cohen (Eds.), *Understanding other minds: Perspectives from autism.* Oxford: Oxford University Press.

Tager-Flusberg, H. (1996). Current theory and research on language and communication in autism. *Journal of Autism and Developmental Disorders, 26,* 169–172.

Tager-Flusberg, H. (1999). A psychological approach to understanding the social and language impairments in autism. *International Review of Psychiatry, 11,* 325–334.

Tager-Flusberg, H. (2000). The challenge of studying language development in children with autism. In L. Menn & N. Bernstein Ratner (Eds.), *Methods for studying language production* (pp. 313–332). Mahwah, NJ: Lawrence Erlbaum Associates Inc.

Tager-Flusberg, H., Calkins, S., Nolin, T., Baumberger, T., Anderson, M., & Chadwick-Dias, A. (1990). A longitudinal study of language acquisition in autistic and Downs syndrome children. *Journal of Autism and Developmental Disorders, 20,* 1–21.

Tager-Flusberg, H., & Cooper, J. (1999). Present and future possibilities for defining a phenotype for specific language impairment. *Journal of Speech, Language, and Hearing Research, 42,* 1001–1004.

Tager-Flusberg, H., & Sullivan, K. (1995). Attributing mental states to story characters: A comparison of narratives produced by autistic and mentally retarded individuals. *Applied Psycholinguistics, 16,* 241–256.

Tomblin, J.B. & Zhang, X. (1999). Language patterns and etiology in children with specific language impairment. In H. Tager-Flusberg (Ed.), *Neurodevelopmental disorders* (pp. 361–382). Cambridge, MA: MIT Press/Bradford Books.

Tomblin, J.B., Freese, P.R., & Records, N.L. (1992). Diagnosing specific language impairment in adults for the purpose of pedigree analysis. *Journal of Speech & Hearing Research, 35,* 832–843.

Tsai, L., & Beisler, J.M. (1984). Research in infantile autism: A methodological problem in using language comprehension as the basis for selecting matched controls. *Journal of the American Academy of Child Psychiatry, 23,* 700–703.

Ventner, A., Lord, C., & Schopler, E. (1992). A follow-up study of high-functioning autistic children. *Journal of Child Psychology and Psychiatry, 33,* 489–507.

Volkmar, F.R., & Klin, A. (1998). Asperger syndrome and nonverbal learning disabilities. In E. Schopler, G.B. Mesibov, & L.J. Kunce (Eds.), *Asperger syndrome or high-functioning autism?* (pp. 107–121). New York: Plenum Press.

Wetherby, A. (1986). Ontogeny of communication functions in autism. *Journal of Autism and Developmental Disorders, 16,* 295–316.

Wilkinson, K. (1998). Profiles of language and communication skills in autism. *Mental Retardation and Developmental Disabilities Research Reviews, 4,* 73–79.

Wiig, E.H., Secord, W., & Semel, E. (1992). *Clinical Evaluation of Language Fundamentals–Preschool.* San Antonio: The Psychological Corporation, Harcourt Brace & Co.

Williams, K.T. (1997). *Expressive Vocabulary Test.* Circle Pines, MN: American Guidance Service.

LANGUAGE AND COGNITIVE PROCESSES, 2001, *16* (2/3), 309–331

Divergence of verbal expression and embodied knowledge: Evidence from speech and gesture in children with specific language impairment

Julia L. Evans, Martha W. Alibali and Nicole M. McNeil

University of Wisconsin, Madison, USA

It has been suggested that phonological working memory serves to link speech comprehension to production. We suggest further that impairments in phonological working memory may influence the way in which children represent and express their knowledge about the world around them. In particular, children with severe phonological working memory deficits may have difficulty retaining stable representations of phonological forms, which results in weak links with meaning representations; however, nonverbal meaning representations might develop appropriately due to input from other modalities (e.g., vision, action). Typically developing children often express emerging knowledge in gesture before they are able to express this knowledge explicitly in their speech. In this study we explore the extent to which children with specific language impairment (SLI) with severe phonological working memory deficits express knowledge uniquely in gesture as compared to speech. Using a paradigm in which gesture-speech relationships have been studied extensively, children with SLI and conservation judgement-matched, typically developing controls were asked to solve and explain a set of Piagetian conservation tasks. When gestures accompanied their explanations, the children with SLI expressed information uniquely in gesture more often than did the typically developing children.

Requests for reprints should be addressed to Julia L. Evans, Waisman Center, University of Wisconsin-Madison, 1500 Highland Avenue, Madison, WI 53705-2280, USA.

This research was supported by a Clinical Investigator's Development Award from NIDCD to Julia Evans, by an NIMH Research Fellowship for Undergraduates to Nicole M. McNeil, and by the Undergraduate Research Initiative at Carnegie Mellon University. Portions of these data were presented at the 1998 Symposium for Research on Children with Language Disorders, Madison, Wisconsin. Special thanks are extended to all the children who participated in this study. We also thank Erin Pitts Alexander for contributions to the design of the study, Cecilia Chang and Martha Scott for assistance with data collection, Kert Viele for statistical advice, and Lisa Gershkoff-Stowe, Susan Goldin-Meadow, Jill F. Lehman, Donna Thal, and Asli Özyürek for helpful discussions and thoughtful comments on previous versions of the manuscript.

---

http://www.tandf.co.uk/journals/pp/01690965.html   DOI: 10.1080/01690960042000049

Further, the children with SLI often expressed *more sophisticated* knowledge about conservation in gesture (and in some cases, distributed across speech and gesture) than in speech. The data suggest that for the children with SLI, their embodied, perceptually-based knowledge about conservation was rich, but they were not always able to express this knowledge verbally. We argue that this pattern of gesture-speech mismatch may be due to poor links between phonological representations and embodied meanings for children with phonological working memory deficits.

Children with specific language impairment (SLI) fail to acquire age-appropriate language skills in the absence of clearly identifiable emotional, neurological, visual, hearing, or intellectual impairments. While it has been suggested that SLI is due to underlying linguistic deficits (e.g., Clahsen, 1989; Gopnik & Crago, 1991; Rice, Wexler, & Cleave, 1995), there is strong evidence to suggest that the language impairments seen in children with SLI are secondary to deficits in processing capacity (e.g., Bishop, 1992, 1997; Ellis Weismer, Evans, & Hesketh, 1999; Gathercole & Baddeley, 1990a; Leonard, 1998). In particular, there is strong evidence to suggest that children with SLI have particular deficits in phonological working memory capacity. Recent studies have shown that children with SLI are significantly worse than age-matched peers on nonword repetition tasks, a paradigm used by Baddeley and colleagues as a direct measure of phonological working memory (Dollaghan & Campbell, 1998; Edwards & Lahey, 1998; Gathercole & Baddeley, 1990b; Montgomery, 1995). Further, research suggests that poor phonological working memory, as measured by these nonword repetition tasks, may be a phenotypic marker of language impairments in these children (Bishop, North, & Donlan, 1996).

Phonological working memory has been argued to be key in the processing and retention of language, in particular, retaining a stable representation of the phonological forms of new words (e.g., Baddeley, 1986; Gathercole & Baddeley, 1993). Plaut and Kello (1999), in a recent connectionist model of language acquisition, have suggested that phonological representations are the key link between language comprehension and production during language acquisition. In the early stages of language learning, before infants can learn to produce the articulatory movements required for comprehensible speech, they must first extract and maintain stable and accurate internal acoustic representations of words from the ongoing stream of speech. These stable acoustic representations must then be mapped onto their meaning representations (e.g., semantics). In addition to linking the acoustic pattern of a word to its meaning, infants also must map the meaning of the word to the articulatory patterns required to produce the word. Plaut and Kello have suggested that phonological representations are what enable the infant to accomplish this link, during comprehension, between acoustic input and meaning representations, and during production, between meaning and articulatory representations.

In Plaut and Kello's model, phonological representations are not predefined, but are distributed representations that evolve over time as a result of the child's active processing of language. It is the distributed nature of the acoustic representations that allows a stable phonological representation to emerge from the highly variable acoustic input. While phonological representations are derived from the acoustic input, Plaut and Kello suggest that semantic representations are derived from input from other modalities (e.g., vision).

The idea that meaning representations are based on input from other modalities (e.g., vision, motor activity, proprioception) is central to embodied accounts of language and cognition. According to these accounts, meaning is grounded in bodily and perceptual experiences, and language comprehension and production are the activation and extraction of these embodied meanings (Gibson, 1966; Glenberg, 1997; Glenberg & Robertson, 1999; Iverson & Thelen, in press; MacWhinney, 1999). If one extends Plaut and Kello's notion of semantic representations to incorporate embodied meaning representations, then language comprehension is the mapping of acoustic input onto stable, embodied meaning representations via phonological representations. Production is the expression of embodied meanings via articulatory movements derived from phonological representations.

But what happens if a part of the developmental process is disrupted? In particular, what happens to the child with SLI who has poor phonological working memory abilities? It has been suggested that, when confronted with novel words, the listener must rely upon phonological working memory to encode and maintain the novel phonological sequence in an undegraded form long enough to generate a stable long-term memory representation of the sound structures of the words (Gathercole, 1995). Plaut and Kello have suggested further that it is the phonological representations themselves that "instantiate" the memory necessary to map the acoustic patterns of words to meaning representations (p. 385). Presumably then, the child with SLI who has difficulty with nonword repetition tasks might have been a child who, throughout the language learning process, had difficulty maintaining the phonological sequence of novels words long enough to establish the links between meaning representations, acoustic input, and articulatory patterns. However, because other input modalities would not be impaired, the child's meaning representations would continue to develop appropriately.

In spontaneous language, meanings can be conveyed not only through speech, but also through other avenues of communication, such as through gesture. Very young typically developing children often rely on gestures when they are still limited in their verbal abilities (Acredolo & Goodwyn, 1988; Bates, 1979; Butcher & Goldin-Meadow, in press). In older, school-age children, newly emerging knowledge is often expressed in gesture before it is expressed in speech (Church & Goldin-Meadow, 1986; Perry, Church, & Goldin-Meadow, 1988). Further, gestures and speech are often integrated to express a speaker's overall meaning (McNeill, 1992). Iverson and Thelen (in press) have suggested that the tight integration of gestures and speech is a manifestation of the embodiment of thought. In particular, they propose that hand and mouth are tightly coupled in the mutual cognitive activity of language. What does this idea suggest about children with SLI? If these children have meaning representations that are intact but poorly linked to phonological representations, might they express such representations more readily in gestures than in speech?

To date, investigations of gesture use in children with SLI and toddlers at risk for SLI have focused on these children's ability to spontaneously produce or imitate symbolic gestures (Hill, 1998; Thal & Bates, 1988; Thal, O'Hanlon, Clemmons, & Fralin, 1999; Thal & Tobias, 1992; Thal, Tobias, & Morrison, 1991). These studies suggest that both children with SLI and toddlers at risk for SLI may have difficulties generating and imitating symbolic gestures as compared to typically developing peers. However, no studies to date have focused on the nature of the *relationship* between their verbal expression and spontaneous gestures, or more importantly, on the extent to which children with SLI might rely adaptively on the use of spontaneous gestures to express meanings they are unable to express verbally.

One domain in which the relationship between gesture and verbal expression has been extensively studied in typically developing children is Piagetian conservation (Alibali, Kita, & Young, 2000; Church & Goldin-Meadow, 1986). In a conservation task, a child is presented with two objects that have equal quantities (e.g., two identical glasses with the same amount of water). One of the objects is then transformed (e.g., water from one glass is poured into a short, wide dish) and the child is asked to *judge* whether the quantities are still the same or different. After the judgement, the child is then asked to *explain* the judgement (i.e., to provide a rationale for why the quantities are the same or different). When providing such an explanation, children may express their knowledge in speech and in gestures. In some cases, the meaning conveyed in gestures is the same as that conveyed in speech. For example, a child may say, "The dish is *shorter*", and simultaneously indicate the *height* of the dish in gesture by holding a flat palm at the rim of the dish. In this example, both speech and gesture convey information about the height of the dish.

In other cases, the meaning conveyed in children's gestures differs from that conveyed in speech. For example, a child may say, "The dish is *shorter*", but may indicate the *width* of the dish in gesture, by using a cupped hand to demarcate the width of the dish. In this case, the child's gesture conveys a dimension, *width*, that is not expressed at all in the child's verbal explanation. Thus, information about width is conveyed uniquely in the child's gesture. In this latter example, if one considers only the child's speech, one might infer that the child focused only on the object's height, and did not understand that width is also relevant to the quantity judgement. However, if one considers both speech and gesture, one might infer that the child understands the principle of compensating dimensions (i.e., that even though the dish is shorter, it's also wider, so the quantities are the same). In typically developing children, such "mismatches" between gesture and speech indicate their emerging understanding of conservation (Church & Goldin-Meadow, 1986).

The purpose of this study was to investigate the nature of the relationship between speech and gesture in children with SLI. Specifically, the goal of this study was to determine the extent to which children with SLI, who have severe phonological working memory deficits, express knowledge uniquely in gesture as compared to speech in their explanations of Piagetian conservation tasks.

METHOD

Participants

Eight children with SLI (ages 7;0 to 9;4; 4 girls and 4 boys) participated in the study. One girl had difficulty remaining focused on the tasks, so she was excluded from the sample. The children all met the exclusion criteria for SLI: (1) no hearing loss as measured by pure tone audiometry, (2) no behavioural or emotional problems, (3) no demonstrable neurological involvement, (4) no oral motor deficits, and (5) nonverbal IQ at or above chronological age, as measured by the Columbia Mental Maturity Scale (CMMS; Burgemeister, Blum, & Lorge, 1972). The children also had severe expressive language deficits as measured by the Clinical Evaluation of Language Functions–Revised (CELF-R; Semel, Wiig, & Secord, 1989). All children with SLI were in a speech and language resource classroom, were receiving speech and language services, and had not been exposed to natural or artificial sign languages.

In addition, the children with SLI were selected to have severe auditory working memory deficits as measured by the Goldman–Fristoe–Woodcock Test of Auditory Discrimination, a multisyllabic nonsense word repetition task (Goldman, Fristoe, & Woodcock, 1980). A number of cognitive processes are required for a child to successfully complete nonword repetition tasks (e.g., Dollaghan, Biber, & Campbell, 1993; Gathercole, 1995). These include discriminating the acoustic signal, encoding the acoustic information into a phonological representation, and maintaining that acoustic representation in working memory long enough to plan and execute a verbal response. These nonword repetition tasks, regarded as an index of phonological short-term memory, are strong predictors of a child's ability to learn nonword lexical items such as names for toys (Gathercole & Baddeley, 1990b). It has also been argued that, for children with SLI, they may be a reliable measure of children's ability to form and/or store phonological representations in working memory (e.g., Bishop et al., 1996; Dollaghan & Campbell, 1998; Edwards & Lahey, 1998).

While the children's nonword repetition scores were all below the 10th percentile, their scores on a range of other standardised language measures varied. The additional standardised language measures for each child included: (1) the Peabody Picture Vocabulary Test (PPVT–R; Dunn & Dunn, 1981), (2) the composite receptive language score of the Clinical Evaluation of Language Fundamentals–Revised (CELF–R; Semel et al., 1989), (3) verbal working memory as measured by the Competing Language Processing Task (CLPT; Gaulin & Campbell, 1994), (4) composite expressive language score of the CELF–R, and (5) mean length of utterance (MLU) derived from a separate free play spontaneous language sample. The scores for all of the standardised language test measures for the children with SLI are shown in Table 1.

TABLE 1

Chronological age (CA), Mean Length of Utterance[a] (MLU), percentile scores for Non-Word Repetition task (NWRP)[b] and PPVT–R[c], percent words recalled for CLPT[d], and standard scores for the composite expressive (ELS) and receptive language scores (RLS) on CELF–R[e] for the children with SLI[f]

Child	CA	MLU	NWRP (Percentile)	PPVT–R (Percentile)	CLPT (%)	ELS (ss)	RLS (ss)
1	7;0	4.99	<1	37 (7;7)	48	70	76
2	7;7	3.99	<1	25 (7;6)	40	59	85
3	9;4	3.50	<1	2 (8;4)	50	67	74
4	7;10	1.73	<1	3 (7;11)	52	73	80
5	7;3	2.88	2	1 (7;2)	40	50	74
6	8;10	3.58	6	5 (7;10)	60	62	80
7	8;11	3.65	<1	2 (8;6)	36	64	70

[a] Calculated from a 15-minute freeplay language sample.

[b] Goldman–Fristoe–Woodcock (1980).

[c] Peabody Picture Vocabulary Test–Revised (Dunn & Dunn, 1981).

[d] Competing Language Processing Test (Gaulin & Campbell, 1994).

[e] Clinical Evaluation of Language Fundamentals–Revised (Semel et al., 1989).

[f] With the exception of the PPVT–R, all tests were administered within 6 months of the administration of the experimental tasks used in this study. Age at administration of the PPVT–R is noted in parentheses in the table.

Seven additional children (ages 6;5 to 7;7—5 girls and 2 boys) were also selected to participate. The typically developing children were drawn from a larger sample of children who had taken part in a previous, unpublished study of children learning Piagetian conservation. No additional IQ or standardised language tests were administered to these children; however, they were in age-appropriate classrooms and had no known history of atypical development. Each child with SLI was matched to a typically developing child on the basis of the pattern of same and different judgements they provided for six conservation tasks (see below). Selection of the typically developing children was otherwise random among the typically developing children whose judgement pattern corresponded to each child with SLI. This matching strategy resulted in a typically developing judgement-matched group that was somewhat younger than the language-impaired group (mean chronological ages 7;0 vs. 8;1).

Procedure

Each child completed six Piagetian conservation tasks, including two liquid quantity tasks, two length tasks, and two number tasks. The typically developing children completed these tasks as part of a larger set of 18 conservation tasks, whereas the children with SLI completed the six conservation tasks only. All six tasks used the same procedure, which was based on that used by Church and Goldin-Meadow (1986), and which has previously been used to study gesture production in children with unilateral brain damage (Alexander, 1999). First, the child was presented with two identical quantities (i.e., two identical glasses each containing the same amount of water, two sticks of the same length, or two rows of six checkers spaced approximately 1" apart). The experimenter then asked, "Are these two (glasses of water, sticks, sets of checkers) the same or different (amounts, lengths, numbers)?" After the child verified that the quantities were the same, the experimenter then transformed one of the quantities. The six transformations used in the study are listed in Table 2. After the transformation, the experimenter asked, "Now, are these two (glasses of water, sticks, sets of checkers) the same or different (amounts, lengths, numbers)?" The child's response to this question is termed the child's *judgement*. The experimenter then asked the child to explain his or her judgement ("How can you tell?" or "Why are they the same (different)?"). The experimenter probed the child for additional explanations ("How else can you tell?" or "Any other reason?") until the child stopped providing explanations. The child's responses to these questions are termed the child's *explanations*.

To assess the relationship between speech and gesture in children's explanations, we used the procedure developed by Church and Goldin-

TABLE 2
Tasks used in study

Quantity	Transformation
Liquid quantity (water)	Pour contents of one glass into a taller, thinner container
	Pour contents of one glass into a shorter, wider container
Length (sticks)	Move one stick so that its endpoint extends approximately two inches beyond that of the other stick
	Move one stick so that it is perpendicular to the other stick
Number (checkers)	Spread or compress the checkers in one row, so that the two rows differ in both length and density
	Form one row of checkers into a circle shape

Meadow (1986), which involves independently evaluating the content of the verbal and gestured explanations.

Coding verbal explanations

Children's verbal explanations of the conservation tasks were transcribed, and the content of the verbal explanations was coded using Church and Goldin-Meadow's (1986) system. Eight different types of strategies were identified in children's spoken explanations. Definitions and examples are presented in Table 3. Conserving strategies (e.g., Identity, Compensation) argue that the two quantities are the same after the transformation. Non-conserving strategies (e.g., Comparison, Transformation) argue that the two quantities are different after the transformation.

Coding gestured explanations

Children's gestured explanations were transcribed and coded using the system developed by Church and Goldin-Meadow (1986). The stream of manual movement was segmented into individual gestures based on changes in the shape, orientation, placement, or motion of the hand(s). A meaning was assigned to each individual gesture. Strings of gestures were then assigned to strategy categories. Six different types of strategies were identified in children's gestured explanations. Examples are presented in Table 3.

Coding the relation of gesture to speech

For each explanation, the relation of gesture to speech was classified into one of four categories: (1) *speech alone*, in which no gesture accompanies the verbal explanation, (2) *gesture used to indicate only*, in which gesture simply indicates the objects described in the accompanying speech, but does not convey substantive information about the objects, (3) *all gestured*

TABLE 3
Strategies expressed in verbal and gestured explanations

Strategy	Definition	Speech example	Gesture example
Nonconserving strategies			
Description	Focus on one attribute of one task object	*Number task, SLI* 'Cause that's small (Description: size) *Length task, SLI* Because this one's down and this one's up (Comparison: placement)	*Number task, Typical* 1. RH & LH palms at endpoints of U row (Description: length) *Water task, SLI* 1. LH palm at level of T glass 2. RH palm at level of U glass (Comparison: level)
Comparison	Focus on one attribute on both task objects	*Water task, Typical* 'Cause this is more round, this is more skinny (Missed compensation: shape, width)	*Length task, SLI* 1. RH & LH palms at endpoints of U stick 2. LH point at left endpoint of T stick (Missed compensation: length, placement)
Missed compensation	Focus on two different, non-compensating attributes on one or both task objects		
Transformation	Focus on the transformation	*Length task, Typical* 'Cause you pushed that one up	*Number task, Typical* 1. RH & LH in neutral space mime putting checkers into a circle
Conserving strategies			
Identity	Focus on the current or initial identity of quantity	*Number task, Typical* They're still the same number (Identity: number)	*Length task, SLI* 1. RH & LH palms at endpoints of U stick 2. RH & LH palms at endpoints of T stick (Identity: length)
Reversibility	Focus on the reversibility of the transformation	*Water task, SLI* If you dump that back in there, then it will be the same	Not observed in gesture in this study
Compensation	Focus on two, compensating dimensions on one or both task objects	*Water task, SLI* It's taller than this one. This one is skinny and this one is fat (Compensation: height, width)	*Water task, SLI* 1. RH curved handshape around T glass, moves up 2. RH curved handshape around U glass, moves up (Compensation: width, height)
Add–Subtract	Focus on the fact that nothing was added or taken away	*Number task, Typical* 'Cause you didn't add any, and you didn't take any away	Not observed in gesture in this study

T = transformed object; U = untransformed object; LH = left hand, RH = right hand.

information also in speech, in which gesture conveys substantive information that is also conveyed in speech, or (4) *some information unique to
gesture*, in which gesture conveys some substantive information that is not
conveyed at all in speech.

Next, explanations in which some information was expressed uniquely in
gesture were further classified into one of three categories: (a) *specific*, in
which gesture provides more specific information than speech, (b) *overlap*,
in which gesture expresses some of the information expressed in speech as
well as some additional, unique information, or (c) *disjoint*, in which
gesture expresses information that is completely distinct from that
expressed in speech. Examples of explanations in each of these categories
are presented in Table 4.

Reliability of coding procedures

Reliability was established by having a second coder evaluate a subset of
the data. Agreement between coders was 94% ($N = 70$ explanations) for
coding strategies expressed in speech and 91% ($N = 43$ explanations) for
coding strategies expressed in gesture. Agreement was 88% ($N = 50$
explanations) for coding the relationship between gesture and speech.

RESULTS

The pattern of same and different judgements provided by each child
across the liquid, length and number conservation tasks is presented in
Table 5. As described above, the children with SLI and the typically
developing controls in this study were matched on their pattern of same
and different judgements across the tasks, so the pattern of judgements in
the control children was identical to that of the children with SLI. From
the set of 18 tasks administered to the children in the control group, the six
that we used in our analysis (those that corresponded to the tasks
administered to the children with SLI) were tasks, 1, 3, 4, 5, 6, and 9. No
differences were observed between children's performance on the ninth
task and their performance on the other tasks. Children provided a
comparable number of explanations on the ninth task as on the other five
tasks ($M = 1.28$ on the ninth task vs. $M = 1.26$ on the others). Thus, there
was no evidence that the number of explanations dropped off as children
progressed through the set of tasks. Further, the rate at which children
produced gestures was comparable on the ninth task, which was a liquid
quantity task, and the first task, which was the other liquid quantity task
($M = 0.27$ gestures per word vs. $M = 0.20$ gestures per word), $F(1, 17) =
1.04$, $p = .32$. Thus, there was no evidence that the pattern of gesture use
changed as children progressed through the set of tasks.

TABLE 4

Examples of different types of gesture–speech relationship

Relationship	Speech	Gesture
Speech alone	Because it's the tallest bottle (Description: height)	No gesture
Speech plus indicating gesture	Because this is bigger than this one (Comparison: size)	1. RH point to side of transformed glass (T glass) 2. LH point to side of untransformed glass (U glass) (Indicate glasses)
All gestured information also in speech	Because this one is only up to here, and this one is only up to here (Comparison: level)	1. RH palm at water level of transformed glass (level T) 2. LH palm at water level of untransformed glass (level U) (Comparison: level)
Different information in gesture and speech–specific	Because this smaller and this bigger (Comparison: size)	1. RH palm at top edge of transformed glass (height T) 2. LH palm at top edge of untransformed glass (height U) (Comparison: height)
Different information in gesture and speech–overlap	This is thinner and this is fatter (Comparison: width)	1. RH cupped around transformed glass, moves up (width + height T) 2. RH cupped around untransformed glass, moves up (width + height U) (Compensation: width + height)
Different information in gesture and speech–disjoint	You put that into here (Transform)	1. RH & LH palms facing near experimenter (width of original glass) 2. RH & LH palms facing at top edge of transformed glass (width + height T) (Compensation: width + height)

Note: All examples are drawn from children with SLI explaining one of the two water tasks.

TABLE 5
Number of same judgements (out of two) on the three types of
conservation tasks for children with specific language impairment
(SLI) and typically developing judgement-matched children (JM)

Child	Liquid	Length	Number
SLI/JM			
1	0	0	2
2	0	0	1
3	2	0	2
4	0	0	2
5	0	0	0
6	0	0	0
7	0	0	2

The results are organised around three main questions. First, do children with SLI produce gestures at a rate comparable to typically developing judgement-matched children? Second, do children with SLI express information uniquely in gesture more often than do typically developing judgement-matched children? Third, do children with SLI express more advanced understanding of conservation in their gestures than in their speech? Note that all of the data analyses focus on children's *explanations* (i.e., their responses to the "How can you tell?" question), which followed their conservation judgements. All of the children spontaneously produced gestures with at least some of their verbal explanations.

Before exploring the nature of the speech-gesture relationship in the two groups, we first examined the number of explanations children provided for each task. The children with SLI were much more likely than the judgement-matched typically developing children to provide additional explanations when they were probed after their initial explanation. Children with SLI provided an average of 2.55 explanations per task, whereas judgement-matched children provided only 1.29, $t(12) = 5.39, p <$ .001. These data suggest that, with prompting, children with SLI had more to say about the conservation tasks than they expressed in their initial explanations.

Do children with SLI produce gestures at a rate comparable to judgement-matched typically developing children?

Each *explanation* was coded as including gestures or not including gestures. Children with SLI produced a greater proportion of explanations without gesture than typically developing judgement-matched (JM) children (SLI, 19%; JM, 8% of all explanations); however this difference was not significant, $t(12) = 1.84$, *ns*, two-tailed. Across both groups, explanations that did not include gestures tended to be very brief, "minimal" explanations of five words or fewer, such as, "because I counted them" or "it got big one". Such brief explanations were more common in children with SLI than in judgement-matched typically developing children (SLI, $M = 23\%$; JM, $M = 8\%$ of all explanations).

For explanations that included gestures, we then examined the rate at which children in the two groups produced gestures. The rate of gestures per 10 words was comparable in both groups (SLI, $M = 2.40$, $SE = .13$; JM, $M = 2.14$, $SE = .09$), $F(1, 13) = 2.76$, $p = .12$.

Do children with SLI express information uniquely in gesture more often than judgement-matched typically developing children?

When children produced gestures, they could use gestures to indicate the objects, to convey information that they also expressed in speech, or to convey information that they did not express at all in speech. Figure 1

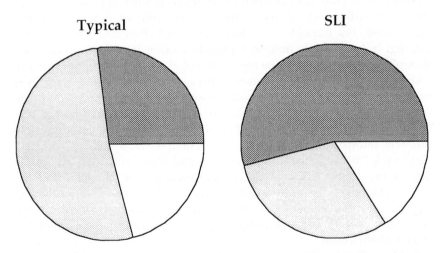

☐ Gesture used only to indicate

▨ All gestured information also in speech

▩ Some information unique to gesture

Typical   SLI

Figure 1. Distribution of explanations that include gesture for children with SLI and younger judgement-matched typically developing children, classified according to whether gesture serves only to indicate the task objects (☐), gesture conveys information that is also expressed in speech (   ), or gesture conveys unique information not expressed in speech (▓).

presents the mean proportion of explanations of each of these three types across all explanations that included gesture. As seen in the figure, when they produced gestures, children with SLI more often expressed some information unique to gesture than did judgement-matched typically developing children (SLI, $M = 54\%$; JM, $M = 29\%$), $t(12) = 2.58, p < .02$, one-tailed. These data are complicated by the fact that the proportions are based on different numbers of responses for different children, with low Ns in some cases. Therefore, to confirm this finding, we also compared the two groups using a non-parametric test, the median test, which compares the number of children in each group who are above versus at or below the grand median. More of the children with SLI were above the median in the proportion of explanations they produced that included some information unique to gesture (SLI, $N = 6$; JM, $N = 2$), $p < .05$, Fisher's Exact (see Siegel & Castellan, 1988).

For explanations in which gesture conveyed information not expressed in speech, we next examined the gesture-speech relationship at a finer grain. As noted above, the gesture-speech relationship was classified as *specific* for explanations in which the information expressed in gesture was more specific than that expressed in speech. For example, on a water task, one child said, "because this is bigger and this is smaller" while pointing to the water level in the tall, thin glass, and then to the water level in the untransformed glass. In this example, gesture conveys a more specific dimension (level) than speech (size). The gesture–speech relationship was classified as *overlap* for explanations in which gesture expressed some of the information expressed in speech, as well as some additional information. For example, on a water task, one child said, "because you put that in here" while making a pouring motion into the tall glass, and then placed his flat palm at the top of the tall glass. In this example, gesture conveys some of the information expressed in speech (the water was poured into the tall glass), as well as some additional information (the height of the tall glass). Finally, the gesture–speech relationship was classified as *disjoint* for explanations in which gesture conveyed completely different information from speech. For example, on a number task, one child said, "because these still have six and these still have six" while tracing the round shape of the transformed row of checkers and the straight shape of the untransformed row of checkers. In this example, speech conveys information about the number of checkers in each of the rows, and gesture conveys completely different information about the shapes of the rows.

Table 6 displays the proportion of explanations that included gesture that were classified into each of these three categories. As seen in the table, children with SLI produced overlapping information in gesture three times as often as judgement-matched typically developing children (median test,

TABLE 6

Proportion of explanations (mean and standard errors) that included gestures characterised by each type of gesture–speech relationship for specifically language impaired (SLI) and typically developing judgement-matched (JM) groups

Type of explanation	SLI M (SE)	JM M (SE)
Specific	0.14 (.05)	0.13 (.06)
Overlap	0.18 (.04)	0.06 (.06)
Disjoint	0.23 (.05)	0.11 (.05)

$p < .02$, Fisher's Exact), and disjoint information in speech and gesture twice as often as judgement-matched children (median test, $p = .13$, Fisher's Exact).

Thus, children with SLI expressed information uniquely in gesture more often than judgement-matched typically developing children. We have suggested that this pattern of gesture-speech mismatch seen in the children with SLI can be attributed to their poor phonological working memory, on which basis the participants were selected. This pattern of gesture use might alternatively relate more strongly to severity of impairment in some other language domain, such as receptive vocabulary. Pearson pairwise correlation coefficients revealed that none of the correlations between the standardised language indices (see Table 1) and the proportion of explanations in which children with SLI expressed information uniquely in gesture were significant (PPVT, $r = .63$, ns; MLU, $r = .38$, ns; CLPT, $r = -.48$, ns; ELS, $r = -.09$, ns; RLS, $r = -.16$, ns).

Do children express more advanced reasoning in speech and gesture together than in speech alone?

The preceding analyses indicate that children with SLI have knowledge about conservation that is expressed in gestures but not speech. We next examined the nature of this "hidden knowledge" about conservation. Would children's gestures reveal more advanced knowledge about conservation than their speech? To address this question, we examined when and how often children expressed *conserving* knowledge in their explanations. As noted above, conserving strategies are strategies that justify why the quantities have the same amount. They include strategies that focus on the *identity* or *initial equality* of the quantities, the *compensation* of two dimensions, or the *reversibility* of the transformation. Examples of conserving strategies are presented in Table 3.

We first counted the number of times that children expressed conserving strategies in their verbal explanations of the tasks. As seen in Figure 2 (left

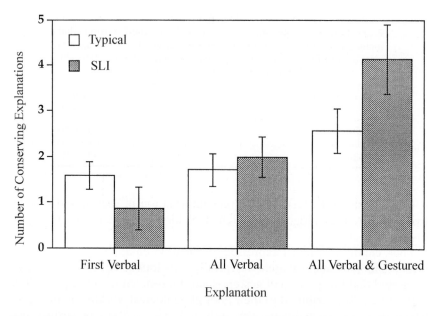

Figure 2. Number of conserving strategies (means and standard errors) expressed by children with SLI and younger judgement-matched typically developing children across the set of six tasks, in the first verbal explanation for each task (left), in all verbal explanations (middle), and in all verbal and gestured explanations (right).

set of bars), on the first explanation for each task, children with SLI produced slightly (though not significantly) *fewer* conserving strategies than the younger judgement-matched children, $t(12) = 1.31$, $p = 0.22$. When all verbal explanations were considered (middle set of bars), children with SLI produced slightly (though not significantly) *more* conserving strategies than the younger judgement-matched children, $t(12) = 0.51$, $p = .62$.

The crucial comparison considers whether children's gestures revealed conserving strategies that they did not express in speech. We assessed the number of conserving strategies that each child produced when both modalities (speech and gesture) and all explanations were considered. In this analysis, we included both conserving strategies that children expressed *uniquely in gesture* (e.g., on a water task, gesturing about *both the height and width* of a particular container while talking about *only the height* of the container) and conserving strategies that were *distributed across speech and gesture* in a single explanation (e.g., on a water task, gesturing about *only the width* of a particular container while talking about *only the height* of the container). As seen in Figure 2, in their explanations, when both speech and gesture were considered, children with SLI produced more conserving strategies than when only verbal explanations were considered, paired $t(6) = 3.38$, $p < .02$. Further, when both modalities were considered, children with SLI produced significantly more conserving strategies in their explanations as compared to the younger judgement-matched children, $t(12) = 1.73$, $p = .05$, one-tailed.

DISCUSSION

This study investigated the relationship between gesture and speech in Piagetian conservation tasks for children with SLI who had phonological working memory deficits and for judgement-matched typically developing children. While the children with SLI produced slightly more brief explanations that did not include gestures, when they produced gestures, the children with SLI expressed unique information in gesture significantly more often than did judgement-matched children. Thus, the nature of the relationship between speech and gesture appears to differ in children with SLI who have deficits in phonological working memory as compared to typically developing children. Further, in this study, the children with SLI often expressed *more sophisticated* knowledge about conservation in gesture (and in some cases, distributed across speech and gesture) than in speech. Thus, our data suggest that for these children with SLI, their embodied, perceptually-based knowledge about conservation was rich, but they were not always able to express this knowledge verbally. We have argued that this pattern of gesture-speech mismatch may be a result of poor links between phonological representations and embodied meanings for children with phonological working memory deficits like the participants in this study.

Church and Goldin-Meadow (1986) have observed a similar pattern of mismatch between speech and gesture in typically developing children who are on the brink of learning to conserve. They found that children who frequently conveyed additional information in gesture were particularly receptive to instruction about conservation. In their view, frequent mismatches of speech and gesture are an index of transitional knowledge states (see also Perry et al., 1988). One interpretation of Church and Goldin-Meadow's findings is that children whose knowledge is "transitional" have knowledge about the tasks that is represented in a nonverbal, perceptual format. According to this view, children initially acquire knowledge in a nonverbal format, and over developmental time, this knowledge then becomes re-represented in an explicit, verbalisable form. Indeed, the redescription of knowledge from one format to another may be a hallmark of transitional knowledge states (Alibali & Goldin-Meadow, 1993; Karmiloff-Smith, 1986, 1992). Thus, Church and Goldin-Meadow argued that the relation between gesture and speech might serve as an index not only of children's "readiness" to learn about conservation, but more broadly as an index of transitional knowledge.

It is possible that the children with SLI in this study, who also frequently conveyed additional information in gesture, were in a similar transitional knowledge state with regard to their conservation knowledge as well. Previous studies have documented delays in the acquisition of conservation among children with language impairments, even when conservation is assessed using nonverbal tasks. For example, Siegel and colleagues used an operant conditioning paradigm to test concrete operational reasoning in children with SLI and age-matched peers (Siegel, Lees, Allan, & Bolton, 1981). They found that children with SLI were less likely to demonstrate concrete operational reasoning on conservation and seriation tasks than peers. Similarly, Kamhi (1981) found that 5-year-old children with SLI showed poorer understanding of number conservation than age-matched peers. However, Johnston and Ramstad (1983) found that some children with SLI do eventually acquire explicit, verbal knowledge about conservation, but at a much slower rate than typically developing children.

One possibility is that, for both children with SLI and typically developing children, the mismatch between knowledge conveyed in gestures and in speech may signal somewhat weak links between embodied knowledge and verbally explicit representations. We suggest that, for children with SLI, embodied meaning representations may evolve in advance of and possibly independently of phonological representations, due to input from other modalities. According to Plaut and Kello (1999), the typically developing child's phonological representations evolve over time through repeated exposure to speech input. It might be that for children with SLI who have poor phonological working memory deficits, their exposure to speech input has been insufficient to develop stable phonological representations. Thus children with SLI might require more exposure to speech input as compared to their typically developing peers before they are able to develop stable phonological representations that can then be linked to embodied meanings, resulting in a prolonged state of transitional knowledge for these children. There is support for this idea in studies of lexical learning in children with SLI. While there is some inconsistency in the findings (Dollaghan, 1987), it has been reported that these children are less likely to incidentally learn new words quickly as compared to their age-matched peers (Rice, Buhr, & Nemeth, 1990). In particular, research suggests that these children require increased exposures to a new word before they show evidence of learning it (Rice, Buhr, & Oetting, 1992). Thus, children with SLI may express different information in speech and gesture for an extended period of time because they need increased exposure to language input in order to translate embodied knowledge into a more explicit verbal format. We plan to explore this hypothesis in future work.

Alternative accounts of SLI have been put forth that suggest that the deficits observed in linguistic and non-linguistic tasks in children with SLI are not due to phonological working memory deficits, but are due to limitations in general processing capacity (e.g., Johnston, 1994; Leonard, 1998). For example, Leonard (1998) has suggested that the deficits seen in children with SLI are secondary to impairments in their ability to simultaneously process the acoustic patterns of bound morphemes and derive their grammatical function before the acoustic pattern disappears from memory. In addition, Johnston and colleagues (e.g., Johnston & Smith, 1989) have proposed limited processing capacity as an account of *cognitive* deficits seen in children with SLI, arguing that overall information processing factors may be more critical than language specific factors. These limited processing accounts of SLI are not incompatible with the findings from this study. It has been argued that gestures may help speakers manage resource demands (Goldin-Meadow, in press). In particular, it has been suggested that gestures externalise some information, which helps speakers to manage cognitive load (Alibali & DiRusso, 1999). Further, some evidence suggests that speakers produce gestures that mismatch speech whey they are working at the limits of their processing capacity (Goldin-Meadow, Nusbaum, Garber, & Church, 1993). It may be that the children with SLI in this study often produced gestures that conveyed different information from speech because they were at the limits of their processing capacity, due to the cognitive and conversational demands of the task.

In particular, it is noteworthy that the children with SLI were more likely than the typically developing children to provide additional explanations when they were probed after their initial explanation ("How else can you tell?"). It might be that the children with SLI were unable to simultaneously process the verbal request of the examiner and verbally formulate their entire conceptual understanding of the task in a single response, and they needed the additional probes on the part of the examiner to express their full conceptual knowledge. This is consistent with studies of the conversation abilities of children with SLI. In particular, in conversations with adults, children with SLI are more likely to respond to an adult with a minimal, elliptic response (Johnston, Miller, Curtiss, & Tallal, 1993). However when given additional opportunities to respond, or when conversational demands are reduced, children with SLI are more likely to add information in their subsequent responses (e.g., Evans, 1996; Leonard, 1986; Van Kleeck & Frankel, 1981). Alternatively, however, it is possible that in this study the children in the two groups interpreted the communicative intent of the additional probe questions differently (see

Siegal, 1997; Siegal & Waters, 1988, for discussion). The children with SLI may have interpreted the experimenter's repeated questioning as an indication that their initial explanation was inadequate, so they may have attempted to provide another (hopefully more adequate) explanation. The typically developing children appeared to interpret the experimenter's probe question as a simple request for additional information, and they seemed quite comfortable indicating that they had no other reasons for their judgement. This issue needs to be explored further in future work.

In this paper, we have suggested that phonological working memory deficits critically affect the developmental organisation of phonological representations and their links to embodied knowledge for children with SLI. Further, we have suggested that impairments in phonological working memory may play a role in the extent to which children with SLI express knowledge uniquely in gesture. These suggestions should be taken tentatively. First, the protocol was not completely identical for both groups of children (as noted above, the judgement-matched group completed the tasks as part of a larger study). Second, although the correlations between the degree of gesture-speech mismatch and language indices were not significant for the children with SLI, one cannot rule out the possibility that language indices other than phonological working memory might be related to the unique gesture-speech profile seen in these children. For example, receptive language abilities have been shown to be highly correlated with nonword repetition abilities in prior work (e.g., Gathercole & Baddeley, 1990a). In the current study, for two of the children with SLI, receptive vocabulary abilities were assessed approximately a year prior to the completion of the conservation tasks. One would anticipate that for these two children, even very low PPVT–R scores would improve over the course of the school year. Thus, it is possible that receptive language abilities might also relate to the unique gesture-speech profile seen in these children. Future research is needed to replicate the findings in this study with a larger group of children with SLI who have a wider range of phonological working memory abilities, and with an identical protocol for both groups of children.

In sum, this study showed that, when they produced gestures, children with SLI expressed knowledge uniquely in gesture more often than judgement-matched typically developing children. Thus, patterns of gesture-speech integration differ in children with SLI and children who are developing typically. Further, children with SLI often conveyed more advanced reasoning in gesture than in speech. Our results suggest that phonological working memory deficits may have consequences for children's ability to translate embodied knowledge into a verbally explicit format. Based on these findings, we suggest that children with SLI may represent their knowledge in a format that is more readily accessible to gesture, and less readily accessible to verbal expression. As a result, children with language impairments may express their knowledge in ways that are qualitatively different from typically developing children.

REFERENCES

Acredolo, L.P., & Goodwyn, S.W. (1988). Symbolic gesturing in normal infants. *Child Development, 59*, 450–456.

Alexander, E.P. (1999). *Language and gesture production in normal and congenitally, left-hemisphere-damaged individuals: A developmental study.* Unpublished doctoral dissertation, University of Chicago.

Alibali, M.W., & DiRusso, A.A. (1999). The function of gesture in learning to count: More than keeping track. *Cognitive Development, 14*, 37–56.

Alibali, M.W., & Goldin-Meadow, S. (1993). Transitions in learning: What the hands reveal about a child's state of mind. *Cognitive Psychology, 25*, 468–523.

Alibali, M.W., Kita, S., & Young, A. (2000). Gesture and the process of speech production: We think, therefore we gesture. *Language and Cognitive Processes, 15*, 593–613.

Baddeley, A. (1986). *Working memory.* Oxford, UK: Oxford University Press.

Bates, E. (1979). *The emergence of symbols: Cognition and communication in infancy.* New York: Academic Press.

Bishop, D.V.M. (1992). The underlying nature of specific language impairment. *Journal of Child Psychology and Psychiatry, 33*, 1–64.

Bishop, D.V.M. (1997). *Uncommon understanding: Development and disorders of language comprehension in children.* Hove, UK: Psychology Press.

Bishop, D.V.M., North, T., & Donlan, C. (1996). Nonword repetition as a behavioural marker for inherited language impairment: Evidence from a twin study. *Journal of Child Psychology and Psychiatry, 37*, 391–403.

Burgemeister, B., Blum, L.H., & Lorge, I. (1972). *Columbia Mental Maturity Scale.* Harcourt, Brace, Jovanovich, Inc.

Butcher, C., & Goldin-Meadow, S. (in press). Gesture and the transition from one- to two-word speech: When hand and mouth come together. In D. McNeill (Ed.), *Language and gesture: Window into thought and action.* Cambridge, UK: Cambridge University Press.

Church, R.B., & Goldin-Meadow, S. (1986). The mismatch between gesture and speech as an index of transitional knowledge. *Cognition, 23*, 43–71.

Clahsen, H. (1989). The grammatical characterization of developmental dysphasia. *Linguistics, 27*, 897–920.

Dollaghan, C. (1987). Fast mapping of normal and language-impaired children. *Journal of Speech and Hearing Disorders, 52*, 218-222.

Dollaghan, C., Biber, M., & Campbell, T. (1993). Constituent syllable effects in a nonsense-word repetition task. *Journal of Speech and Hearing Research, 36*, 1051–1054.

Dollaghan, C., & Campbell, T.F. (1998). Nonword repetition and child language impairment. *Journal of Speech, Language, and Hearing Research, 41*, 1136–1146.

Dunn, L., & Dunn, D. (1981). *Peabody Picture Vocabulary Test-Revised.* Minneapolis: American Guidance Service.

Edwards, J., & Lahey, M. (1998). Nonword repetitions of children with specific language impairment: Exploration of some explanations for their inaccuracies. *Applied Psycholinguistics, 19*, 279–309.

Ellis Weismer, S., Evans, J.L., & Hesketh, L.J. (1999). An examination of verbal working memory capacity in children with Specific Language Impairment. *Journal of Speech, Language, and Hearing Research, 42,* 1249–1260.

Evans, J. (1996). SLI subgroups: Interaction between discourse constraints and morpho-syntactic deficits. *Journal of Speech and Hearing Research, 39,* 655–660.

Gathercole, S.E. (1995). Is nonword repetition a test of phonological memory or long-term knowledge? It all depends on the nonwords. *Memory and Cognition, 23,* 83–94.

Gathercole, S.E., & Baddeley, A.D. (1990a). Phonological memory deficits in language-disordered children: Is there a causal connection? *Journal of Memory and Language, 29,* 336–360.

Gathercole, S.E. & Baddeley, A.D. (1990b). The role of phonological memory in vocabulary acquisition: A study of young children learning arbitrary names of toys. *British Journal of Psychology, 81,* 439–454.

Gathercole, S.E., & Baddeley, A.D. (1993). *Working memory in language processing.* Hove, UK: Lawrence Erlbaum Associates Ltd.

Gaulin, C., & Campbell, T. (1994). Procedure for assessing verbal working memory in normal school-age children: Some preliminary data. *Perceptual and Motor Skills, 79,* 55–64.

Gibson, J.J. (1966). *The senses considered as perceptual systems.* Boston, MA: Houghton Mifflin.

Glenberg, A.M. (1997). What memory is for. *Behavioral and Brain Sciences, 20,* 1–55.

Glenberg, A.M., & Robertson, D.A. (1999). Indexical understanding of instructions. *Discourse Processes, 28,* 1–26.

Goldin-Meadow, S. (in press). Giving the mind a hand: The role of gesture in cognitive change. In J.L. McClelland & R.S. Siegler (Eds.), *Mechanisms of change in cognitive development: Behavioral and neural perspectives.* Mahwah, NJ: Lawrence Erlbaum Associates Inc.

Goldin-Meadow, S., Nusbaum, H., Garber, P., & Church, R.B. (1993). Transitions in learning: Evidence for simultaneously activated strategies. *Journal of Experimental Psychology: Human Perception and Performance, 19,* 1–16.

Goldman, R.W., Fristoe, M., & Woodcock, R.W. (1980). *Goldman–Fristoe-Woodcock test of auditory discrimination.* Circle Pines, MN: American Guidance Service.

Gopnik, M., & Crago, M. (1991). Familial aggregation of a developmental language disorder. *Cognition, 39,* 1–50.

Hill, E.L. (1998). A dyspraxic deficit in specific language impairment and developmental coordination disorder: Evidence from hand and arm movements. *Developmental Medicine and Child Neurology, 40,* 388–395.

Iverson, J.M., & Thelen, E. (in press). Hand, mouth, and brain: The dynamic emergence of speech and gesture. In R. Nunez & W.J. Freeman (Eds.), *Reclaiming cognition: The primacy of action, intention, and emotion.* Thorverton, UK: Imprint Academic.

Johnston, J.R., Miller, J., Curtiss, S., & Tallal, P. (1993). Conversations with children who are language impaired: Asking questions. *Journal of Speech and Hearing Research, 36,* 973–978.

Johnston, J.R., & Smith, L.B. (1989). Dimensional thinking in language impaired children. *Journal of Speech and Hearing Research, 32,* 33–38.

Johnston, J.R. (1994). Cognitive abilities of children with language impairment. In R.V. Watkins & M.L. Rice (Eds.), *Specific language impairments in children.* Baltimore, MD: Brookes.

Johnston, J.R., & Ramstad, V. (1983). Cognitive development in preadolescent language-impaired children. *British Journal of Disorders of Communication, 18,* 49–55.

Kamhi, A. (1981). Nonlinguistic symbolic and conceptual abilities of language-impaired and normally developing children. *Journal of Speech and Hearing Research, 24,* 446–453.

Karmiloff-Smith, A. (1986). From meta-processes to conscious access: Evidence from children's metalinguistic and repair data. *Cognition, 23,* 95–147.

Karmiloff-Smith, A. (1992). *Beyond modularity: A developmental perspective on cognitive science.* Cambridge, MA: MIT Press.

Leonard, L. (1986). Conversational replies of children with specific language impairment. *Journal of Speech and Hearing Research, 29,* 114–119.

Leonard, L. (1998). *Children with specific language impairment.* Cambridge, MA: MIT Press.

MacWhinney, B. (1999). The emergence of language from embodiment. In B. MacWhinney (Ed.), *The emergence of language* (pp. 213–256). Mahwah, NJ: Lawrence Erlbaum Associates Inc.

McNeill, D. (1992). *Hand and mind: What gestures reveal about thought.* Chicago: University of Chicago Press.

Montgomery, J. (1995). Sentence comprehension in children with specific language impairment: The role of phonological working memory. *Journal of Speech and Hearing Research, 38,* 177–189.

Perry, M., Church, R.B., & Goldin-Meadow, S. (1988). Transitional knowledge in the acquisition of concepts. *Cognitive Development, 3,* 359–400.

Plaut, D.C., & Kello, C.T. (1999). The emergence of phonology from the interplay of speech comprehension and production: A distributed connectionist approach. In B. MacWhinney (Ed.), *The emergence of language* (pp. 381–415). Mahwah, NJ: Lawrence Erlbaum Associates Inc.

Rice, M., Buhr, J., & Nemeth, M. (1990). Fast mapping word learning abilities of language delayed preschoolers. *Journal of Speech and Hearing Disorders, 55,* 33–42.

Rice, M., Buhr, J., & Oetting, J. (1992). Specific-language-impaired children's quick incidental learning of words: The effects of a pause. *Journal of Speech and Hearing Research, 35,* 1040–1048.

Rice, M., Wexler, K., & Cleave, P.L. (1995). Specific language impairment as a period of extended optional infinitive. *Journal of Speech and Hearing Research, 38,* 850–863.

Semel, E., Wiig, E., & Secord, W. (1989). *The Clinical Evaluation of Language Fundamentals–Revised.* Texas: The Psychological Co., Harcourt, Brace, Jovanovich, Inc.

Siegal, M. (1997). *Knowing children: Experiments in conversation and cognition.* Hove, UK: Psychology Press.

Siegal, M., & Waters, L.J. (1988). Misleading children: Causal attributions for inconsistency under repeated questioning. *Journal of Experimental Child Psychology, 45,* 438–456.

Siegel, L.S., Lees, A., Allan, L., & Bolton, B. (1981). Nonverbal assessment of Piagetian concepts in preschool children with impaired language development. *Educational Psychology, 2,* 153–158.

Siegel, S., & Castellan, N.J., Jr. (1988). *Nonparametric statistics for the behavioral sciences.* New York: McGraw-Hill, Inc.

Thal, D.J., & Bates, E. (1988). Language and gesture in late talkers. *Journal of Speech and Hearing Research, 31,* 115–123.

Thal, D.J., O'Hanlon, L., Clemmons, M., & Fralin, L. (1999). Validity of a parent report measure of vocabulary and syntax for preschool children with language impairment. *Journal of Speech, Hearing, and Language Research, 42,* 482–496.

Thal, D.J., & Tobias, S. (1992). Communicative gestures in children with delayed onset of oral expressive vocabulary. *Journal of Speech and Hearing Research, 35,* 1281–1289.

Thal, D.J., Tobias, S., & Morrison, D. (1991). Language and gesture in late talkers: A 1-year follow-up. *Journal of Speech and Hearing Research, 34,* 604–612.

Van Kleeck, A., & Frankel, T. (1981). Discourse devices used by language disordered children: A preliminary investigation. *Journal of Speech and Hearing Disorders, 46,* 250–257.

Subject Index

Author Index